Charles Henry Crandall

Representative sonnets by American poets

with an essay on the sonnet, its nature and history, including many notable

sonnets of other literatures

Charles Henry Crandall

Representative sonnets by American poets
with an essay on the sonnet, its nature and history, including many notable sonnets of other literatures

ISBN/EAN: 9783743328907

Manufactured in Europe, USA, Canada, Australia, Japa

Cover: Foto ©Thomas Meinert / pixelio.de

Manufactured and distributed by brebook publishing software
(www.brebook.com)

Charles Henry Crandall

Representative sonnets by American poets

REPRESENTATIVE SONNETS
BY AMERICAN POETS

WITH

AN ESSAY ON THE SONNET, ITS NATURE AND
HISTORY, INCLUDING MANY NOTABLE
SONNETS OF OTHER
LITERATURES

ALSO

BIOGRAPHICAL NOTES, INDEXES, ETC.

BY

CHARLES H. CRANDALL

BOSTON AND NEW YORK
HOUGHTON, MIFFLIN AND COMPANY
The Riverside Press, Cambridge
1890

This Work

IS AFFECTIONATELY DEDICATED

TO

THE MEMORY OF MY WIFE,

KATHERINE,

WHO RENDERED LOVING ASSISTANCE

IN ITS PREPARATION.

A sonnet is a moment's monument.
                           D. G. ROSSETTI.

It is a little picture painted well.
                           R. W. GILDER.

A sonnet is a wave of melody.
                           THEODORE WATTS.

It hath a subtile music, strangely sweet.
                           JULIA C. R. DORR.

A sonnet should be like a cygnet's cruise.
                           EDITH M. THOMAS.

The thing became a trumpet.
                           WORDSWORTH.

PREFATORY NOTE

THE design of this work is to group as many of the best sonnets in American literature as can be included in a volume of convenient size, and to make the selection as widely representative as possible while giving to the most eminent sonnet-writers a proper prominence by more numerous examples of their work. The editor has endeavored to apply to every sonnet the test of merit: first, for genuine poetic thought; second, for melodious expression and a reasonable regard for the accepted forms. Sonnets of merit in imagination and structure have been rejected in some cases because they contained some repellent idea or discordant note. Again, it has seemed well to allow some subjects to be represented by several sonnets in order to secure the best work of each author, regardless of subject, as well as to give the additional interest of comparing the various views of the same theme. Generally it has been intended to place the finest of an author's sonnets at the head, but occasionally it has been put at the close or elsewhere, when the exceptional arrangement enhanced the general effect. A considerable number of the sonnets have been revised since their first appearance, especially for this book; titles have been supplied where they were lacking. Not a few of the sonnets are printed now for the first time, and it has been intended to include as many good sonnets of biographical and personal interest, by or about famous people, as possible. The systematic indenting of lines will enable readers to see at a glance whether the form is Petrarcan, Shakespearean, or irregular, thus contributing to the enjoyment of the reading.

Being convinced of the superiority of the Petrarcan style of sonnet, the compiler at first determined to admit no other form, at least from living poets, but the frequent fine poems modeled on the Shakespearean or other patterns constrained him to make frequent exceptions to the rule. The older poets, especially, often used irregular arrangements, and it has seemed only fair and hospitable to welcome their poesy, and let the question of superiority of form be referred to the reader.

In making selections and preparing a study of the sonnet the author acknowledges his indebtedness to the Hunt-Lee "Book of the Sonnet," as well as to English treatises, among many sources of material. The uniform courtesy of publishers and authors in granting copyright is cordially acknowledged. Proper request has been made, whenever practicable, for the use of each sonnet, and as no author has refused permission it is hoped that any oversight will not be construed as intended discourtesy. The compiler has profited by the generous assistance of a number of well-known students and critics whose names are passed in silence, though in sincere gratitude.

INDEX.

I. OPENING CHAPTER AND APPENDIX.

	PAGE
ALDRICH, THOMAS BAILEY.	
"Enamored architect of airy rhyme"	18
ARNOLD, MATTHEW.	
Immortality	75
BROWNING, ELIZABETH BARRETT.	
For Love's Sake only	72
Broken Idols	72
BUCHANAN, ROBERT.	
"When we are all asleep"	83
BUONNAROTI, MICHAEL ANGELO.	
"Dante" (tr. by Longfellow)	35
BYRON, GEORGE GORDON, LORD.	
The Prisoner of Chillon	66
CAMOENS, LUIS DE.	
"Os olhos onde o casto Amor ardia" (tr. by Higginson)	41
COLERIDGE, SAMUEL TAYLOR.	
Kosciusko	60
Fancy in Nubibus	61
CRAIK, DINAH M. MULOCK.	
Guns of Peace	74
DANTE ALIGHIERI.	
"Tanto gentile e tanto onesta pare" (English and Italian) (tr. by Miss Guiney)	28
"Io mi sentii svegliar dentro allo core" (tr. by Miss Guiney)	29
DOBSON, AUSTIN.	
Don Quixote	85
DORR, JULIA C. R.	
The sonnet, To a Critic	17
The sonnet, To a Poet	17
DRAYTON, MICHAEL.	
Love's Last Word	52

II. REPRESENTATIVE SONNETS.

* Sonnets now first published.
P. — Sonnets with Petrarcan octave.
S. — Shakespearian quatorzains.
I. — Irregular sonnets.
G. — Guittonian sonnets.
Sp. — Spenserian sonnets.

(NOTE. — A number of the sonnets marked "Irregular" are mainly Petrarcan in form, but have a third rhyme in the octave.)

ABBEY, HENRY.
* Faith's Vista (I) 93
ADAMS, OSCAR FAY.
   Renunciation (P) 94
ALBEE, JOHN.
   Fading Barriers (P) 94
   Recreation in Love (P) 95
   Keats' Love-Letters (P) 95
ALCOTT, AMOS BRONSON.
   Thoreau (I) 96
   To Mrs. Alcott (S) 96
   To L. M. Alcott (I) 97
   Read at Emerson's Funeral (I) 97
ALDEN, HENRY MILLS.
   A Child shall lead Them (P) 98
ALDRICH, THOMAS BAILEY.
   Sleep (P) 98
   Miracles (P) 99
   Fredericksburg (P) 99
   Three Flowers (P) 100
   England (P) 100
   "Even this will pass away" (P) 101
ALLSTON, WASHINGTON.
   Coleridge (I) 101
ARNOLD, JENNIE PORTER.
   Penitence (P) 102
AURINGER, OBADIAH CYRUS.
   Confession (P) 102
   On the Bridge at Glenn's (P) 103
   Emerson — Carlyle (P) 103

BACON, T. R.
   Deus Immanens (I) 104
BAIRD, CHAMBERS.
   Atlantis (P) 104
   After Many Years (P) 105

BARTLETT, MARY RUSSELL.
  Land Ahead (P) 105
BASHFORD, HERBERT.
  *An Autumn Night (P) 106
BATCHELDER, SAMUEL FRANCIS.
  *February (P) 106
BATES, ARLO.
  Our Dead (P) 107
  A Consolation (P) 107
BATES, KATHARINE LEE.
  Felices (P) 108
  Songs of the Future (P) 108
BAUDER, LEVI F.
  *Wait (P) 109
BAYLIS, SAMUEL M.
  Our Birthright (P) 109
BEERS, HENRY AUGUSTIN.
  Waiting for Winter (P) 110
  The Singer of One Song (P) 110
BENHAM, IDA WHIPPLE.
  The Scarlet Pimpernell (P) 111
BENJAMIN, PARK.
  New York Harbor (I) 111
BENSEL, JAMES BERRY.
  A Portrait (P) 112
BENTON, JOEL.
  Dahkota (I) 112
  At Chappaqua (I) 113
BLOEDE, GERTRUDE ("STUART STERNE").
  Transformation (P) 113
  Solitude (P) 114
  Silence (P) 114
BOKER, GEORGE HENRY.
  On a Threatened Invasion (P) 115
  Love Defended (P) 115
  To the Memory of M. A. R. (P) 116
  Love and Philosophy (P) 116
  The Tariff (P) 117
  To England. I. (P) 117
  To England. II. (P) 118
BONER, JOHN HENRY.
  Easter Advent (P) 118
  The Old Guard (P) 119
BOTTA, ANNE LYNCH.
  Vita Nuova (I) 119
  Largess (I) 120
  Unrest (I) 120

BOWKER, R. R.
　Thomas À Kempis (P) 121
BOYESEN, HJALMAR HJORTH.
　Evolution (I) 121
　The Lily (I) 122
　Prescience of Death (I) 122
BOYNTON, JULIA.
　Divided (P) 123
BRADLEY, MARY.
　To R. H. Stoddard (P) 123
BROTHERTON, ALICE WILLIAMS.
　Shakespeare (P) 124
BRUCE, WALLACE.
　A Star-eyed Daisy (I) 124
BRYANT, WILLIAM CULLEN.
　October (I) 125
　To Cole, the Painter, departing for Europe (I) 125
　Mutation (Sp) 126
BUEL, CLARENCE CLOUGH.
　Emerson (P) 126
　Poet and Actress (P) 127
BUNNER, H. C.
　A Poem in the Programme (P) 127
BURLEIGH, WILLIAM H.
　Rain (I) 128
"BURROUGHS, ELLEN." See JEWETT.
BURTON, RICHARD E.
　In a Library (P) 128
　The Poet (P) 129
　An Unpraised Picture (P) 129
BURTON, SARAH E.
　Longing (P) 130
BUTTS, MARY F.
　Homesickness (P) 130

CARRUTH, WILLIAM HERBERT.
　"O Grave, where is thy Victory?" (P) 131
CHADWICK, JOHN WHITE.
　"Why this Waste?" (P) 131
　The Hardest Lot (P) 132
　The King's Diary (P) 132
CHANLER, AMÉLIE RIVES. See RIVES.
CHANNING, WILLIAM ELLERY.
　The Day is Done (P) 133
　Hearts of Eternity (I) 133
CHENEY, JOHN VANCE.
　The Skillful Listener (P) 134
　Music (P) 134

CLARKE, SIMEON TUCKER.
  My Prayer (P) 135
CLYMER, ELLA DIETZ.
  Penelope (P) 135
COAN, TITUS MUNSON.
  * The Watch-fire (P) 136
COATES, FLORENCE EARLE.
  Morning (P) 136
  * Let me Believe (P) 137
  Sappho (P) 137
COLEMAN, CHARLES WASHINGTON.
  * Open Sesame (P) 138
  * Locality (P) 138
COLLIER, THOMAS S.
  Not Lost (P) 139
  Venus (P) 139
CONE, HELEN GRAY.
  The Torch-Race (P) 140
  On First Reading Landor's Hellenics (P) . . . 140
  Henry Wadsworth Longfellow (I) 141
  Ellen Terry's Beatrice (P) 141
  The Resolve (P) 142
COOKE, ROSE TERRY.
  Concerning Dead Love (I) 142
COOLBRITH, INA DONNA.
  Beside the Dead (I) 143
"COOLIDGE, SUSAN" (SARAH C. WOOLSEY).
  Tokens (I) (See Introduction) 143
CORNWELL, HENRY S.
  To the Katydid (P) 144
CRANCH, CHRISTOPHER PEARSE.
  Life and Death. I. (P) 144
  Life and Death. VIII. (P) 145
  Old Age. III. (P) 145
  The Lady's Sonnet (P) 146
CRANDALL, CHARLES H.
  Waiting (P) 146
  Adelaide Neilson (P) 147
CROSBY, MARGARET.
  Sappho to Phaon (I) 147
  The Phœnix (P) 148
CROSS, ALLEN E.
  To Emma Lazarus (P) 148
CURRAN, LULU.
  * A Vision of Night (P) 149
CURTIS, GEORGE WILLIAM.
  The Jersey Prison Ship (S) 149

DAVENPORT, JAMES PIERPONT.
 * To Julian M. Sturtevant, D. D. (P) 150
 * To A. B. Davenport (P) 150
DAVENPORT, WILLIAM C.
 The Judgment of Love (P) 151
 Beecher (P) 151
DAY, RICHARD EDWIN.
 Spain (P) 152
DAZEY, CHARLES T.
 The Poet's Art (P) 152
 Storm-Music (I) 153
DeKAY, CHARLES.
 Night on the River (P) 153
 The City Transfigured (I) 154
 Be thou My Sun (P) 154
 Her Apparition (I) 155
DENTON, FRANKLIN EVERT.
 Night Influence (P) 155
 Presage of Autumn (P) 156
DODGE, MARY MAPES.
 The Human Tie (I) 156
 The Stars (P) 157
 Over the World (P) 157
DORGAN, JOHN A.
 Life and Death (S) 158
DORR, JULIA C. R.
 Silence (P) 158
 Darkness (P) 159
 Mercédès (P) 159
 To-morrow. (P) 160
 Resurgamus (P) 160

EGAN, MAURICE FRANCIS.
 Maurice de Guérin (P) 161
 Of Flowers (P) 161
ELLET, ELIZABETH FRIES.
 The Good Shepherd (Sp) 162

FAWCETT EDGAR.
 Other Worlds (P) 162
 Bees (P) 163
 Sleep's Threshold (P) 163
 Earthquake (P) 164
 Victor Hugo Dead (P) 164
 Longfellow in Westminster Abbey (P) 165
 Transformation (G) 165
FEARING, LILLIAN BLANCHE.
 The Snow (P) 166

FELLOWES, CAROLINE WILDER.
  A Volume of Dante (P) 166
FIELDS, ANNIE ADAMS (MRS. J. T. FIELDS).
  Not Strand but Sea (I) 167
FORMAN, EMILY SHAW.
  Cactus (I) 167
  Golden Rod (P) 168
  The Cardinal Flower (I) 168
FOSTER, WILLIAM PRESCOTT.
  The Sea's Voice. I. (P) 169
  The Sea's Voice. II. (I) 169
  In November (P) 170
FULLER, MARGARET. See OSSOLI.

GARRISON, WENDELL PHILLIPS.
  The Vision of Abraham Lincoln (P) 170
  Post-Meridian. I. (P) 171
  Post-Meridian. II. (P) 171
GARRISON, WILLIAM LLOYD.
  Freedom of the Mind (S) 172
GATES, LEWIS E.
  The Silent Life (P) 172
GIBSON, WILLIAM.
  Pisa (P) 173
GILDER, JOSEPH B.
  Land and Sea (P) 173
GILDER, RICHARD WATSON.
  The Celestial Passion (S) 174
  Holy Land (P) 174
  Day unto Day (P) 175
  The Life-Mask of Lincoln (P) 175
  Weal and Woe (P) 176
  Call me not Dead (I) 176
GOODALE, DORA READ.
  Confession (P) 177
GOODALE, ELAINE.
  An Ice Storm (P) 177
GOODWIN, HENRY M.
  The Sistine Madonna (I) 178
GOODWIN, HOPESTILL.
  Love's Imagining (P) 178
GREENE, HOMER.
  Aphelion (I) 179
GUINEY, LOUISE IMOGEN.
  Winter Boughs (P) 179
  Sleep (P) 180
  April Desire (P) 180
  Twofold Service (P) 181
  Among the Flags (P) 181

HALL, ELIZA CALVERT.
  Her Choice (I) 182
  One Way of Love (P) 182
HAY, JOHN.
  In the Dim Chamber (P) 183
HAYNE, PAUL HAMILTON.
  The Poet's Mind (P) 183
  A Comparison (P) 184
  A Longing (P) 184
HEAVYSEGE, CHARLES.
  Winter Skies (S) 185
HENDERSON, WILLIAM J.
  Eve (P) 185
  The Wandering Jew (P) 186
"H. H." See JACKSON.
HIBBARD, GEORGE A.
  Terra Incognita (P) 186
HIGGINSON, THOMAS WENTWORTH.
  To Duty (P) 187
  Since Cleopatra Died (P) 187
  To the Memory of "H. H." (P) 188
HILLARD, KATHARINE.
  The Best Gift. I. (I) 188
  The Best Gift. II. (I) 189
HINCKLEY, ABBY S.
  Motherhood (P) 189
HOLLAND, JOSIAH GILBERT.
  Two Homes (P) 190
HOLMES, OLIVER WENDELL.
  "Songs in Many Keys" (Proem) (I) 190
  The Dead Singer (Longfellow) (P) 191
  Joseph Warren, M. D. (P) 191
  Harvard ("Veritas") (P) 192
HOUGHTON, GEORGE W. W.
  Columbus (P) 192
HOWELLS, WINIFRED.
  Past (I) 193
HUMPHREYS, COLONEL DAVID.
  The Soul (I) 193
HUNTINGTON, WILLIAM R.
  Tellus (P) 194
  George Zabriskie Gray (P) 194

INNSLEY, OWEN. See JENNISON.
IRELAND, MARY E.
  * Elysian Hours (P) 195
  * Sympathy (P) 195

JACKSON, HELEN HUNT.
  Ariadne's Farewell (P) 196
  Thought (P) 196
  Emigravit (P) 197
  Fame (P) 197
  October. I. (P) 198
  October. II. (P) 198
  The Victory of Patience (P) 199
JENNISON, LUCY W. ("OWEN INNSLEY").
  Communion (P) 199
  In a Letter (P) 200
  Whom He loveth He chasteneth (P) 200
JEWETT, SOPHIA ("ELLEN BURROUGHS").
  Separation (P) 201
JOHNSON, ROBERT UNDERWOOD.
  Noblesse Oblige (P) 201
  Amiel (P) 202
JONES, EDITH.
  St. Martin's Summer (P) 202
JONES, MARIA W.
  Paradise Regained (I) 203

KEESE, WILLIAM L.
  George Eliot (P) 203
KEMBLE, FRANCES ANNE.
  What is my Lady like? (I) 204
KENYON, JAMES BENJAMIN.
  A Sea Grave (P) 204
  Cleopatra to Antony (P) 205
  Romeo to Juliet (P) 205
KIMBALL, HARRIET MCEWEN.
  "He opened not his mouth" (P) 206
  To J. G. Whittier (P) 206
KING, EDWARD.
  Bulgarian ("War Contrasts") (I) 207
  Turk ("War Contrasts") (I) 207
KINNEY, ELIZABETH C.
  William Cullen Bryant (P) 208

LAIGHTON, ALBERT.
  Night (I) 208
LAMBORN, EMMA TAYLOR.
  In Weimar (I) 209
  Karnac (I) 209
LAMPMAN, ARCHIBALD.
  Outlook (I) 210
  A Prayer (P) 210
  Knowledge (I) 211

    The Railway Station (P) 211
    Midsummer Night (P) 212
LANIER, SIDNEY.
    The Mocking-Bird (P) 212
    Acknowledgment (S) 213
    In Absence (S) 213
    Laus Mariæ (S) 214
    The Harlequin of Dreams (P) 214
LARCOM, LUCY.
    The Wood-Thrush (P) 215
LATHROP, GEORGE PARSONS.
    In Absence (P) 215
    Immanent Imperfection (P) 216
LAWTON, WILLIAM C.
    In Athens (P) 216
LAYARD, NINA F.
    A Snow Sonnet (P) 217
LAZARUS, EMMA.
    The Taming of the Falcon (I) 217
    Sympathy (I) 218
    Venus of the Louvre (P) 218
    Life and Art (I) 219
    The New Colossus (P) 219
    Symphonic Study, The Undines' Dance (I) . . . 220
    The Sea of Life (I) 220
LEARNED, WALTER.
    To a Firefly (I) 221
LIPPMANN, JULIE M.
    Solace (P) 221
    Stone Walls (I) 222
LONGFELLOW, HENRY WADSWORTH.
    Charles Sumner (P) 222
    Washington Irving (P) 223
    The River of To-morrow (P) 223
    Giotto's Tower (P) 224
    Holidays (P) 224
    Possibilities (P) 225
    Nature (P) 225
LORD, AUGUSTUS M.
    * Aurea Mediocritas (I) 226
LOWELL, ANNA MARIA.
    Love in Winter (I) 226
LOWELL, JAMES RUSSELL.
    To Whittier (P) 227
    The Spiritual in the Real (S) 227
    The Eye's Treasury (P) 228
    To Jeffries Wyman (P) 228
    Bon Voyage! (P) 229

With an Armchair (P) 229
To Miss D. T. (P) 230
LÜDERS, CHARLES HENRY.
   Egypt (P) 230
   The Haunts of the Halcyon (P) 231
LUNT, ANN PARSONS.
   Minot's Light (I) 231
LUNT, GEORGE.
   The Philosophers (I) 232

MACE, FRANCES LAUGHTON.
   Alcyone. I. (P) 232
   Alcyone. II. (P) 233
   Alcyone. III. (P) 233
   St. Cecilia (P) 234
MARKHAM, CHARLES EDWIN.
   The Cricket (I) 234
   Love's Vigil (P) 235
   In High Sierras (P) 235
MARSH, JULIET C.
   The Pines' Thought (I) 236
MASON, CAROLINE A.
   May (P) 236
   June (P) 237
MASON, MARIE.
   "That Lass o' Lowrie's" (P) 237
MASSEY, SUSANNA.
   The Rival of the Roses (P) 238
MATTHEWS, JAMES NEWTON.
   October (P) 238
   Death — What is it? (P) 239
MAY, CAROLINE.
   Early Morn (P) 239
   Patience (I) 240
MCKAY, JAMES T.
   The Thunder Cloud (P) 240
   The Whispering Gallery (P) 241
MCKENZIE, WILLIAM P.
   Sorrow (P) 241
MELLISH, JOHN H.
   * Sonnet and Acrostic (P) 242
MITCHELL, LANGDON ELWYN.
   Decoration Day (I) 242
   Love Deathless (S) 243
   Natural Nuptials (S) 243
MONROE, HARRIET.
   With a Copy of Shelley (P) 244

MORRIS, HARRISON S.
  To Poverty (I) 244
  A Greek Panel (P) 245
  Homer (I) 245
MORSE, JAMES HERBERT.
  Friends (P) 246
  Sense (P) 246
  H. W. Longfellow (P) 247
  Immortality (P) 247
MOULTON, LOUISE CHANDLER.
  The Last Good-bye (I) 248
  A Cry (P) 248
  Sister Sorrow (P) 249

NOYES, CHARLES ("CHARLES QUIET").
  Comfort (I) 249

O'DONNELL, JESSIE F.
  Reflections (P) 250
OSSOLI, MARGARET FULLER.
  Orpheus (S) 250

PARKER, THEODORE.
  The Life, the Truth, the Way (S) 251
  * The Pilgrim's Star (I) 251
PARSONS, THOMAS WILLIAM.
  To a Poet in the City (I) 252
PECK, SAMUEL MINTURN.
  Sleep (S) 252
PERCIVAL, JAMES GATES.
  My Love (P) 253
  Night (I) 253
PERRY, LILLA CABOT.
  In Answer to a Sonnet (P) 254
PIATT, JOHN J.
  Abraham Lincoln (P) 254
PINNEY, NORMAN.
  The Return (I) 255
POE, EDGAR ALLAN.
  To Science (Sp) 255
PONTE, DA, C. E.
  A Lover's Sonnet (P) 256
POWERS, HORATIO NELSON.
  To Robert Collyer (P) 256
PRESTON, MARGARET J.
  The Cathedral (P) 257
  "Conviva Satur" (P) 257
  "Sit, Jessica" (P) 258

Hawthorne (P) 258
"Philip My King" (P) 259

REALF, RICHARD.
  The Spirit of Nature (I) 259
  Discord (I) 260
REESE, L. WOODWORTH.
  Tell Me Some Way (P) 260
RICHARDS, WILLIAM C.
  Monosyllables (P) 261
RICKETSON, DANIEL.
  To R. W. Emerson (I) 261
RILEY, JAMES WHITCOMB.
  When She comes Home (P) 262
RIVES, AMÉLIE (MRS. CHANLER).
  Surrender (I) 262
ROBERTS, CHARLES G. D.
  Midwinter Thaw (P) 263
  The Potato Harvest (P) 263
  The Cow Pasture (P) 264
ROBINSON, FANNY RUTH.
  * Love's Sovereignty (P) 264
  An Order for a Cameo (I) 265
ROBINSON, HARRIET H.
  The Thyme-Leaved Sandwort (P) 265
RUBLE, ZULEMA A.
  * The Infinite Curve (P) 266

SALTUS, FRANCIS SALTUS.
  Originality (P) 266
  The Bayadere (P) 267
SANBORN, F. B.
  Pilgrim Love (I) 267
  The Gentle Heart (I) 268
  Hampton Beach (S) 268
SARGENT, EPES.
  The Planet Jupiter (S) 269
SAVAGE, MINOT J.
  The Mystic Hope (P) 269
  * Her Eyes (P) 270
  Ralph Waldo Emerson (P) 270
SAXE, JOHN G.
  Love's Sovereignty (P) 271
  Mnemosyne (P) 271
SAXTON, ANDREW B.
  Midsummer (P) 272
  The Overflowing Cup (P) 272

SCOLLARD, CLINTON.
  Pomona (P) 273
  Memnon (P) 273
  Wild Coreopsis (P) 274
SCOTT, JOHN M.
  * The Human Love Divine (S) 274
  A Marsh Melody (P) 275
SHERMAN, FRANK DEMPSTER.
  A Butterfly in Wall Street (P) 275
SILL, EDWARD ROWLAND.
  Recall (P) 276
  Quem Metui Moritura (P) 276
  Her Explanation (P) 277
SMITH, ELIZABETH OAKES.
  Charity, Not Justice (P) 277
SNOW, FLORENCE L.
  Victor Hugo (P) 278
SPALDING, SUSAN M.
  Dear Hands (P) 278
  A Desire (P) 279
STEDMAN, EDMUND CLARENCE.
  A Mother's Picture (P) 279
  Hope Deferred (I) 280
  To Bayard Taylor (P) 280
STOCKARD, HENRY J.
  * Indian Summer (P) 281
  Do You Remember? (P) 281
STODDARD, RICHARD HENRY.
  Abraham Lincoln (S) 282
  To Edmund Clarence Stedman (P) 282
  To Bayard Taylor (P) . . , ... 283
  To the Memory of Keats (S) 283
  To Mary Bradley (I) 284
STORY, W. W.
  Little We Know what Secret Influence (P) 284
  After Long Days of Dull Perpetual Rain (P) 285

TAIT, JOHN R.
  Poets (I) 285
TAYLOR, BAYARD.
  Nubia (I) 286
  To a Persian Boy (I) 286
  A Wedding Sonnet (P) 287
  From the North (P) 287
  To E. C. S. (P) 288
THAXTER, CELIA.
  Beethoven (I) 288
  Mozart (I) 289

Modjeska (I) 289
The Sounding Sea (I) 290
THAYER, JULIA H.
Respice Finem (P) 290
THAYER, STEPHEN HENRY.
Heart of Gold (P) 291
Greeting (P) 291
Betrothed (P) 292
THOMAS, EDITH M.
The Fountains of The Rain (P) 292
Frost (P) 293
A Sonnet on a Sonnet (P) 293
A Revenge (P) 294
The Return to Nature (P) 294
THOMPSON, MAURICE.
Aphrodite (I) 295
Eros (I) 295
TILTON, THEODORE.
The Dead Poet (I) 296
TIMROD, HENRY.
If Life were all Love (I) 296
Elusive Nature (I) 297
TOWNSEND, JAMES B.
To Ellen Terry as " Beatrice " (I) 297
TROWBRIDGE, JOHN TOWNSEND.
Providence (P) 298
TUCKERMAN, HENRY THEODORE.
Love Sonnet (S) 298
To One Deceived (S) 299
TYRRELL, HENRY.
To a Debutante (P) 299
Idylls (P) 300

VERY, JONES.
Enoch (S) 300
Thy Beauty Fades (S) 301
Labor and Rest (S) 301
The Frost (S) 302
The Invitation (S) 302

WALSH, HENRY C.
Love's Gold (P) 303
WASSON, DAVID ATWOOD.
Love against Love (S) 303
Royalty (I) 304
Defiance (S) 304
WEBB, CHARLES HENRY (" JOHN PAUL ").
" Last Night in Blue My Little Love was dressed " (P) . . 305

WEEKS, ROBERT KELLEY.
　By the Brook (I) 305
　In the Meadow (I) 306
WHITING, CHARLES GOODRICH.
　Shakespeare (P) 306
WHITTIER, JOHN GREENLEAF.
　Bayard Taylor. I. (I) 307
　Bayard Taylor. II. (I) 307
　Forgiveness (I) 308
　Adjustment. I. (I) 308
　Adjustment. II. (I) 309
WILCOX, ELLA WHEELER.
　Friendship after Love (P) 309
　The Saddest Hour (I) 310
WILDE, RICHARD HENRY.
　To the Mocking Bird (I) 310
WILKINSON, WILLIAM C.
　My Open Polar Sea. I. (P) 311
　My Open Polar Sea. II. (P) 311
WILLIAMS, FRANCIS HOWARD.
　Decoration Day (P) 312
　An Early-April Morning (P) 312
　Earth and Night (P) 313
WILLIS, NATHANIEL PARKER.
　Evening Glow (I) 313
　Acrostic Sonnet (I) 314
WILSON, ROBERT BURNS.
　Sunrise (P) 314
WOODBERRY, GEORGE E.
　At Gibraltar. I. (P) 315
　At Gibraltar. II. (P) 315
WOOLSEY, SARAH CHAUNCEY. See "COOLIDGE."

RECAPITULATION.

　Petrarcan Sonnets 304
　Shakespearian Sonnets 30
　Irregular Sonnets 108
　Spenserian Sonnets 2
　Guittonian Sonnets 1
　　Total 445

REPRESENTATIVE SONNETS.

THE SONNET.

ONE must needs be in a rarely appreciative mood fully to enjoy the privilege of listening to an old violin that bears the autograph inscription of Antonius Stradivarius, knowing that the legend, *Faciebat Anno 1720*, is a true one, and that the soul of music embodied by the genius of Cremona has since been wooed and won by a Paganini or an Ole Bull. There are times when one is not attuned to the full appreciation of choice old ware of any sort; but again we become enthusiastic connoisseurs, and can almost worship through the medium of an old missal or miniature. In this latter spirit one should approach the consideration of a gem in the domain of literature which has outlasted seven centuries, and has glowed with the choicest thoughts of such souls as Dante and Shakespeare, Milton and Wordsworth, by the chrism of whose genius its hope of immortality may be as well founded as almost any emanation of the human mind.

There must be unusual strength and excellence in the artistic structure of the sonnet to give it an endurance, which, for so intricate and elaborate a form, is unparalleled in literature. The lays of minnesingers and troubadours, the eddas of the North, the ballad, the improvisations of the Celtic minstrel to the twanging of his harp, — hymn and psalm and war-song, — have all left their impress on literature. But for preserving its own form and spirit, and retaining its popularity with readers and writers of to-day, the staunch-built little sonnet outsails all the literary craft of time. One feels like substituting the name of Petrarch in Aldrich's happy couplet: —

"What mighty epics have been wrecked by time
Since Herrick launched his cockle-shells of rhyme!"

The large number of fantastic conceits in the line of short poems, which have long ago foundered, only emphasizes the sea-going qualities of the sonnet. As for Herrick, he did not write sonnets, finding his debonair muse better suited with a shorter stanza and livelier line. But the most confirmed sonneteer will not think any less of Herrick for choosing to do what he could do best.

The "fourteen facets" of the sonnet touch so many points of sympathy, and throw out such alluring rays into all the regions of history, biography, language, and poetic lore, that one is tempted to digress. In the works of Tasso will be found a whole lecture devoted to the consideration of a single sonnet by Casa, a poetic successor of Petrarch, the typical sonneteer of Italy. One can imagine that one of the rhymed texts by later and greater sonneteers might easily furnish an hour of profitable elucidation. It is apparent, then, that we cannot pursue our subject to the limits of its interest and yet complete a comprehensive glance at the sonnet's character and development within the few pages at our command.

It should be stated at the outset, and afterward borne in mind, that the peculiar form of poem under consideration is a product of a remote time and land. Could one be transported to Italy, and the last six centuries be restored to future time, the sonnet might be heard as a snatch of song, sentimental, witty, or amorous, trolled by dusky Neapolitans or Florentines for the amusement of themselves, or their loves or lovers. It is this ancient relic of melody, recalling by its chiming rhymes the throb of its old companions, stringed instruments, which forms the present study. As we glance over its history, world-renowned names, varying ages and literatures, poems lofty, exquisite, tender, will rise before us to demonstrate that the sonnet is a word to conjure with.

Let the novice, if there be such, first form a sympathetic acquaintance with the sonnet, and afterward he will feel the greater interest in tracing its career. To acquire this appreciation, there is no better mode than that of a friendly introduction to a sonnet, such as this one by Longfellow, the acknowledged master among American poets of this style of stanza: —

A SUMMER DAY BY THE SEA.

The sun is set, and in his latest beams
  Yon little cloud of ashen gray and gold,
  Slowly upon the amber air unrolled,
The falling mantle of the Prophet seems.
From the dim headlands many a lighthouse gleams,
  The street lamps of the ocean; and behold
  O'erhead the banners of the night unfold;
The day hath passed into the land of dreams.

> O summer day beside the joyous sea!
> O summer day, so wonderful and white,
>   So full of gladness and so full of pain!
> Forever and forever shalt thou be
> To some the gravestone of a dead delight,
>   To some the landmark of a new domain.

It will be seen at once that this lovely little poem has fourteen lines; that it is written in iambic pentameter, or ten-syllable verse, the accent falling on the second and each alternate syllable. Next it will be noted that the first eight lines have but two rhymes, the first, fourth, fifth, and eighth rhyming together; while the second, third, sixth and seventh lines iterate and reiterate the other rhyme. So far, all the distinctions noted are absolutely necessary to the formation of a true sonnet,— that is, the Petrarcan type. The arrangement of the rhymes in the sestet, or last six lines, is often varied, and almost any arrangement is now accepted, and the poem called a sonnet, if the octave, or first eight lines, be only in proper form. This looseness of requirement that is tolerated regarding the sestet is a serious mistake, however, and has led to the deterioration of many sonnets. The arrangement of rhymes in the sestet of the sonnet quoted is to be preferred, because most symmetrical and subtly musical as a balance to the octave. That it is the favorite arrangement with an artist like Longfellow, appearing in most of his best sonnets, is alone a strong indorsement. But it may be added that it is one of the oldest arrangements. The rhymes, it will be seen, rhyme in tercets, as,— one, two, three; one, two, three. This forms an echo-like repetition of sounds, just indistinct enough in nowise to obtrude on the thought, which here in the sestet should be at its height, alluring the reader by some half-seen suggestion toward the full idea of the writer, which is, in the last line, to flood the whole path with a transfiguring light. This delicate rhyme-repetition should strike on the reader as bird-notes in the tree-tops do on a rapt and eager traveler.

Another musical, as well as frequent, arrangement of the sestet is to have but two rhymes, rhyming interwoven couplets, as, — one, two; one, two; one, two. Still another form of the sestet is to write the first four lines as an alternate-rhymed quatrain, like a stanza of "Gray's Elegy," and to make the last two lines an independent-rhyming couplet. This style cannot be highly recommended, as the quatrain and couplet jar on the reader after becoming accustomed to the Petrarcan style of the octave; while the two changes in rhyme-arrangement in the sestet give an unpleasant surprise. The rhyming couplet also has the effect of isolating the last two lines, they having no rhyme connection with the rest, while they give so undeserved an emphasis to the last two rhyme-words that it obtrudes on the thought, or at least unpleasantly intrudes the mechanism of the verse. If any further objection need be made to this style of sestet, it is that the favorite way of describing the effect of the last two lines is to say, as many writers have, that it "clinches" the sonnet. Certainly one wants no "clinching" about a poem, if it is to be poetical.

Still another way of writing the sestet is to

write the first four lines as a Petrarcan quatrain, the first rhyming with the fourth, second with third, the two last as a couplet. This seems, if anything, still more objectionable. The Petrarcan quatrain has done full duty in the first eight lines, and to continue it is to make it monotonous, and detract from the beauty of the octave by the repetition.

For any who like to give "infinite variety" when writing the sestet, it may be stated that there are eighteen different ways in which it may be arranged with the two or the three rhymes. Dante Gabriel Rossetti is said to have preferred the rhymes of the sestet in the following order, when it could be fortunately contrived so as not to hamper the thought; namely, one, two; two, one; two, one. This gives something of the "dying fall" effect. One of the faintest of rhyme-values is obtained by writing the sestet with rhymes as follows: one, two, three; three, two, one. But there is risk in expecting much value from rhyme-words separated by more than three lines, unless the same rhyme is continued otherwise, and given a cumulative effect. The eighteen possible rhyme arrangements of the sestet, allowing that no terminal lacks its fellow rhyme-word, may be easily worked out or noted in the examples in this book. It may be remarked that the most of these irregular arrangements are of doubtful value, and they should only be adopted by writers when the rhyme exigencies demand it, and when the unusual strength of lines so arranged atone for the irregularity. A single strong objection to irregularity in the sestet is that it disappoints one who is accustomed to expect one of the few favorite arrangements, and causes one instinctively and apprehensively to "feel his way" for the rhyme when he should have all his attention concentrated on the essential thought. Such sestets are often productive of unsupported couplets and far-sundered rhyme-words, which operate against the symmetrical unity characteristic of a model sonnet. It may be said that, without a rhythmical order or musical arrangement of the succession of rhymes, the latter lose half their value.

When we remember that we are considering the national type of poem of a most musical, artistic, and poetic people, it seems absurd to suppose that at this late day we can better the sonnet structure. Guittone, who wrote in the thirteenth century the first regular Italian sonnets, perfected it; for, though most of his sonnets have the octave with lines rhyming alternately on two rhymes, he also wrote a number with the regular arrangement, current to-day, and successively indorsed by the practice of Dante, Petrarch, Milton, and Wordsworth. It is only natural that a form that was educed by the aid of the mandolin and lute, to which sonnets were sung in Italy, should be as harmoniously perfect as possible.

Having mastered the rhyme requirements of the sonnet, and learned their preferred arrangement, let us see what else is necessary to a good sonnet. Certainly (as regards form), good, strong, flexible, rightly-accentuated iambic pentameter verse is indispensable. In the sonnet, especially in the octave, it is a great beauty to have a strong movement to the lines; no feeling the way or undue compression, inversion, or ellipsis, but a sure movement and a prompt response of the rhyme-word, such as a bell gives to the bellman's rope. Note Longfellow's sonnet on "Possibilities," and see how the rhymes jump to their places, and the word "strong" rings in at the end of the octave as if it had been held all the while in reserve, waiting at the full-stretched power of the bowstring! Such a sonnet seems to make its own music by its rushing movement. Fertile, sonorous rhymes are therefore to be chosen, and they should not repeat the same vowel-sound, either in the octave or sestet. How many times a sonneteer has purposed to write a regularly formed sonnet, but has run out of rhyme-words, and put in an extra rhyme at the end of the sixth and seventh lines! Then the poor eighth line rhyme limps in like a lost sheep looking for its fellows of the first quatrain, from which it is separated by two strangers. A feminine rhyme, or dissyllabic terminal, is often a beauty when rightly treated and supported by vigorous lines; and it is the usual one in the musical sonnets of Italian literature, where even trisyllabic rhymes are common. For excellent examples of sonnets with feminine rhymes, see Longfellow's "River of To-morrow," Mr. Tyrrell's "Idylls," or Mrs. Arnold's "Penitence."

And while on the subject of rhyme, can we not find in it alone a secret of the sonnet's power? Let the rhymes of Longfellow's sonnet, "A Summer Day by the Sea," be separated and considered alone. Pronounce the words: " beams — gold-rolled — seems — gleams — hold — fold — dreams — sea — white — pain — be — light — main." Is there not the germ of music in them, borrowed from the old Italian mandolins; a chiming iteration and reiteration in the octave, then an echo-like repetition of sound in the sestet? If one repeats the words again and again, he will be apt unconsciously to give each rhyme a musical note, making, perhaps, the second rhyme in the octave a note considerably higher on the scale than the first. In the sestet, three other notes may be given to the rhymes at harmonic intervals, in an ascending or descending scale. Step to the piano and select notes to correspond with them, and it will be found to produce as pleasant a bit of sound-arrangement as can well be produced with so few strokes on so few notes. It will be noticed also that only three or four of the preferred orders of rhyme in the sestet preserve any semblance to melody when put to this test.

Fully believing that poetry is one thing and music another, we perceive they yet pervade each other so that no one can say where the influence of one on the other stops. Sidney Lanier has made the most exhaustive study of this subtle correspondence in his "Science of Verse," but probably he did not fully apprehend the relationship, nor could he make others fully understand it. It is just as well, perhaps, that the musical value of words and the musical notation of language in poetry should remain unanalyzed, an elusive secret, felt rather than known. This we do know, that the greatest poets put a singing quality in their verse; that it is this language-music, combined with great thought, that makes great poems; and that the "inner beauty of the line" is as charming in its way as the inner beauty of the thought itself.

Aside from its rhyme arrangement, the sonnet might be written as simply fourteen lines of blank verse, excepting of course the usual break between octave and sestet and the occasional *volte* or cæsura in the middle of the sestet, at the end of the eleventh line. In its rhyme arrangement, therefore, is its vitality and individuality, the chime-music that Francesca Petrarca set ringing for all time! Yet dissatisfied poets will persist in tampering with this time-tested form of the sonnet.

But the sonnet has a fortunate construction in other respects. It is dignified, owing to its ten-syllable verse, and is well suited to convey either religious, philosophical, or amatory thought. Its length is happily prescribed, since it gives ample room to frame the picture of one impassioned thought, and throw, in the sestet, a side-light of suggestion or higher application thereon. As Leigh Hunt says, the fourteen lines are "not a rule without a reason, but a harmonious necessity."

I am tempted here to quote from a correspondent — Mr. W. C. Lawton — a clever characterization of the sonnet's scope and power: "In the few and rare occasions when versification seems a necessity, the intellectual and mechanical effort required to mould one's thoughts into so elaborate a form seems to exorcise a haunting fancy more thoroughly and finally than any other process."

Henry Timrod, who wrote well in the sonnet as well as about it, says: "The sonnet is often called artificial, but it is so only as all verse is artificial. Its very restriction, by its brevity, forces the artist to condensation, which the artist knows is an advantage. The whole power of a poet has sometimes been exemplified within its narrow bounds as completely as within the compass of an epic!"

This is a strong argument for the sonnet in these busy days. Who wishes to read a long, attenuated poem to get no more poetry that Longfellow puts in a single sonnet?

Any one must notice, in reading a collection of choice sonnets, the number of lines which have become familiar by quotation, and which demonstrate that living poetry can be cast in the sonnet's intricate form as well as in simpler stanzas. The late George H. Boker, a most enthusiastic and extensive writer of the sonnet, put such warm praise of it in a recent letter as must please all lovers of the poem. He writes: —

"It is a satisfaction to me to notice that the literary men of this country are at length doing at least partial justice to that wonderful little poem, the sonnet. Wonderful it certainly is, in its best specimens, and it fills a place in poetry which can be occupied by no other poem, whether in form or spirit."

The sonnet, naturally, when most closely adapted to the Petrarcan form, is a double poem; a picture and a reflection, a song and an echo. That is what its structure especially suits, though beautiful poems are written in its lines without showing but one side to the thought, — merely direct delineation of idea. A great many of the finest sonnets, however, are in the nature of syllogisms, elaborated similes, or metaphors. In the octave, the outline of the idea, the main lines or framework, are worked out with ever so dainty and sure an art; every word and its position, every rhyme and its order, carefully (or by the fortunate impulse that outstrips care) weighed, and adjusted to the best result. There should be utmost clearness of outline, and yet a fine reserve of the central inspiration. The rhyme-words should grow rather than decrease in value, and help, not hinder, the movement and thought.

Whether or not there should be a break in the grammatical construction and the flow of thought between the octave and sestet, must depend on the poem and the scheme of it. The "Miltonic" sonnet, so called, carries thought and language, at least grammatical connection, from octave to sestet without break; but where this calls for evident effort the dragging of a few words across the gap only breaks rhythm and arrests the interest. As a rule, the Petrarcan idea of a break at the end of the eighth line seems a happy one, particularly where the poem takes the nature of a syllogism, or the treatment of the thought changes from a lower to a higher plane.

It is easier to write a good octave than a good sestet. One may have to crowd his thought to get it all in at the last six lines, or he may have run out of his best material and have to put in inferior work. Either produces a bad effect, for it is necessary that the sestet be especially dignified, adequate, and sustained,—in short the culmination of the sonnet. Poetically, the sestet should at least balance in value the eight lines preceding. It should sustain the interest to the last line and word, and if the last line or word is the key to the whole poem, so much the better. Suggestion is better than a didactic style in the sestet; and the effect at the close should be as if one had heard music played by unseen fingers, or seen the veil lifted from a masterpiece of painting or sculpture, without catching a glimpse of the hand that did it; as if a window had suddenly opened for us, and we looked out on a lovely, never-dreamed-of landscape, —

"Swelling loudly up to its climax and then dying proudly."

The first, eighth, and last lines of a sonnet should be especially strong ones. They give not only an appearance of ripe design, but real strength, binding it and making it memorable. They are main beams in the structure. The Italian sonneteers often make a break or *volte* at the end of the third line in the sestet, and musically it is of value, especially where the "one, two, three, one, two, three," order of rhymes is used. A rhyme-word should be a word of value, of force of meaning and sound, as its position gives it a double emphasis, and the rhymes in octave and sestet should offer pleasing contrasts of sound. It should not be forgotten that unity is essential to the sonnet. A single thought, well worked out, will fill its little limits, and be far better than dividing the attention by numerous unrelated images or ideas. It is unity that makes the sonnet memorable. The desirability of climax is emphasized by Petrarch, who says the thought " should be borne in on the reader at the close." This need not lead to any baldness of epigrammatic statement; such would be unpoetical. Leigh Hunt, also, states that the close should be "equally impressive and unaffected." Grammatical inversions are somersaults of construction which always hinder the flow of thought, cumber the mind, and are most mischievous when they allow of two interpretations of the meaning.

Of minor defects in sonnet structure may be instanced a sequence of small, weak words in a line, or a multiplicity of ponderous ones; a too great number of grammatical breaks, which necessitate numerous dashes, semicolons, colons, or periods, especially in the middle of the line, where they detract from the rhyme values. Not but that an occasional break in a line is a relief, and often helps instead of hinders musical effect. In short, the rules of versification should be observed in the sonnet with special care, as a defect shows all the more plainly in so short a poem.

While all these small points should be observed where possible, it is true that many of the best sonnets contain one or more such faults. One has to make the most of his material, and not sacrifice his thought to correct a minor defect in form. It would not do to change the form of a statue for the sake of cutting out a minute flaw. And yet, by selecting new rhymes and working a rearrangement, one sometimes will even improve on his own ideal. Several writers on the sonnet have formulated a number of rules for writing the poem. The essence of those rules has been given in what has preceded, and to put them in a category seems too much like invading the domain of mechanics, and inviting an increase of the class of sonnets which are written by rule and not by inspiration. If the reader can gather herein a sympathy with the character of the sonnet, and familiarity with its forms, as he proceeds, he need not look up a list of rules in order to detect a true sonnet, nor consult a category of recipes in order to write a sonnet, should he have the inspiration and versifying talent which should precede the task.

Leigh Hunt has put one of the fundamental requirements of the sonnet in excellent shape. He says: "The student is to bear in mind that the music of the lines is to be at once as sweet and as strong and as varied as possible, and that there should be something of a difference discernible in the major and minor portions, as there is in the divisions of music so called, or in the two strains of an air or melody." A good sonnet can be well described as *luminous:* the thought shines out, it has life and movement and proclaims its right to exist.

It must be admitted that it is more pleasant to study poetry through object-lessons than by fine-spun theories. These notes from the sonnet-lute will tell in music all that we have been laboriously learning; the place of honor being given to Wordsworth's familiar but mighty composition: —

THE SONNET.

Scorn not the sonnet. Critic, you have frowned,
  Mindless of its just honors. With this key
  Shakespeare unlocked his heart; the melody
Of this small lute gave ease to Petrarch's wound;

A thousand times this pipe did Tasso sound;
  With it Camoens soothed an exile's grief;
  The sonnet glittered a gay myrtle-leaf
Amid the cypress with which Dante crowned
His visionary brow; a glow-worm lamp,
  It cheered mild Spenser, called from Fairyland
To struggle through dark ways; and when a damp
  Fell round the path of Milton, in his hand
The thing became a trumpet, whence he blew
Soul-animating strains, — alas! too few.

This sonnet on the sonnet by Mr. Gilder would be charming as a poem, even if it were not full of suggestive ideas of the sonnet, closing as it does with a fine description of Nature in the last line : —

A SONNET ON THE SONNET.

WHAT is a sonnet? 'T is the pearly shell
  That murmurs of the far-off murmuring sea;
  A precious jewel carved most curiously;
It is a little picture painted well.
What is a sonnet? 'T is the tear that fell
  From a great poet's hidden ecstasy;
  A two-edged sword, a star, a song — ah me!
Sometimes a heavy-tolling funeral bell.
This was the flame that shook with Dante's breath;
  The solemn organ whereon Milton played,
  And the clear glass where Shakespeare's shadow falls:
A sea this is, — beware who ventureth!
  For like a fjord the narrow floor is laid
  Mid-ocean deep to the sheer mountain walls.

Another American sonneteer, — a lady of whom it has been said that "the sonnet is her native language," — Mrs. Dorr, has shown how the sonnet should be regarded by the critic, and how by the poet, as follows : —

THE SONNET.

I. TO A CRITIC.

"It is but cunning artifice," you say?
    "To it no throb of nature answereth?
    It hath no living pulse, no vital breath,
This puppet, fashioned in an elder day,
    Through whose strait lips no heart can cry or pray?"
    O deaf and blind of soul, these words that saith!
    If that thine ear is dull, what hindereth
That quicker ears should hear the bugles play

And the trump call to battle? Since the stars
    First sang together, and the exulting skies
        Thrilled to their music, earth hath never heard,
Above the tumult of her worldly jars,
    Or loftier songs or prayers than those that rise
        Where the high sonnet soareth like a bird!

II. TO A POET.

Thou who wouldst wake the sonnet's silver lyre,
    Make thine hands clean! Then, as on eagle's wings,
    Above the soiling touch of sordid things,
Bid thy soul soar till, mounting high and higher,
It feels the glow of pure celestial fire,
    Bathes in clear light, and hears the song that rings
    Through heaven's high arches when some angel brings
Gifts to the Throne, on wings that never tire!

It hath a subtile music, strangely sweet,
    Yet all unmeet for dance or roundelay,
        Or idle love that fadeth like a flower:
It is the voice of hearts that strongly beat,
    The cry of souls that grandly love and pray,
        The trumpet-peal that thrills the battle-hour!

This graceful object-lesson in sonnetry must also be included, though we borrow it from across the sea, and from an eminent sonnet-writer, now still further "Beyond Sea" —

THE SONNET.

A SONNET is a moment's monument, —
  Memorial from the soul's eternity
  To one dead, deathless hour. Look that it be,
Whether for lustral rite or dire portent,
Of its own arduous fullness reverent;
  Carve it in ivory or in ebony,
  As Day or Night may rule; and let Time see
Its flowering crest impearled and orient.

A sonnet is a coin: its face reveals
  The soul, — its converse to what Power 't is due, —
Whether for tribute to the august appeals
Of Life, or dower in Love's high retinue,
It serve; or, 'mid the dark wharf's cavernous breath,
In Charon's palm it pay the toll to Death.
                  DANTE GABRIEL ROSSETTI.

This may be the best place to insert Mr. Aldrich's poetic philosophy, which applies very well to sonnet-writing, and, once read, should be always remembered: —

ENAMORED ARCHITECT OF AIRY RHYME.

ENAMORED architect of airy rhyme,
  Build as thou wilt; heed not what each man says.
  Good souls, but innocent of dreamers' ways,
Will come, and marvel why thou wastest time;
Others, beholding how thy turrets climb
  'Twixt theirs and heaven, will hate thee all their days;
  But most beware of those who come to praise.
O Wondersmith, O worker in sublime

And heaven-sent dreams, let art be all in all;
    Build as thou wilt, unspoiled by praise or blame,
    Build as thou wilt, and as thy light is given:
Then, if at last the airy structure fall,
    Dissolve, and vanish, take thyself no shame.
    They fail, and they alone, who have not striven.

Perhaps the following sonnet is also pertinent to the poet's art, and it is put in as a counter-weight to so much technical lore which has preceded. As it is written in deprecation of too laborious verse-making, — that which may embody form, but, forgetting the aim of art, does not preserve the spirit, — it may be tolerated in the loose, easy quatrains of the Shakespearean model: —

THE SINGING THOUGHT.

It is the Thought that, like a bird, doth sing, —
    So ran the fancy of an earlier song, —
The words are but the gilded wires that ring
    Around the spirit-voice to hold it strong,
And keep it within sound of human ears;
    Yet some upon their verse so long have wrought,
The singing voice within one never hears,
    Because the cage hath hushed the captive Thought.

Were it not better far that we should weave
    Our lines so light, like fretted work of frost,
The soul within might never think to grieve,
    But sing out bold, in fancied freedom lost?
So that the song but help a single heart,
The world beside may criticise the art!

These poets, it is seen, do not exalt the form of poetry above its spirit, even in so intricate a poem as the sonnet. Nor is it any more incumbent on the poet to write a sonnet in a masterly manner than it is to form a simple couplet or quatrain in the best possible way. Poetry is an art that crowns at the last nothing but the highest workmanship, and the only sure test for immortality in a poem is, that it shall put a truly precious thought in a form that has never been and never can be surpassed. The sonnets, the poems, that live prove this true. In this line, then, runs the true development of the sonnet; not in a change of form, but in an enlargement of its original scope. This book alone will show what varied chords of love, joy, grief, patience, hope, faith, worship, prayer, — what divers notes from nature — may be struck on the instrument. One can hardly define that mystic form and quality of thought which has been termed "adequate sonnet-motive." But as the sonnet is a form of great dignity and artistic compass, it would be well not to task it with any theme that is not deeply felt, intrinsically beautiful, or of a lofty and precious significance. Fortunate for the sonnet if all three qualities are present!

> Be sure your song is from the heart,
> Not every theme is worth your art!
> Seems, then, your subject worthy still?
> Then give it nought but finest skill.

There is, indeed, a small class of objectors who maintain that the sonnet (*i. e.*, the Petrarcan type) does not take kindly to the English tongue. They hold that because we cannot reproduce the liquid, wave-like words and the dulcet, dissyllabic and trisyllabic rhymes of the Italian serenader we should let the sonnet alone, leave it to the land of its origin.

It is readily admitted that we cannot in the English tongue reproduce the native tone and coloring which make the sonnet most at home in the country of its birth. But the argument that would prevent our borrowing the scheme of its construction and melody, its form and scope, would prevent the writing of English poetry at all. The sonnet has an inner music. It matters not greatly whether we hear the "Trovatore" sung in the Italian or English words, so we hear the melodies that perpetuate the soul of the composer. We may not be able to translate Heine satisfactorily, though it has been nearly accomplished, but that does not prevent enjoyment from many of his translated poems, nor does it furnish the least reason why an English writer may not write in Heine's stanzas. And we have the same right to the Italian forms of composition. No one can deny that as great sonnets have been written in English as in Italian. The best of Dante, Michael Angelo, Tasso, Petrarch, are no more than worthy to be compared with the best of Milton, Wordsworth, Keats, Mrs. Browning, or Longfellow. It is apparently with some a pet habit to lament the limitations of the tongue that Shakespeare spoke. There is a music of the pine as well as of the palm. The rugged melodies of the wind-struck harp of the forest, which are latent in the Anglo-Saxon tongue, should not be so neglected that we must needs satisfy our *ennui* by the languorous cadences of a language spoken where the air merely pulses on the terraced vineyards, or is gently heaved in slumber on the Mediterranean.

The writers of English may not improve the

sonnet's structure or melody, nor may they equal the charm as a serenade or love-song which it bears in the Italian. But as an expression of the loftiest thought, has not its usefulness been extended, if not enlarged? If its tone be not quite as mellow as in its old home, has not the instrument thrilled to inspirations that it would never have known in its native air?

Our acknowledgment of our debt to Italy for the origin of the sonnet must be frank and grateful. To Italy we must go to find its beginning and trace its development, as well as to discover some of the finest specimens ever penned. Italian literature is so studded with sonnets that all who are familiar with it scarcely need any guidance to follow the path of the sonnet from the thirteenth century to the present time,—a path which we shall but briefly outline, knowing it to be so attractive as to lure to further study all lovers of the sonnet.

It may be remarked first that the word "sonnet" is a true index of the character of the poem. It is the equivalent of the Italian word *sonetto*, meaning "a little sound," or short melody. It is the diminutive of *suono*, that is, "sound." Music is "sounded" in the Italian, and therefore the word has a fuller meaning in this connection than does our word "sound." The sonnet is of similar derivation to the delightful compositions of a sister art, the sonata of music.

That some other stanza formed the basis on which the sonnet was built is altogether likely, though no authentic line of connection has been traced between them. Leaving out the supposition that the sonnet is an outgrowth of the Greek epigram, — a mere unsupported theory, — one may stop to consider the *stornello* as a possible germ of the sonnet. This dainty Liliput of a poem had always one grace, — that of brevity, being composed of two lines, containing a single metaphor. From its simplicity it became decidedly popular, and was sung by all classes. The other Italian stanzas — the *sestina rima*, quatrain and couplet; *ottava rima*, six lines on two rhymes alternating and a concluding couplet; the *rispetto*, a system of quatrains and couplets returning to one theme, all apparently grew from the *stornello*.

In Italian sonnet collections, the leading sonnet is attributed to Ludovico della Vernaccia, and bears date of 1200, but there seems to be some doubt as to his claim to be the sonnet pioneer. The sonnet is Petrarcan in form, and has five rhymes. Provence claims the origin of the sonnet, tracing its connection to the French word *sonnette*, and points out the resemblance of the recurrent rhymes to the lulling bells of the woolly flocks. It would seem, however, that Sicily was more probably its birthplace. The first near approach to a sonnet is credited to Pier delle Vigne, the state secretary of Frederick II. of Sicily. His sonnet, "Pero'ch'amore," is in regular form except that the quatrains are of the alternate, not the Petrarcan arrangement. It rhymes as *a–b, a–b, a–b, a–b; c–d–e, c–d–e*. And so the first sonnet was, true to its character, a poem of love! Giving all due credit to this pioneer, recently discovered by J. A. Symonds, we must place the crown of the first sonneteer on the head of that musical brother of the Church, Fra Guittone, who has reflected added renown on his town of Arezzo. It may have been that for years the sonnet had been gradually assuming its permanent form and tone-structure as it was gradually moulded to the music of mandolin or lute. Be this as it may, for all that is known, Fra Guittone may have been the very first man to write a sonnet of the present orthodox type, and thus his honors are as sure as those of Columbus. His sonnets are creditable, too, as poems. He wrote during the latter half of the thirteenth century, and his sonnets, with others, sixteen varieties in all, are mentioned in the "Poetica Vulgare" of Antonio di Tempo, a judge of Padua. The manuscript bears the date 1332, and is preserved at Milan.

The sonnet-lyre was taken up by Cino da Pistoja and Guido Cavalcante, lyrists of genuine quality, who led up to the lofty poetry of their common friend, the great Florentine, Dante Alighieri. It is pleasant to think of the mighty saturnine poet as one of the earliest lovers of the sonnet, for he wrote specimens of wonderful promise in his teens, and later disclosed, as unmistakably in his sonnets as elsewhere, his overshadowing imagination, while some reveal a rarely tender nature. Hunt gives the superiority of Dante's sonnets over Petrarch's as being one of grace over mere elegance, "of the inner spirit of the beautiful over the outer, of unstudied over studied effect." It seems a matter of regret that Longfellow did not translate more of the Italian sonnets, particularly Dante's, as he had so rare a touch for this work. Indeed, he became so permeated with sympathy for the Italian language, and especially for the genius of Dante, that his six sonnets on the "Divina Commedia" impress one as the joint effluence of the spirits of the two poets.

It seems most appropriate to print here these six superb sonnets on the great poem of Italy : —

THE DIVINA COMMEDIA.

I.

OFT have I seen at some cathedral door
   A laborer, pausing in the dust and heat,
   Lay down his burden, and with reverent feet
Enter, and cross himself, and on the floor
Kneel to repeat his paternoster o'er :
   Far off the noises of the world retreat ;
   The loud vociferations of the street
Become an indistinguishable roar.

So, as I enter here from day to day,
   And leave my burden at this minster gate,
Kneeling in prayer, and not ashamed to pray,
   The tumult of the time disconsolate
To inarticulate murmurs dies away,
   While the eternal ages watch and wait.

II.

How strange the sculptures that adorn these towers!
   This crowd of statues, in whose folded sleeves
   Birds build their nests ; while, canopied with leaves
Parvis and portal bloom like trellised bowers,
And the vast minster seems a cross of flowers !
   But fiends and dragons on the gargoyled eaves
   Watch the dead Christ between the living thieves,
And, underneath, the traitor Judas lowers !

Ah! from what agonies of heart and brain,
   What exultations trampling on despair,

What tenderness, what tears, what hate of wrong,
What passionate outcry of a soul in pain,
  Uprose this poem of the earth and air,
    This mediæval miracle of song!

III.

I enter, and I see thee in the gloom
  Of the long aisles, O poet saturnine!
    And strive to make my steps keep pace with thine.
The air is filled with some unknown perfume;
The congregation of the dead make room
  For thee to pass; the votive tapers shine;
    Like rooks that haunt Ravenna's groves of pine,
The hovering echoes fly from tomb to tomb.

From the confessionals I hear arise
Rehearsals of forgotten tragedies,
  And lamentations from the crypts below,
And then a voice celestial that begins
With the pathetic words, "Although your sins
  As scarlet be," and ends with "as the snow."

IV.

With snow-white veil, and garments as of flame,
  She stands before thee, who so long ago
    Filled thy young heart with passion and the woe
From which thy song in all its splendors came;
And while with stern rebuke she speaks thy name,
  The ice about thy heart melts as the snow
    On mountain heights, and in swift overflow
Comes gushing from thy lips in sobs of shame.

Thou makest full confession; and a gleam
  As of the dawn on some dark forest cast
    Seems on thy lifted forehead to increase;
Lethe and Eunoe — the remembered dream

And the forgotten sorrow — bring at last
   That perfect pardon which is perfect peace.

V.

I lift mine eyes, and all the windows blaze
   With forms of saints and holy men who died,
   Here martyred and hereafter glorified;
And the great Rose upon its leaves displays
Christ's Triumph, and the angelic roundelays,
   With splendor upon splendor multiplied;
   And Beatrice again at Dante's side
No more rebukes, but smiles her words of praise.

And then the organ sounds, and unseen choirs
   Sing the old Latin hymns of peace and love
      And benedictions of the Holy Ghost;
And the melodious bells among the spires
   O'er all the housetops and through heaven above
      Proclaim the elevation of the Host!

VI.

O star of morning and of liberty!
   O bringer of the light whose splendor shines
   Above the darkness of the Apennines,
Forerunner of the day that is to be!
The voices of the city and the sea,
   The voices of the mountains and the pines,
   Repeat thy song till the familiar lines
Are footpaths for the thought of Italy!

Thy fame is blown abroad from all the heights,
   Through all the nations; and a sound is heard,
      As of a mighty wind, and men devout,
Strangers of Rome, and the new proselytes,
   In their own language hear thy wondrous word,
      And many are amazed and many doubt.

One of Dante's sonnets in the Italian is inserted as an example of such notable handiwork, welcome to all who are familiar with the language, and no doubt of curious interest to others: —

> Tanto gentile, e tanto onesta pare
>   La donna mia, quand' ella altrui saluta,
>   Ch' ogni lingua divien tremando muta,
> E gli occhi non l' ardiscon di guardare.
>
> Ella sen va, sentendosi laudare,
>   Umilmente d' onestà vestuta;
>   E par che sia una cosa venuta
> Di cielo in terra a miracol mostrare.
>
> Mostrasi sì piacente a chi la mira,
>   Che dà per gli occhi una dolcezza al core,
> Che'ntender non la può chi non la pruova.
>
> E par, che dalla sua labbia si mova,
>   Uno spirito soave, pien d' amore,
> Che va dicendo all' anima: sospira.

Miss Louise Imogen Guiney has translated this sonnet so well that it must be given in English also; and here the merits of the two languages may be compared: —

> So chaste, so noble looks that lady mine
>   Saluting on her way, that tongues of some
>   Are mute a-tremble, and the eyes that clomb
> High as her eyes, abashed, their gaze decline.
> Thro' perils of heard praise she moves benign,
>   Armored in her own meekness, as if come
>   Hither from Heaven, to give our Christendom
> Even of a miracle the vouch divine.

So with beholders doth her worth avail,
  It sheds, thro' sight, a sweetness on the soul,
    (Alas! how told to one that felt it never?)
And from her presence seemeth to exhale
  A breath, half solace and of love the whole,
    That saith to the bowed spirit "Sigh!" forever.

This sonnet also is by Dante, Miss Guiney's translation: —

IO MIA SENTII SVEGLIAR DENTRO ALLO CORE.

Within my bosom from long apathy
  Love's mood of tenderness extreme awoke,
  And, spying him far off, mine eye bespoke
Love's self, so joyous scarce it seeméd he,
Crying: "Now, verily, pay thy vows to me!"
  And bright thro' every word his smile outbroke.
Then stood we twain, I in my liege lord's yoke,
Watching the path he came by, soon to see
The Lady Joan and Lady Beatrice
  Nearing our very nook, each marvel close
    Following her peer, all beauty else above;
And Love said, in a voice like Memory's:
  "The first is Spring; but she that with her goes,
    My counterpart, bears my own name of Love!"

Here we will note the fashions in form which the first masters of the sonnet followed and established. The sonnets of Guittone number 217, all but eight of which have the first eight lines rhymed on two rhymes alternately. The other eight observe the Petrarcan arrangement of the octave previously described. Of these, 158 have only four rhymes, and 59 have five. Of the 80 sonnets attributed to Dante, many of them doubtfully, only ten have the two rhymes of the octave alternate, while

70 octaves have the two rhymes in the Petrarcan arrangement. When we consider Petrarch, the classic master of sonnet form, we find that, of the 317 sonnets in the "In vita di M. Laura" and the "In Morte di M. Laura," every octave is rhymed on two rhymes only, and only fifteen of them are rhymed by alternate lines, the balance being in the true Petrarcan arrangement.

When we study the arrangement of sestets, we find the rhyme-order of one-two-three, one-two-three, preferred in 116 examples. In 107 sonnets the sestets rhyme as one-two, one-two, one-two, previously mentioned as the second-best arrangement. It is to Petrarch, then, that credit must be given for indorsing what was best in the rhyme arrangements of his predecessors, Guittone and Dante. The latter has 52 sonnets with five rhymes and 28 with four, and 12 close with couplets. Taking up Michael Angelo, the next great Italian genius, it is seen that seven eighths of his sonnets are in the strict Petrarcan type. One cannot ask a clearer judgment on sonnet form than the record of practice by masters of the sonnet, writing in the sonnet's native language, who stamped their names in indelible association with the poem.

Guido Guinicelli helped to fill the interval between Dante and Petrarch, a name that irresistibly brings up visions of "lovely Laura in her light green dress," and all the amorous conceits that throng the three hundred odd sonnets of her faithful poet, produced in a period of thirty-two years. Petrarch, says Foscolo in his "Essays on Petrarch" (1823), had a sweet, flexible voice of great compass, and composed and sang his sonnets to his lute, which he left by will to a friend. Some of the memoranda made by the poet on the manuscript of his sonnets are well worth perpetuating, for the glimpse afforded of this famous serenader working behind the scenes in his metrical studio.

Says Petrarch, "I began this by the impulse of the Lord, 10th September, at the dawn of day, after my morning prayers."

"I must make these two verses over again, singing them, — *cantando*, — and I must transpose them: 3 o'clock A. M. 19th October."

"I like this (*Hoc placet*)."

"I shall return to this again. I am called to supper."

(Sensible Petrarch!)

Another soliloquy gives a hint to future sonneteers, as follows: —

"Consider this. I had some thoughts of transposing these lines, and of making the first verse the last, but I have not done so for the sake of harmony. The first would then be more sonorous, and the last less so, which is against rule; for the end should be more harmonious than the beginning."

One learns from manuscripts of sonnets by contemporaries of Petrarch, preserved in Florence, that he was not alone in composing by the aid of musical accompaniment. Some of these show that the poet suggested the melody to which his words were to be sung, and several are indorsed as having been sung by Franco, a celebrated singer of the day.

It must be observed, however, that not lutes or mandolins, nor a mere passion for music or poetry, have inspired the most famous sonnets which have been written as a series; but instead of these an absorbing tender passion, and that often for ladies somewhat separated, socially, from the poets. One cannot pass by the curious circumstance that the great love sonnets of literature have often been addressed by the poets to other men's wives. Is it that the ideal and poetical conception of love can only find expression when the object is separated from the prosaic round of everyday life; and is it only the unattainable — the lost or the imagined love — that draws the founts of feeling to the surface? Whether or not these instances are merely accidental, it yet must be confessed that Dante's Beatrice had a husband, although her marriage occurred after their first acquaintance; that Petrarch's Laura had a similar incumbrance. Casa's adored one was a matron outside of his family; Alfieri sonnetized the wife of the second English Pretender; the gallant Sidney knew well that his "Stella" was a Lady Rich, — however poor a stick of a husband she had, — and no one supposes it was Anne Hathaway who called out the ruby sonnet-drops from Shakespeare's heart!

Genuine loves they would appear to have been, for the love poems of the great Italian poets of the fourteenth century are still popular in Italy, as the others are immortal in English literature. Petrarch especially gained the favor of the ladies, it would seem, by his delicate flatteries and compliments, his insinuating pleasantry, yet tender and sincere sentiment. In short, he made love like a gentleman, and was perhaps instrumental in raising the plane of courtship in an age not noted for the finest sensibility in this regard. Boccaccio was a friend of Petrarch, and probably the dissimilarity that is often noticed between friends was emphasized in the story-teller and the poet, to judge from their literary relics.

The following sonnets by Petrarch should be read with interest, two being addressed to Laura living, and one after she is dead. The translations by Colonel Higginson are especially admirable: —

SONNET (NO. 223).
Qual donna attende a gloriosa fama.

DOTH any maiden seek the glorious fame
  Of chastity, of strength, of courtesy?
  Gaze in the eyes of that sweet enemy
Whom all the world doth as my lady name!
How honor grows, and pure devotion's flame,
  How truth is joined with graceful dignity,
  There thou mayst learn, and what the path may be
To that high heaven which doth her spirit claim;

There learn that speech beyond all poets' skill,
  And gracious silence, and those holy ways
    Unutterable, untold by human heart.
But the infinite beauty that all eyes doth fill,
  This none can learn! because its lovely rays
    Are given by God's pure grace, and not by art.
      (TRANSLATED BY T. W. HIGGINSON.)

THE PERISHING HEART.
Mille fiate o dolce mia guerrera.

A THOUSAND times, sweet warrior, to obtain
  Peace with those beauteous eyes I've vainly tried,
  Proffering my heart; but with that lofty pride
To bend your looks so lowly you refrain:

Expects a stranger fair that heart to gain,
   In frail, fallacious hopes will she confide:
   It never more to me can be allied;
Since what you scorn, dear lady, I disdain.

In its sad exile if no aid you lend,
   Banished by me; and it can neither stay
   Alone, nor yet another's call obey:
Its vital course must hasten to its end:
   Ah me, how guilty then we both should prove,
   But guilty you the most, for you it most doth love!
                (TRANSLATED BY NOTT.)

SONNET (No. 261).
Levommi il mio pensiero.

DREAMS bore my fancy to that region where
   She dwells whom here I seek, but cannot see.
   'Mid those who in the loftiest heavens be
I looked on her, less haughty and more fair.
She took my hand; she said, "Within this sphere,
   If hope deceive not, thou shalt dwell with me:
   I filled thy life with war's wild agony;
Mine own day closed ere evening could appear.

"My bliss no human thought can understand;
   I wait for thee alone, and that fair veil
      Of beauty thou dost love shall yet retain."
Why was she silent then, why dropped my hand
   Ere those delicious tones could quite avail
      To bid my mortal soul in heaven remain?
             (TRANSLATED BY T. W. HIGGINSON.)

For a period of nearly a century the Italian sonneteers were feeble or extravagant imitators and followers of Petrarch.

Michael Angelo (1475–1564), — a sonnet of whose is quoted in the preceding essay, — is conspicuous not only for sonnets of a rare order, but because he united his gift of poetry to genius in art. For a blending of rare religious feeling with a self-deprecating, pure affection, the love sonnets of Angelo are unrivaled. His mistress, or rather his friend, Vittoria Colonna, walks far above the plane of his own worthiness, as he imagines it, as indeed Beatrice does to Dante; but, as far as their sonnets indicate, the latter lover had perhaps the more mundane feeling of the two. In short, the poetry of the great painter and sculptor was in fine harmony with the lofty, sacred character of his other art-work.

The following sonnet by Angelo is, like many by Milton, Keats, Wordsworth, and later poets, of peculiar biographical interest. It is an estimate of the greatest of Italian poets, by one of the next in importance, translated by America's greatest sonneteer: —

DANTE.

WHAT should be said of him cannot be said;
   By too great splendor is his name attended;
   To blame is easier those who him offended,
Than reach the faintest glory round him shed.
This man descended to the doomed and dead
   For our instruction; then to God ascended;
   Heaven opened wide to him its portals splendid,
Who from his country's, closed against him, fled.

Ungrateful land! To its own prejudice
   Nurse of his fortunes; and this showeth well,
     That the most perfect most of grief shall see.
Among a thousand proofs let one suffice,
   That as his exile hath no parallel,
     Ne'er walked the earth a greater man than he.
         (TRANSLATED BY LONGFELLOW.)

Next for consideration is a sonnet-writer who was a most valued patron of Angelo's. This versatile Florentine, Lorenzo de' Medici, statesman, wit, and philosopher, beguiled his time with sonnets which were at least good imitations in Petrarch's style. Boiardo, author of the "Orlando Innamorato," kept up the love-lorn line of sonnets. The Lombard poet, whose work ranks among Italy's great romantic poems, yields place to the Cardinal, Bembo, and he is outshone by his friend Ariosto, in the line of sonneteers. The latter wrote but thirty-six, marked by a luxuriance of feeling, if not by striking originality. The Archbishop Giovanni della Casa followed his brother ecclesiastic, Ariosto, and by his harsher but stronger verse worked an innovation among the languorous followers of the early sonneteers. Costanzo, the historian of Naples, wrote sonnets, fair, indifferent, and sometimes ridiculous; and contemporary with him were three lady devotees of the sonnet, — the famous Vittoria Colonna, Marchioness of Pescara; Veronica Gambara; and Gaspara Stampa. In Tasso we have a sonnet-writer well worthy of study, a writer of stately, dignified poems. Leigh Hunt has given the next prominent sonnet-maker, Marini, so thorough a castigation for his flippancies, extravagancies, and ludicrous conceits, that he may as well be considered a poetic corse, and dismissed as such.

The Italians have a proverb to the effect that an Italianized Englishman is a very devil; from which one might go on to infer that his doubtful majesty is a good sonneteer, as are not a few Italianized Englishmen. At any rate the chronological order of writers of notable sonnets in the Italian brings us next to Milton, who visited Manso, the Marquis of Villa, about twelve years after Marini's death. Manso was the patron of this latter poet, as well as of Tasso; and it is related that Milton had to use all his adroitness in order to appear to compliment them both, while in his heart he must have disapproved strongly of Marini's style. Milton has left evidence, in a canzone, of his failure to please the Italian taste with his sonnets, which were doubtless too austere and self-contained, even in their love passages, to suit the luxurious taste of his entertainers. After Milton's visit, there flourished another group of sonnet-writers in Italy. Redi wrote the pleasing "Bacco in Toscana," Menzini was a satirist, Maggi and Lemene were both chivalrous and humorous in their rhyming; but all aided to combat the taste for Marini's acrobatic poetry. Of all, Filicaja was perhaps the truest poet, winning as he has the praise of Wordsworth, while he evidently attracted Longfellow, as is witnessed by this translation of a lovely sonnet from the Italian's works: —

TO ITALY.

Italy! Italy! thou who 'rt doomed to wear
   The fatal gift of beauty, and possess
   The dower funest of infinite wretchedness,
Written upon thy forehead by despair;
Ah! would that thou wert stronger, or less fair,
   That they might fear thee more, or love thee less,
   Who in the splendor of thy loveliness
Seem wasting, yet to mortal combat dare!
Then from the Alps I should not see descending
   Such torrents of armed men, nor Gallic horde
   . Drinking the wave of Po, distained with gore,

> Nor should I see thee girded with a sword
>   Not thine, and with the stranger's arm contending,
> Victor or vanquished, slave forevermore.

In 1690 was formed the society of "Arcadians," under the leadership of Crescimbeni, poet and historian, and the organization has survived to the present time. Founded for the purpose of cultivating a pure taste in poetry as opposed to the Marinesque order, it appears not to have encouraged greatness in the lyric art. Its members enjoyed idyllic meetings in those old days, wearing the names and garb of shepherds and shepherdesses, granting each other tracts of land in an imaginary Greek Arcadia, and gathering in sylvan groves or gardens to recite poetry. The idea appears ridiculous to all who have not seen the countrymen of Boccaccio, social, frolicsome, impulsive, ready to throw all the heart into such simple amusement as would only provoke a disdainful smile from more phlegmatic peoples. Still, not a few English scholars of Italian literature were made members of the "Arcadia." Pius VI. gave it a room in the Vatican, and so the Arcadians have drifted fortunately down the years, building Castilian mansions on imaginary estates in Greece.

Of later Italian poets of virility, may be mentioned Alfieri, Foscolo, Pindemonte, and Monte. These, with Leopardi and Manzoni, stand out from many lesser lights, including the Italianized "Della Cruscan" Englishmen who doubtless fell under the sweeping denunciation of the proverb already alluded to.

Treading these stepping-stones, or century-stones, formed by a mere category of prominent poets of Italy, one gets some impression of how the sonnet grew when grafted upon the strongest stocks of Italian genius. But, of the minor sonneteers, one can only ask the imagination to picture their under-chorus of song; the little, love-laden compositions that may have flowered and died in a single night, sung in gondolas rocking in moonlight under latticed windows, in serenades borne up to languorous Dulcineas on the strains of the lute. Bard and serenader, and lovely lady and impassioned sonnet, sleep in oblivion; but the charm of their one hour of glory and passion and music may still seem to invest the little poem for those who can detect its spirit as well as its form.

It has been observed that the periods of the greatest brilliance in English poetry have been times when there was the greatest interest in Italian literature. It seems as if many of the best sonnet-writers have owed a debt to an infusion in one way or other of Italian study or feeling. One need but instance Milton, who visited Italy and wrote sonnets in Italian; Mrs. Browning, a Florentine by adoption; Keats, who died in Italy; Rossetti, of Italian blood; and Longfellow, the translator of the Divine Comedy. Instances of the apparent benefit of Italian study or sojourn would be easy to select also from living sonneteers.

Before passing to the sonnet field of English literature, so surpassing in its interest, especially to the American student, one can but glance at the conquests of the sonnet in other lands and tongues. It adorns French literature, sometimes distorted in form and trivial in spirit, and again memorably fine. The French sonnet has usually an octave of Petrarcan arrangement and a sestet of three rhymes, the first two lines rhyming together in a couplet. Bellay, Ronsard, and others helped to foster the sonnet at first in France. Felix Arvers has written a celebrated sonnet, "Mon ame a son secret," and De Musset inscribed one of pleasing quality to Victor Hugo. The grace and courtliness of the spirit of old Pierre Ronsard is embalmed in a sonnet, of which there follows a faithful and clever translation, by Miss Katherine Hillard, not heretofore published. Béranger and Thackeray have both paraphrased the sonnet, which is as follows: —

TO HÉLÈNE.

WHEN by the fire, grown old, with silv'ry hair,
   You spin by candle-light, with weary eyes,
   Humming my songs, you'll say with still surprise,
"Ronsard once sang of me when I was young and fair."
Then as your maidens hear the well-known sound,
   Though half asleep after the toils of day,
   Not one but wakes, and, as she goes her way,
Blesses your name, with praise immortal crowned.
I shall be dead and gone, a fleshless shade,
   Under Elysian bowers my head be laid;
While you, crouched o'er your fire, grown old and gray,
   Sigh for my love, regret your past disdain.
   Live now, nor wait for love to come again,
Gather the roses of your life to-day!
                        (PIERRE RONSARD.)

The genius of Camoens makes the sonnet a perennial delight in Portuguese literature, where over three hundred appear of his composition. It has bloomed since the sixteenth century in Spain under the tendance of no less a hand than Lope de Vega, one of whose sonnets must be imbedded here : —

THE GOOD SHEPHERD.

SHEPHERD ! who with thine amorous, sylvan song
    Hast broken the slumber that encompassed me,
    Who mad'st thy crook from the accursed tree
On which thy powerful arms were stretched so long !
Lead me to mercy's ever-flowing fountains ;
    For thou my shepherd, guard, and guide shalt be ;
    I will obey thy voice, and wait to see
Thy feet all beautiful upon the mountains.
Hear, Shepherd ! thou who for thy flock art dying,
    O, wash away these scarlet sins, for thou
    Rejoicest at the contrite sinner's vow.
O, wait ! to thee my weary soul is crying,
    Wait for me ! Yet why ask it, when I see,
    With feet nailed to the cross, thou 'rt waiting still for me !
        (TRANSLATED BY LONGFELLOW.)

Here, too, is an excellent translation of a sonnet by Camoens, praising the eyes of his inamorata, Catarina Cornaro, who has received a fine tribute in Mrs. Browning's poem, "Sweetest eyes were ever seen."

SONNET BY CAMOENS (No. 186).

Os olhos onde o casto Amor ardia.

THOSE eyes from whence chaste love was wont to glow,
    And smiled to see his torches kindled there ;
    That face within whose beauty strange and rare
The rosy light of dawn gleamed o'er the snow ;

That hair which bid the envious sun to know
  His brightest beams less golden rays did wear;
  That pure white hand, that gracious form and fair, —
All these into the dust of earth must go.

O perfect beauty in its tenderest age!
  O flower cut down ere it could all unfold
    By the stern hand of unrelenting Death!
Why did not Love itself quit Earth's poor stage,
  Not because here dwelt beauty's perfect mould,
    But that so soon it passed from mortal breath?
            (Translated by T. W. Higginson.)

Nor was the sonnet neglected in German literature, when that literature was at its best. Goethe's sonnets are charming to read, not only in the original but in the translations of Bowring, and it is amusing to hear him, when nearly sixty, acknowledge his surrender to the sonnet as follows: —

NEMESIS.

When through the nations stalks contagion wild,
  We from them cautiously should steal away.
  E'en I have oft with ling'ring and delay
Shunn'd many an influence, not to be defiled.

And e'en though Amor oft my hours beguiled,
  At length with him preferr'd I not to play,
  And so, too, with the wretched sons of clay,
When four and three lined verses they compiled.

But punishment pursues the scoffer straight,
  As if by serpent-torch of furies led
    From hill to vale, from land to sea to fly.

I hear the genie's laughter at my fate;
  Yet do I find all power of thinking fled
    In sonnet-rage and love's fierce ecstasy.

Goethe's are all love-sonnets, graceful and gallant, and written in the years 1807 and 1808. In one he alludes to Petrarch as suffering a long penitential Good Friday of unrequited love, and so betrays his familiarity with the Italian whose model in form he copies. Friedrich Ruckert (1788-1866) writes "Sonnets in Armor" on the war of the Liberation; and Count von Platen (1796-1835) intersperses sonnets and ghazels, being, like Ruckert, of Oriental and classic tastes. Schiller ignored the sonnet, though the stanzas of the "Artists" strongly suggest them at times. Heine, however, pours forth his mingled love, pathos, and cynicism in a baker's dozen of sonnets.

A short, quick flight through English literature, barely touching the most important nests of sonnet-lore, must suffice to impress the sonneteers of the New World with the greatness of the predecessors in whose aërial wake they are winging. Flying high and strong from its southern home, over alps or seas, the sonnet seems to have been out of sight and hearing to " Dan Chaucer, —

> That first warbler, whose sweet breath
> Preluded those melodious bursts that fill
> The spacious times of great Elizabeth
> With sounds that echo still."

Strange is it that so blithe a minstrel of love, who revered Dante; eulogized and possibly had met Petrarch; and who wrote the "Canterbury Tales," so suggestive of the latter's friend Boccaccio, — strange that this poet should have overlooked the sonnet! We can imagine what fresh, witty, audacious, musical, love-laden sonnets they would have been. But if there were any Italian sonnets in England in Chaucer's day, they were as yet a strange bird, and the poet probably did not know them.

So we come down to Sir Thomas Wyatt (1503–1542), the cotemporary of Casa in Italy, for the first English sonnet-writer. He wrote thirty-two sonnets, only one being other than in Petrarcan form, though slightly irregular in their closing couplets. Sir Thomas and his young friend, Henry Howard, Earl of Surrey (1517–1547), had traveled in Italy, and so had become enamored of the sonnet. But the younger man immediately forsook the Petrarcan model, and wrote either all on two rhymes, except the ending couplet, or else in the form generally known as the "English" or Shakespearean sonnet. Had he foreborne to write the fatal sonnet, "On the Life and Death of Sardanapalus," he might not have excited the anger of King Henry VIII. and lost his head at the age of thirty. One cannot but sincerely lament this young knight, whose poetic relics are embalmed in Tottle's Miscellany, "*The Songs and Sonnettes written by the ryght honourable lorde Henry Howard, late Earle of Surrey, and other.*"

Here is one of Surrey's sonnets, and it deserves attention because we now first strike the "Shakespearean" sonnet in literature. This form is also called often the "illegitimate" sonnet, though there are more irregular forms that better deserve the name!

EPITAPH ON HIS SQUIRE, THOMAS CLERE.

Norfolk sprung thee, Lambeth holds thee dead;
Clere, of the Count of Cleremont, thou hight;
Within the womb of Ormond's race thou bred,
And saw'st thy cousin crownèd in thy sight.[1]
Shelton for love, Surrey for lord thou chase [2]
(Ay me! whilst life did last, that league was tender);
Tracing whose steps thou sawest Kelsal blaze,
Landrecy burnt, and battered Boulogne render,
At Montreuil gates, hopeless of all recure,
Thine Earl, half dead, gave in thy hand his will,
Which cause did thee this pining death procure,
Ere summers four times seven thou couldst fulfill.
 Ah, Clere! if love had booted care, or cost,
 Heaven had not won, nor earth so timely lost.

It will be seen that three quatrains, like the stanzas of Gray's Elegy, having no similarity in rhymes, are joined together, with a concluding couplet having a seventh rhyme, in one poem. It was doubtless formed in imitation of the Petrarcan sonnet, and in the English language is much easier to write, as the latter has more numerous but less fertile rhymes than the Italian. At the same time it is, as Leigh Hunt observes, the least artistic form of sonnet.

 Next in order is the chivalrous Sir Philip Sidney (1554–1586), snaring the sonnet with his fluent verse and gallant, poetic thoughts. The dream of the coterie of shepherds and shepherdesses in Italy gives title to his poem, "The Arcadia," and he summons his muse in the person of "Stella," as Petrarch did in the beloved "Laura."

---

[1] Anne Boleyn.   [2] Chose.

Having borne himself to victory in the jousts, the versatile knight sits down and dutifully pens this sonnet to his lady, and so makes history forget what sort of prize it was that he won by his arms: —

HAVING this day my horse, my hand, my lance
  Guided so well, that I obtained the prize,
  Both by the judgment of the English eyes
And of some sent from that sweet enemy, France;
Horsemen my skill in horsemanship advance;
  Townfolks, my strength; a daintier judge applies
  His praise to sleight, which from good use doth rise;
Some lucky wits impute it but to chance;
Others, because, of both sides, I do take
  My blood from them who did excel in this,
Think nature me a man of arms did make.
  How far they shot awry! The true cause is,
Stella looked on; and from her heavenly face
Sent forth the beams which made so fair my race.

In another sonnet he has embalmed the line, —

> Our life is but a step in dusty way.

The literature of sleep, likewise, he has enriched by a sonnet with such charming characterization that room must be made for it. What could be better than the first, third, fourth, tenth, and eleventh of these lulling lines?

COME Sleep, O Sleep, the certain knot of peace,
  The baiting place of wit, the balm of woe,
The poor man's wealth, the prisoner's release,
  The indifferent judge between the high and low.
With shield of proof shield me from out the prease [1]
  Of those fierce darts Despair at me doth throw;
O make in me those civil wars to cease:

[1] Press.

I will good tribute pay, if thou do so.
Take thou of me smooth pillows, sweetest bed,
  A chamber deaf to noise and blind to light,
  A rosy garland, and a weary head;
And if these things, as being thine by right,
Move not thy heavy grace, thou shalt in me
Livelier than elsewhere Stella's image see.

Still another sixteenth century sonneteer appears in sword and buckler, — Sir Walter Raleigh, — and one begins to feel that a sonneteer is a man who can carve a foe as well as cut a cameo poem. In connection with this Memory sings mischievously the lines of Emerson : —

> No jingling serenader's art
> Nor tinkle of piano-strings
> Can make the warm blood start
> In its mystic springs.

Yet here is the sonnet already the poem of soldiers! It must be undergoing a transformation, for it drops the languor of a mere serenade, and thrills soon to the world-music of Shakespeare, to celestial diapasons of Milton's mind, to haunting melodies of Wordsworth's windy hills.

Raleigh's most notable sonnet is a generous tribute to his friend's "Faërie Queene."

The gentle Spenser comes "pricking o'er the plain" as another of the sonneteers of Queen Elizabeth's time. The peculiar form of his sonnets demands special attention. It is an innovation on the "English" sonnet of Surrey, the last rhyme of one quatrain following as the first rhyme of the next, and in this respect improving on Surrey's sonnets, inasmuch as more unity and rhyme-relation is given to the poem. Spenser was so successful in his special stanza, used in the "Faërie Queene" and now called after him, that he must needs invent a special form of sonnet for himself. This form he uses in many examples, the character of the sonnets being generally amatory, and marked by the graceful fancy, easy style, and charming picture-painting which characterize this author. The following is a fair example of Spenser's sonnets:—

> In that proud port, which her so goodly graceth,
> Whiles her faire face she reares up to the skie,
> And to the ground her eie-lids low embaseth,
> Most goodly temperature ye may descry,
> Myld humblesse, mixt with awfull majestie;
> For, looking on the earth, whence she was borne,
> Her minde remembreth her mortalitie,
> Whatso is fayrest shall to earth returne;
> But that same lofty countenance seemes to scorne
> Base thing, and thinke how she to heaven may clime;
> Treading downe earth as lothsome and forlorne,
> That hinders heavenly thoughts with drossy slime.
>   Yet lowly still vouchsafe to looke on me;
>   Such lowlinesse shall make you lofty be.

Spenser wrote eighty-eight of these sonnets. He was born in 1552, and his death in 1599 brings us to the Seventeenth Century.

One should devote no little study to the next poet we consider, a sonnet-writer of the first magnitude, no other than William Shakespeare (1564–1816). We have spoken of the "Shakespearean" sonnet as an imitation of the Petrarcan, more easily composed but artistically inferior. Yet Shakespeare's poems in this form prove that, after all, it is the material and workmanship, more than the exterior form of architecture, which tell for permanence in poems as in buildings. It has been inferred by good scholars that Shakespeare did not closely study contemporary Italian literature, and probably never visited Italy. The *sestina rima* used in his long poems is apparently his only debt in that direction as regards forms of stanza. As for the Petrarcan sonnet, it was not yet popular in England. That the sonnets were written in his younger days, and published after his retirement from the stage, is well known. Some of them are addressed apparently to a lady with whom he was enamored, but others, as the sonnets indicate, were soliloquies, and others still were addressed to a male friend. The example of Shakespeare has been the great cause of what popularity this form of sonnet retains. It may be that he knew and admired the form of the Petrarcan sonnet; yet it is not strange that, writing as voluminously as he did, and addicted to the use of simple stanzas, as shown in his poems and songs, he should have chosen the "English" form in which to write his hundred and a half of sonnets. It would have been strange, under the circumstances, had he done otherwise. And now, as we have subjected the Petrarcan system of rhymes to the test of music, one can, if he cares to, give a distinct note to each of the rhymes in an "English" sonnet. But the result would be most flat and monotonous, — one, two, one, two; three, four, three, four; five six, five six, seven, seven!

The sonnet that we quote next is so pertinent to the foregoing remarks that one cannot emphasize them better than by including it. It would seem almost as if Shakespeare had prevision of how the Petrarcan sonnet would vindicate its superiority over the vehicle he chose, and in this sonnet had written his own excuse! The italics are his own.

SONNET XXXII.

If thou survive my well-contented day,
    When that churl Death my bones with dust shalt cover,
And shalt by fortune once more re-survey
    These poor rude lines of thy deceased lover,
Compare them with the bettering of the time;
    And though they be outstripped by every pen,
Reserve them for my love, not for their rhyme,
    Exceeded by the height of happier men.
O then vouchsafe me but this loving thought!
    Had my friend's muse grown with this growing age,
A dearer birth than this his love had brought,
    To march in ranks of better equipage:
But since he died, and poets better prove,
    Theirs for their style I'll read, his for his love.

And, true enough, whatever the merits of their "style" or form, this uneven but collectively magnificent series of sonnets continues to be read for their rare revelation of love! Shakespeare makes still another apology in sonnet LXXVI.: —

    Why is my verse so barren of new pride?
        So far from variation or quick change?
    Why, with the time, do I not glance aside
        To new-found methods and to compounds strange?

And yet what glorious poetry has been written by Shakespeare in this form, as for instance this sonnet! —

FULL many a glorious morning have I seen
   Flatter the mountain tops with sovereign eye,
Kissing with golden face the meadows green,
   Gilding pale streams with heavenly alchemy,
Anon permit the basest clouds to ride
With ugly rack on his celestial face,
And from the forlorn world his visage hide,
   Stealing unseen to west with this disgrace.
Even so my sun one early morn did shine
   With all triumphant splendor on my brow;
But out! alack! he was but one hour mine;
   The region cloud hath masked him from me now.
      Yet him for this my love no whit disdaineth;
      Suns of the world may stain when heaven's sun staineth.

Who that is familiar with the natural picture in the first four lines can forget this sonnet? But there are four pictures in it,—the morning in its glory, the day in its clouded gloom, the poet's life in the glory of youthful feeling, and his after life stained with the inevitable impact of misfortune, sorrow, and sin; while all are bound together by the thought that love can see the lovable through the sinful, and that man must inevitably be "stained" just as the sun must be clouded. Indeed, the poet would excuse man in the example of the mighty "heavenly sun." So much has been said because it is the editor's favorite of all Shakespeare's sonnets, and yet it bears in the Hunt-Lee collection of sonnets this absurd caption:—

"HE LAMENTS THAT THE COUNTENANCE OF SOME GREAT AND WORTHY PATRON SEEMS TO BE DIVERTED FROM HIM."

It is curious how Hunt, who calls the sonnet "loftily beautiful," could put on it so clumsy and mistaken a title. Rather let the sonnet stand without title, for it requires a title as long as the sonnet — the sonnet itself — fitly to entitle it!

Room must be made for another of his great sonnets which is "true love" in a nutshell.

TRUE LOVE.

LET me not to the marriage of true minds
    Admit impediments. Love is not love
Which alters when it alteration finds,
    Or bends with the remover to remove.
Oh no ; it is an ever fixèd mark,
    That looks on tempests and is never shaken :
It is the star to every wandering bark,
    Whose worth's unknown, although his height be taken.
Love's not Time's fool, though rosy lips and cheeks
    Within his bending sickle's compass come ;
Love alters not with his brief hours and weeks,
    But bears it out even unto the edge of doom.
    If this be error, and upon me proved,
    I never writ, nor no man ever loved.

It would be pleasant to quote such wholly charming sonnets as Nos. CII. and CVI., but other though lesser sonneteers press for a hearing. Space must be granted to quote the subtle sonnet which is the masterpiece of Michael Drayton, (1563–1631) : —

LOVE'S LAST WORD.

SINCE there's no help, come let us kiss and part, —
    Nay I have done, you get no more of me ;
And I am glad, yea, glad with all my heart,
    That thus so cleanly I myself can free ;

Shake hands forever — cancel all our vows —
  And when we meet at any time again,
Be it not seen in either of our brows
  That we one jot of former love retain.

Now at the last gasp of Love's latest breath,
  When, his pulse failing, Passion speechless lies,
When Faith is kneeling by his bed of death,
  And Innocence is closing up his eyes, —
Now if thou would'st, when all have given him over,
  From death to life thou might'st him yet recover!

While he was no mean poet, the above is doubtless one of the best poems that Drayton wrote.

Rare Ben Jonson, Shakespeare's boon companion, had to write a sonnet of remonstrance before the king, Charles I., would grant the tierce of sack which was one of the perquisites of wearing the laurel of court poet. He wrote other sonnets, also, of which two are Petrarcan in model. Donne, of a quaint and sober piety, the friend of Jonson, follows the legitimate style in twenty-five sonnets, the finest being the one on Death. Samuel Daniel (1562–1619) has a fine sonnet on Sleep, beginning,

  "Care-charmer Sleep, son of the sable Night."

Overlooking less notable sonneteers, we find William Drummond, of Hawthornden (1585–1649), born, living, and dying in his manor-house; his life an ideal for a man of letters. He uses the pure Italian model so well, and with so much of its native elegance of thought and form, that two examples must be given. If any lines are stronger than others, perhaps the seventh and twelfth will attract special notice in this, his characteristic and beautiful —

PRAISE OF A SOLITARY LIFE.

THRICE happy he who by some shady grove,
   Far from the clamorous world, doth live his own;
   Though solitary, who is not alone,
But doth converse with that eternal love.
   Oh, how more sweet is bird's harmonious moan,
Or the hoarse sobbings of the widowed dove,
   Than those smooth whisperings near a prince's throne,
Which good make doubtful, do the evil approve!

Or how more sweet is Zephyr's wholesome breath,
   And sighs embalmed which new-born flowers unfold,
Than that applause vain honor doth bequeath!
   How sweet are streams to poison drunk in gold!
     The world is full of horrors, troubles, slights;
     Woods' harmless shades have only true delights.

William Alexander (1580-1640), Earl of Stirling, writes sonnets to the number of one hundred, some of them clever. We must now pass over many poets not noted as sonneteers, wishing that Beaumont and Fletcher had put the "Invocation to Sleep" in sonnet form, and so added it to the lovely series of "Sleep" sonnets. William Browne's (1588-1643) arch sonnet on "Palmistry" is noticeable. He was one of the "Sons of Ben Jonson," of the Inner Temple, and friend of Wither and Selden. Carew and Herrick yield nothing in the way of sonnet gems, but Habington writes sonnets, — echoes of Sidney and Petrarch, whom he evidently admired.

The poet of the Church, good George Herbert (1593-1634), did not deem it impious to throw thought in sonnet form; and, though Leigh Hunt has strangely overlooked him, it is interesting to quote a sonnet of his. Though in "English" or illegitimate form, it seems of fine quality: —

LOVE.

IMMORTAL Love, author of this great frame,
  Sprung from that beauty which can never fade,
How hath men parceled out Thy glorious name,
  And thrown it on that dust which Thou hast made,
While mortal love doth all the title gain;
  Which siding with invention, they together
Bear all the sway, possessing all the brain,
  (Thy workmanship) and give Thee share in neither.

Wit fancies beauty, beauty raiseth wit;
  The world is theirs, they two play out the game,
Thou standing by; and though Thy glorious name
  Wrought out deliverance from th' infernal pit,
Who sings Thy praise? Only a scarf or glove
Doth warm our hands and make them write of love.

Leaving this saintly friend of Isaak Walton — the latter should at least have left a sonnet on the trout — we find the little poem out of favor with Crashaw and Vaughan, with Cowley and Waller. But its music is only sleeping to gather again in the trumpet-tones to be blown by John Milton, (1608-1674).

The great Puritan, in many of his sonnets, makes a notable change in the Petrarcan structure by carrying the thought and language from the octave to sestet without any break. This he probably did to insure greater unity, to prevent the sonnet dividing in half. Yet he frequently writes a sonnet that changes in treatment, by a reverse or rise of the thought, in the eighth or ninth lines, thus preserving the double character of the sonnet, a thought and its reflection or transfiguration. This is seen in the sonnet on his blindness, "To Cromwell," and several other sonnets. It has been overlooked by some writers, who maintain that Milton made no such division in his sonnets. Though the innovation by Milton has led to the treatment by some writers of a separate class of sonnets — "Miltonic sonnets" — the change which he made is not important enough to warrant a separate classification. Practically he used and indorsed the Petrarcan sonnet, as did Wordsworth, Mrs. Browning, and most of the best sonneteers who have written since their time. Milton, like Wordsworth, used the sonnet for the expression of his most impassioned thought and lofty poetry. Indeed, when we consider the subject, the author, the wide-winged imagination, the vivid picturing, the conception of the Divine nature, one may well believe the following to be the finest sonnet ever written : —

MILTON'S SONNET ON HIS BLINDNESS.

WHEN I consider how my light is spent
   Ere half my days, in this dark world and wide,
   And that one talent which is death to hide
Lodged with me useless, though my soul more bent
To serve therewith my Maker, and present
   My true account, lest he, returning, chide;
   "Doth God exact day-labor, light denied?"
I fondly ask. But Patience, to prevent
That murmur, soon replies, "God doth not need
   Either man's work, or his own gifts. Who best

Bear his mild yoke, they serve him best. His state
Is kingly; thousands at his bidding speed,
  And post o'er land and ocean without rest;
  They also serve who only stand and wait."

The next sonnet is not only graceful, but has much historical interest, being written when the house where the poet lived was in danger from the soldiery of Charles I. The mighty Milton here uses the little sonnet as a shield of defense.

WHEN THE ASSAULT WAS INTENDED TO THE CITY.[1]

Captain, or Colŏnel, or Knight in arms,
  Whose chance on these defenseless doors may seize,
  If deed of honor did thee ever please,
Guard them, and him within protect from harms:
He can requite thee; for he knows the charms
  That call fame on such gentle acts as these,
  And he can spread thy name o'er land and seas,
Whatever clime the sun's bright circle warms.
Lift not thy spear against the Muses' bower:
  The great Emathian conqueror bid spare
The house of Pindarus, when temple and tower
  Went to the ground; and the repeated air
Of sad Electra's poet had the power
  To save the Athenian walls from ruin bare.

Another sonnet of Milton's, addressed to Cromwell, has something more of the trumpet blast, and is especially memorable for the words, " Peace hath her victories no less renowned than war."

---

[1] Charles the First had arrayed his army against the Republicans at Brentford. The tenth line refers to Alexander. "Electra's poet" obviously refers to Euripides, whose verses were sung at a banquet of generals during the conquest of Lysander.

TO THE LORD GENERAL CROMWELL.

CROMWELL, our chief of men, who through a cloud
   Not of war only, but detractions rude,
   Guided by faith and matchless fortitude,
To peace and truth thy glorious way hath plowed,
And on the neck of crownèd fortune proud
   Hast reared God's trophies, and his work pursued,
   While Darwen stream, with blood of Scots imbrued,
And Dunbar field resounds thy praises loud,
And Worcester's laureate wreath: yet much remains
   To conquer still; Peace hath her victories
   No less renowned than War: new foes arise,
Threatening to bind our souls with secular chains: —
   Help us to save free conscience from the paw
   Of hireling wolves, whose gospel is their maw.

It has been seen that Milton felt free to make a slight change in the grammatical structure of the sonnet, though not to any extent in its form or nature. Meanwhile lesser poets were more daring. Although it seems like belittling the subject to refer to obsolete "varieties" of the sonnet, we follow Leigh Hunt in enumerating the following: 1st, the twelve-syllabled Italian *versi sdruccioli*, or "sliding verses," terminating in dactyls, and styled *Duodenary Sonnets; Mute Sonnets*, that have one-syllable rhymes; *Continuous* or *Iterating Sonnets*, arranged on one rhyme, or with each line beginning and ending with the same word; *Two-rhymed Sonnets*, of which Scott, Gosse, Lord Hanmer, and other English writers have produced examples, also Edgar Fawcett; *Answering Sonnets*, written in reply to others on the same rhymes, but with different meanings; *Retrograde Sonnets*, reading alike forwards or backwards; *Chained or Linked Sonnets*, each verse beginning with the last word of the preceding; *Interwoven Sonnets*, with the rhymes repeated in the body of the lines, (see Mr. Morse's "Immortality"); *Crowning Sonnets*, arranged in a series as a panegyric; *Caudated* or *Tailed Sonnets*, having a number of extra lines, and which naturally degenerated into the *Comic Sonnet*. Leigh Hunt observes that "many of these are puerilities." Perhaps one must recognize them, because Milton's "On the New Forces of Conscience" is a "tailed" or "comic" sonnet. Indeed, Petrarch, Dante, and Tasso are open to the charge of occasionally dallying with such whimsicalities of rhyme. But the consideration of such excrescences is foreign to our purpose, and indeed they are of a short-lived and trivial nature. To see Drollery in the mask of the sonnet seems sacrilege in fact.

The sonnet now goes into retirement for a hundred years, and Dryden and the French school have the field with the restoration of Charles II. Thomas Gray writes an indifferent sonnet on his friend West. Pope sneers at sonnets and "hackney sonneteers." Dryden disdains them, but Mason and Warton keep the form alive. Johnson is, however, tired of sonnets (and who would not tire of poor ones!), and so he derides Warton's muse as

> Tricked in antique ruff and bonnet,
> Ode and elegy and sonnet.

Nevertheless Cowper, dying in the last year of the eighteenth century, writes a creditable sonnet "To Mary Unwin," and gives prelude of the melodious nineteenth, the halcyon period of all sonnet history, lighted by the names of Wordsworth, Keats, and Mrs. Browning.

The chorus is led up to by Sir Samuel Egerton Brydges (1762–1837) and William Lisle Bowles (1762–1850), who write entertaining sonnets, the former's " Echo " and the latter's " Landscape " and " Hope " being excellent examples. Coleridge's sonnets (1772–1834) must attract all sonnet lovers. There is such force and pathos in " Kosciusko," especially in the last line, and such dreamy music in the seaside " Fancy," reminding of Keats, that both are quoted, though one is irregular and one " illegitimate."

ON THE LAST FAILURE OF KOSCIUSKO.

OH, what a loud and fearful shriek was there,
    As though a thousand souls one death-groan poured!
    Ah me! they saw beneath a hireling's sword
Their Kosciusko fall! Through the swart air
(As pauses the tired Cossack's barbarous yell
    Of triumph) on the chill and midnight gale
Rises with frantic burst, or sadder swell,
    The dirge of murdered Hope! while Freedom pale
Bends in such anguish o'er her destined bier,
    As if from eldest time some Spirit meek
Had gathered in a mystic urn each tear
    That ever on a patriot's furrowed cheek
Fit channel found; and she had drained the bowl
In the mere willfulness and sick despair of soul!

FANCY IN NUBIBUS.

(Composed by the seaside, October, 1817.)

Oh, it is pleasant, with a heart at ease,
  Just after sunset, or by moonlight skies,
To make the shifting clouds be what you please,
  Or let the easily persuaded eyes
Own each quaint likeness issuing from the mould
  Of a friend's fancy; or with head bent low,
And cheek aslant, see rivers flow of gold
  'Twixt crimson banks; and then, a traveler, go
From mount to mount, through Cloudland, gorgeous land!
  Or listening to the tide, with closèd sight,
Be that blind bard, who on the Chian strand
  By those deep sounds possessed, with inward light
Beheld the Iliad and the Odyssey
Rise to the swelling of the voiceful sea.

When we come to consider the other great "Lake poet," Wordsworth (1770–1850), we count one of the rarest (if not the very rarest), beads on the sonnet rosary of poets' names. Since he was a writer of sonnets by hundreds, one could not expect them all to be even of second-rate quality; but the pure, clear beauty of his best ones would atone for vapidity in thousands! Nor are his fine sonnets few, and it is pleasant to find his best worthily set in the Petrarcan mould. In letting the sonnet tell its history and triumphs, it would be a pleasure to insert many of Wordsworth's, such as the picturing of sleep "A Flock of Sheep that leisurely pass by;" or the beautiful tribute to girlhood in "It is a Beauteous Evening, calm and free;" "A Volant Tribe of Bards," the sonnet on Westminster Bridge, and many others. But as a sufficient stumbling-block to all "scorners of the sonnet" the following are selected as being adequate examples of Wordsworth's varied power, and as noble signs of the sonnet's scope. Where can they be matched by one author, and where in such brief space can be found so many jewel-like, memorable lines? Well has Emerson called Wordsworth's sonnets "the witchery of language": —

THE QUIET MUSE.

Not Love, not War, nor the tumultuous swell
  Of civil conflict, nor the wrecks of change,
  Nor Duty struggling with afflictions strange,
Not these alone inspire the tuneful shell;
But where untroubled peace and concord dwell,
  There also is the Muse not loath to range,
  Watching the twilight smoke of cot or grange
Skyward ascending from a woody dell.

Meek aspirations please her, lone endeavor,
  And sage content, and placid melancholy;
She loves to gaze upon a crystal river,
  Diaphanous, because it travels slowly.
Soft is the music that would charm forever;
  The flower of sweetest smell is shy and lowly.

The classic building of the following sonnet would have pleased its subject. The qualities of balance, symmetry, acceleration of interest, reserve force, and climax, are all notable: —

MILTON.

Milton! thou shouldst be living at this hour:
  England hath need of thee: she is a fen
  Of stagnant waters: altar, sword, and pen,

Fireside, the heroic wealth of hall and bower,
Have forfeited their ancient English dower
   Of inward happiness. We are selfish men;
   Oh! raise us up, return to us again;
And give us manners, virtue, freedom, power.

Thy soul was like a Star, and dwelt apart:
   Thou hadst a voice whose sound was like the sea:
   Pure as the naked heavens, majestic, free,
So didst thou travel on life's common way,
In cheerful godliness; and yet thy heart
The lowliest duties on herself did lay.

A REPROACH.

WHY art thou silent? Is thy love a plant
   Of such weak fibre that the treacherous air
   Of absence withers what was once so fair?
Is there no debt to pay, no boon to grant?
Yet have my thoughts for thee been vigilant,
   Bound to thy service with unceasing care,
   The mind's least generous wish a mendicant
For nought but what thy happiness could spare.

Speak,—though this soft, warm heart, once free to hold
   A thousand tender pleasures, thine and mine,
Be left more desolate, more dreary cold,
Than a forsaken bird's-nest filled with snow
   'Mid its own blush of leafless eglantine,—
Speak, that my torturing doubts their end may know!

This last sonnet is not often selected by compilers, but it is inserted here not only because it is a personal favorite, but because it betrays in an unguarded moment the susceptible, tender side of the outwardly austere poet.

Southey's sonnets (1794-1843) are not remarkable, many of them not legitimate. Charles Lamb (1775-1834) wrote sonnets that amuse or interest, but largely because they were penned by "Elia." It is to Joseph Blanco White's (1775-1841) sonnet that Milton's on his blindness must look for its most famous rival. Still one may claim that Milton's has the more divine intuition and admirable attitude of spirit. One feels that no one but Milton would have written the one sonnet; that sooner or later some one would have written the one "To Night." Yet is it a noble sonnet, and with fine climax and surprise at the close. It appeared first in the "Bijou" (Pickering), 1828; again in the "Gentleman's Magazine," 1835. As it now stands, it shows many corrections from the first version as given in Mr. Main's notes. It has also become allowable to substitute "flower" for "fly" in the eleventh line, as otherwise there is a bad repetition, — "insect." Of English and Spanish blood, this otherwise obscure writer seems to have fused the genius of Lope de Vega and Milton into one sonnet; and one sonnet makes his name immortal: —

NIGHT AND DEATH.

MYSTERIOUS Night! when our first parent knew
   Thee from report divine, and heard thy name,
   Did he not tremble for this lovely frame,
This glorious canopy of light and blue?
Yet 'neath a curtain of translucent dew,
   Bathed in the rays of the great setting flame,
   Hesperus with the host of heaven came,
And, lo! creation widened in man's view.

Who could have thought such darkness lay concealed
   Within thy beams, O Sun! or who could find,
Whilst flower and leaf and insect stood revealed,
   That to such countless orbs thou mad'st us blind?
Why do we, then, shun death with anxious strife?
If light can thus deceive, wherefore not life?

As Leigh Hunt and Coleridge have both pronounced the above to be the finest sonnet in the language in their day, it is of interest to insert here, taken from the "Treasury of English Sonnets," an earlier reading of this famous sonnet, which Mr. Main obtained from the Rev. Dean R. Perceval Graves, of Dublin, who, some fifty years ago, copied it either from an autograph or from an early printed copy:—

MYSTERIOUS Night! when the first man but knew
   Thee by report, unseen, and heard thy name,
   Did he not tremble for this lovely frame,
This glorious canopy of light and blue?
Yet 'neath a curtain of translucent dew,
   Bathed in the rays of the great setting flame,
   Hesperus with the host of heaven came,
And, lo! creation widened on his view!

Who could have thought what darkness lay concealed
   Within thy beams, O Sun? or who could find,
Whilst fly and leaf and insect stood revealed,
   That to such endless Orbs thou mad'st us blind?
Weak man! why to shun death this anxious strife?
   If light can thus deceive, wherefore not life?

The later version seems to have the advantage in smoothness and simplicity. I gladly add the only other sonnet attributed to White, because it must have a great reflected interest, and because it is a sonnet of considerable power. Of course it must suffer by comparison with the great " Night."

ON FIRST HEARING MYSELF CALLED AN OLD MAN.
(ÆT. 50.)

AGES have rolled within my breast, though yet
  Not nigh the bourn to fleeting man assigned :
  Yes, old ; alas, how spent the struggling mind
Which at the noon of life is fain to set !
My dawn and evening have so closely met
  That men the shades of night begin to find
  Darkening my brow ; and heedless, not unkind,
Let the sad warning drop, without regret.

Gone Youth ! had I thus missed thee, nor a hope
  Were left of thy return beyond the tomb,
I would curse life ; but glorious is the scope
  Of an immortal soul. O Death, thy gloom,
Short, and already tinged with coming light,
  Is to the Christian but a summer's night.

" The most puling, petrifying, stupidly Platonic composition " is Byron's definition of the sonnet, which he follows by writing seven. As a general thing, his wings are too lawless in their sweep to allow him to gyrate in the sonnet's space, but his genius has rested in several, none of which seems so apt and Byronic as the following on Bonnivard, the subject of his immortal poem (1788–1824) : —

THE PRISONER OF CHILLON.

ETERNAL spirit of the chainless mind !
  Brightest in dungeons, Liberty ! thou art ;
  For there thy habitation is the heart, —
The heart which love of thee alone can bind ;

And when thy sons to fetters are consigned, —
   To fetters, and the damp vault's dayless gloom, —
   Their country conquers with their martyrdom,
And Freedom's fame finds wings on every wind.

Chillon ! thy prison is a holy place,
   And thy sad floor an altar ; for 't was trod,
Until his very steps have left a trace
   Worn, as if thy cold pavement were a sod,
By Bonnivard ! May none those marks efface !
   For they appeal from tyranny to God.

One has to be, like Shelley (1792–1822), " in his white ideal, all statue-blind," to see superior excellence in that poet's sonnets ; while to those who confess no great sympathy for his poetry his sonnets must appear particularly tame. Yet his admirers will at once mention " Ozymandias." It is inserted here to show that it is not a sonnet at all, though often classed as one. It must be called, at best, irregularly illegitimate in form ; while its rhymes are atrocious, as note : " stone, frown," " despair, appear " ! And yet one must concede the weird, uncanny strength of the poem : —

OZYMANDIAS.

I MET a traveler from an antique land,
   Who said : " Two vast and trunkless legs of stone
Stand in the desert. Near them, on the sand,
   Half sunk, a shattered visage lies, whose frown,
And wrinkled lip, and sneer of cold command,
   Tell that its sculptor well those passions read
Which yet survive (stamped on these lifeless things)
   The hand that mocked them and the heart that fed ;
And on the pedestal these words appear : —

'My name is Ozymandias, king of kings:
   Look on my works, ye mighty! and despair!'
Nothing beside remains. Round the decay
   Of that colossal wreck, boundless and bare
The lone and level sands stretch far away!"

It is a pleasure to pass the sonnet student on to Leigh Hunt (1784–1859), courtly knight of letters, in whose sonnets may be seen the sympathy and fine knowledge of its capacity and limitations which make his sonnet-study of abiding value. It is true that his poetry is not of the deep, impressive order, but he is bright, sparkling, and entertaining as well as reflective. In his fine sonnet on the Nile he has put Cleopatra's portrait into the eighth line with a rare felicity; while in the sonnet on Milton's hair he gives us almost the pleasure of possessing the relic. One can fancy Hunt, who was a curious manipulator of words, smiling at the unusual spectacle in the last sonnet, where three words form the last line: —

THE NILE.

It flows through old hushed Egypt and its sands,
   Like some grave, mighty thought threading a dream,
   And times and things, as in that vision, seem
Keeping along it their eternal stands, —
Caves, pillars, pyramids, the shepherd bands
   That roamed through the young world, the glory extreme
   Of high Sesostris, and that southern beam,
The laughing queen that caught the world's great hands.

Then comes a mightier silence, stern and strong,
   As of a world left empty of its throng,

And the void weighs on us; and then we wake,
  And hear the fruitful stream lapsing along
'Twixt villages, and think how we shall take
Our own calm journey on for human sake.

ON A LOCK OF MILTON'S HAIR.

It lies before me there, and my own breath
  Stirs its thin outer threads, as though beside
  The living head I stood in honored pride,
Talking of lovely things that conquer death.
Perhaps he pressed it once, or underneath
  Ran his fine fingers, when he leant, blank-eyed,
  And saw, in fancy, Adam and his bride
With their rich locks, or his own Delphic wreath.
There seems a love in hair, though it be dead.
  It is the gentlest, yet the strongest thread
Of our frail plant, — a blossom from the tree
Surviving the proud trunk; as though it said,
  Patience and Gentleness is Power. In me
Behold affectionate eternity.

In spite of the fact that John Keats (1795–1821) left comparatively few sonnets which are wholly admirable, it is not to be denied that he showed a fine facility with the form. Perhaps he wrote it too easily, for in classic form and symmetry his sonnets fall below those of Milton, Wordsworth, and Mrs. Browning. However, he was familiar with the sonnet and loved it, — the only key to success in its use. He counts time by sonnets, as in "I stood tiptoe" he says: "Why, one might read two sonnets," etc. He engages in sonnet contests, now writing about the Nile with Hunt and Shelley, — in which Hunt easily won the wreath, — next championing blue eyes against his friend Reynolds, who advocated brown ones. He leaves a sonnet on Homer on the table after sitting up all night with Chapman's translation; he sends sonnets to ladies; and otherwise makes sonnets his currency, minting his own coin. When he had become independent of the influence of Shakespeare, Spenser, Chaucer, Leigh Hunt, and all others whom he so generously admired, what sonnets he might have written! As it is, there is most excellent work in "O Solitude," his first printed verse, "Give me a Golden Pen," "Glory and Loveliness," "This Pleasant Tale," "On the Sea," "To Sleep," "The Day is gone," etc. One loves to remember such lines as —

> O what a power hath white simplicity,

or, —

> The poetry of earth is never dead.

In selecting his best two, one cannot go outside of the "Homer" and his last sonnet. Of the first, no one would say a better sonnet could be written on the subject. It is, like Homer, unique; a wide vista, a revelation and a surprise. As for the last sonnet, it seems the passionate longing of the sick, weary poet for rest; yet he would have rest blended with love, would breast the unknown sea on undulations of bliss: —

ON FIRST LOOKING INTO CHAPMAN'S "HOMER."

> Much have I traveled in the realms of gold,
>   And many goodly states and kingdoms seen;
>   Round many Western islands have I been,
> Which bards in fealty to Apollo hold.
> Oft of one wide expanse had I been told
>   That deep-browed Homer ruled as his demesne;

Yet did I never breathe its pure serene
Till I heard Chapman speak out loud and bold:

Then felt I like some watcher of the skies,
   When a new planet swims into his ken;
Or like stout Cortes when with eagle eyes
   He stared at the Pacific, and all his men
Looked at each other with a wild surmise —
   Silent, upon a peak in Darien.

HIS LAST SONNET.

BRIGHT Star! would I were steadfast as thou art!
   Not in lone splendor hung aloft the night,
And watching, with eternal lids apart,
   Like Nature's patient, sleepless Eremite,
The moving waters at their priestlike task
   Of pure ablution round earth's human shores,
Or gazing on the new soft-fallen mask
   Of snow upon the mountains and the moors:

No! yet still steadfast, still unchangeable,
   Pillowed upon my fair love's ripening breast,
To feel forever its soft fall and swell,
   Awake forever in a sweet unrest,
Still, still to hear her tender-taken breath,
And so live ever, or else swoon to death.

As we near our own times, the sonnet claims an increasing number of votaries in England, and we pass by the interesting work of Mrs. Hemans, Hartley Coleridge, Thomas Hood, Lord Houghton (see his sonnets on " Happiness " and " The Forest "), and others, to pay tribute to the queen of sonnet-writers, Mrs. Browning (1809–1861). Italy might well claim an interest in her genius; for in her sonnets, especially, it seems as if a more flexible tongue must have blended with her thought, and given that rare fluidity of expression. She delights in a sonnet, as a swallow in a gale, and the harder the rhymes, or the more elusive the thought, the more deftly she turns her wings and beats to heavenward. The "Sonnets from the Portuguese" have had many imitators, and this is high praise, but one must go to the first hands for the ductile, gold continuity of thought, the threaded phrase-jewels. In her we find the sonnet sufficing for a woman's heart, as it did for a man's in Shakespeare. These two sonnets are perhaps no better than many others of Mrs. Browning's. They are both "Miltonic" in treatment: —

FOR LOVE'S SAKE ONLY.

IF thou must love me, let it be for nought
   Except for love's sake only. Do not say
"I love her for her smile . . . her look . . . her way
Of speaking gently, . . . for a trick of thought
That falls in well with mine, and certes brought
   A sense of pleasant ease on such a day;"
   For these things in themselves, Beloved, may
Be changed, or change for thee, — and love so wrought
May be unwrought so. Neither love me for
   Thine own dear pity's wiping my cheeks dry, —
A creature might forget to weep who bore
   Thy comfort long, and lose thy love thereby!
But love me for love's sake, that evermore
   Thou mayest love on, through love's eternity.

BROKEN IDOLS.

AND, O beloved voices, upon which
   Ours passionately call, because erelong
   Ye brake off in the middle of that song

We sang together softly, to enrich
The poor world with the sense of love, and witch
   The heart out of things evil, — I am strong,
   Knowing ye are not lost for aye among
The hills with last year's thrush. God keeps a niche
In Heaven to hold our idols; and albeit
   He brake them to our faces, and denied
     That our close kisses should impair their white,
I know we shall behold them raised, complete,
   The dust shook off their beauty, glorified,
     New Memnons singing in the great God-light.

From so well-known a poet we turn to one little read on this side of the water, Alexander Smith (1830–1867). His sonnets on Christmas are full of the season's feeling, and the following seems a pleasant echo of Keats: —

BEAUTY.

BEAUTY still walketh on the earth and air:
   Our present sunsets are as rich in gold
   As ere the Iliad's music was out-rolled,
The roses of the Spring are ever fair,
'Mong branches green still ring-doves coo and pair,
   And the deep sea still foams its music old;
   So if we are at all divinely souled,
This beauty will unloose our bonds of care.
'T is pleasant when blue skies are o'er us bending
   Within old starry-gated Poesy,
     To meet a soul set to no worldly tune,
   Like thine, sweet friend! Ah! dearer this to me
     Than are the dewy trees, the sun, the moon,
Or noble music with a golden ending.

A few examples must suffice to represent those English poets who have so recently stopped singing, and one must be awarded to a woman who exemplified so much that was tender, womanly, and humane, — Mrs. Mulock-Craik. In many of her poems the thought outruns, and is superior to, the art in the versification, yet the following is evidence enough of her capacity for smooth lines: —

GUNS OF PEACE.
Sunday Night, March 30, 1856.

GHOSTS of dead soldiers in the battle slain,
   Ghosts of dead heroes dying nobler far
   In the long patience of inglorious war,
Of famine, cold, heat, pestilence, and pain, —
All ye whose loss makes up our vigorous gain, —
   This quiet night, as sounds the cannon's tongue,
   Do ye look down the trembling stars among,
Viewing our peace and war with like disdain?

Or, wiser grown since reaching those new spheres,
   Smile ye on those poor bones ye sow'd as seed
   For this our harvest, nor regret the deed?
Yet lift one cry with us to heavenly ears, —
   "Strike with Thy bolt the next red flag unfurl'd,
   And make all wars to cease throughout the world."

This example of the late Matthew Arnold has so much of his gospel of aspiration and hope, amid gloom, that it need hardly be accredited to him. Yet his style of versifying was more like Emerson's, striking "with hammer or with mace," and the sonnet form was perhaps no better suited to him than to the Concord poet. In this sonnet one might fancy the stanza as a gay Italian courtier struggling to bear a heavy coat of mail: —

IMMORTALITY.

Foil'd by our fellow-men, depress'd, outworn,
   We leave the brutal world to take its way,
   And, *Patience! in another life,* we say,
The world shall be thrust down, and we upborne!
And will not, then, the immortal armies scorn
   The world's poor routed leavings? or will they,
   Who fail'd under the heat of this life's day,
Support the fervors of the heavenly morn?

No, no! the energy of life may be
   Kept on after the grave, but not begun!
   And he who flagg'd not in the earthly strife,

From strength to strength advancing, — only he,
   His soul well-knit, and all his battles won,
   Mounts, and that hardly, to eternal life.

Dante Gabriel Rossetti (1828–1882) is highly esteemed in England as a sonneteer. By nature and training he became possessed of great sympathy with the form and used it freely. The "Dark Glass" is one of his strongest, and in it as in many of his poems he paints love and life against a sombre background. While his sonnets are artistic, they do not linger in memory like more spontaneous utterances by Wordsworth, Milton, Keats, Mrs. Browning, etc. But it is doubtless unfair to compare him with such great poets. He was more painter than philosopher or singer, yet he felt keenly, and his lines often throb with stress and pain. He put pretty and graceful work in this sonnet: —

TRUE WOMAN.

To be a sweetness more desired than Spring;
  A bodily beauty more acceptable
  Than the wild rose-tree's arch that crowns the fell;
To be an essence more environing
Than wine's drained juice; a music ravishing
  More than the passionate pulse of Philomel, —
  To be all this 'neath one soft bosom's swell
That is the flower of life, how strange a thing!

How strange a thing to be what Man can know
  But as a sacred secret! Heaven's own screen
Hides her soul's purest depth and loveliest glow;
  Closely withheld, as all things most unseen, —
  The wave-bowered pearl, the heart-shaped seal of green
That flecks the snowdrop underneath the snow.

Here, too, is a fluent, exquisitely subtle sonnet by Miss Rossetti: —

Amor, che ne la mento mi ragiona." — DANTE.
Amor vien nel bel viso di costei." — PETRARCH."

IF there be any one can take my place
  And make you happy whom I grieve to grieve,
  Think not that I can grudge it, but believe
I do commend you to that nobler grace,
That readier wit than mine, that sweeter face;
  Yea, since your riches make me rich, conceive
  I too am crowned while bridal crowns I weave,
And thread the bridal dance with jocund pace.

For if I did not love you, it might be
  That I should grudge you some one dear delight;
  But since the heart is yours that was mine own,
Your pleasure is my pleasure, right my right,

> Your honorable freedom makes me free,
>   And, you companioned, I am not alone.
>   CHRISTINA G. ROSSETTI.

Robert Browning wrote the sonnet rarely, possibly because he disliked its restraints; possibly he purposed to let no lesser light of his shine by the side of the "Sonnets from the Portuguese." The "Helen's Tower" is graceful complimentary and occasional verse, but would not be quoted save for its personal interest. Any one, however, who studies Browning's poetry will see how inapt the sonnet form is for the willful, eccentric orbits in which his genius loved to move.

Lord Tennyson has written the sonnet occasionally, not as a habit. Yet his "Montenegro" is as glorious as Milton's on the massacre in Piedmont; while there is a great deal that is memorable in the natural and moral grandeur of "Night."

MONTENEGRO.

THEY rose to where their sovran eagle sails,
  They kept their faith, their freedom on the height,
  Chaste, frugal, savage, armed by day and night
Against the Turk; whose inroad nowhere scales
Their headlong passes, but his footstep fails,
  And red with blood the crescent reels from fight
  Before their dauntless hundreds, in prone flight
By thousands down the crags and thro' the vales.

O smallest among peoples! rough rock-throne
  Of Freedom! warriors beating back the swarm
    Of Turkish Islam for five hundred years,
Great Tsernogora! never since thine own
  Black ridges drew the cloud and brake the storm
    Has breathed a race of mightier mountaineers.

The sonnet on "Night" is hardly less striking, and is well worth committing to memory as a rune for a lifetime: —

NIGHT.

Though Night hath climbed her peak of highest noon,
   And bitter blasts the screaming Autumn whirl,
   All night through archways of the bridgèd pearl,
And portals of pure silver, walks the moon.
Walk on, my soul, nor crouch to agony,
   Turn cloud to light and bitterness to joy,
And dross to gold with glorious alchemy,
   Basing thy throne above the world's annoy.

Reign thou above the storms of sorrow and ruth
   That roar beneath; unshaken peace hath won thee;
So shalt thou pierce the woven glooms of truth;
   So shall the blessing of the meek be on thee;
So in thine hour of dawn, the body's youth,
   An honorable eld shall come upon thee.

It is beyond the scope of this essay adequately to represent the younger English writers of the sonnet. A commensurate idea of the popularity of the poem in England at present may be gained by consulting the English sonnet anthologies, to all of which I gladly acknowledge more or less indebtedness.

A mere reference to previous writers on the subject may be of interest to sonnet-students who wish to pursue the subject exhaustively. Capel Lofft issued a sonnet anthology in England in 1813. He had an original theory regarding the correspondence between the sonnet's structure and music, which was too elaborate or imaginative to gain favor. He was followed by Housman, in 1833, with a creditable collection and essay. Then came Dyce's small collection and that of Leigh Hunt, whose studious research and artistic sympathy make his essay surpassingly valuable. As a supplement to Hunt's collection, a selection of American sonnets by S. Adams Lee was published with it in 1867. Continuing the succession in England are books of the sonnet by Tomlinson, Dennis, Main (author of the "Treasury of English Sonnets"), Samuel Waddington, compiler of three volumes of sonnets; Hall Caine ("Sonnets of Three Centuries"); and William Sharp ("Sonnets of this Century," and "American Sonnets," the latter not published in this country.) There have been many other writers of essays on the sonnet, including Theodore Watts, Charles Tennyson-Turner, Ashcroft Noble, Edward Dowden, Mark Pattison, editor of Milton's sonnets; Archbishop Trench, editor of Wordsworth's sonnets; J. Addington Symonds, and in this country Henry Timrod, R. H. Stoddard, J. W. Chadwick, J. C. Rowell, and others. One might also instance Dr. Karl Leutzner's sonnet treatise in the German (1886), and two French anthologies by De Veyriéres and Asselineau, beside various Italian anthologies.

Nearly all of these concede the superiority of the Petrarcan octave, and the two or three favorite Italian arrangements of the sestet. Indeed, the practice of the best sonneteers would be hard to combat. Mr. Caine is emphatic in his disapproval of rhymed couplets at the end of a Petrarcan sonnet, while Mr. Sharp says they are only allowable at the end of a "Shakespearean" sonnet. Still it must be confessed that there are Petrarcan sonnets, ending with rhymed couplets, where the thought has seemed to congeal into that as its chosen form, and which one could not change without deterioration. But it is these exceptions that prove the rule.

Theodore Watts formulated the idea that a sonnet, at least one type of the Petrarcan sonnet, of two divisions, has a subtle resemblance to the inflowing and outflowing of a wave on the seashore; and he likens the octave to the flowing, the sestet to the ebbing wave. The simile is happy in some points, but not so generally true as to justify the undiscriminating indorsement it has received by other English critics. A sonnet *should* have a strong, irresistible, beautiful swell of thought, like a wave; and if it be arranged so that the octave states the surface thought and the sestet the underlying one, — the form of a simile, — then it may somewhat resemble a wave in being an action and reaction. The sestet should have the power of the undertow!

But one cannot carry the comparison very far. A sonnet might almost as well be likened to many other alternations of action in natural phenomena. The figure of a wave as applied to the coming and going of the emotion in the poet's own mind is excellent. But as applied to the structure of many sonnets the wave simile is faulty. The wave has a continuous movement, a curve; and as to sound, a crash, a sigh, and a succeeding singing as of a forest of birds, the bubbles dancing like ocean fays as they speed back to the sea: whereas the music of the sonnet is by chiming rhymes, a regular arrangement of notes, and its movement is metrical (*staccato* almost), owing to the accent. It is not that I seek to cross lances with the poet-critic of the London "Athenæum," the poetry and the sonnet essayist in the "Encyclopædia Britannica;" but I think his friends, in zeal to adopt his fancy, have carried it too far.

Thus, Mr. Caine, after his self-imposed task of lifting the burden of "illegitimacy" from the Shakespearean form of sonnet, observes: —

"The Italian form demands two parts to the sonnet-thought, but they are as the two parts of an acorn; the later English form requires also two sides to the sonnet-thought, but they are as the two movements of a wave. In the one, the parts are separate and contrasted, yet united; in the other they are blended, the same in substance, distinct only in movement."

It must be stated that Mr. Caine means the contemporary English sonnet by the "later English;" for he claims as "English" the sonnet as very slightly modified by Milton, the regular Italian form. It is pleasant to cite Mr. Watts's own exposition of his theory. The first line of its sestet is happy and memorable, though we have other as happy characterizations of the sonnet in a single line. That the wave theory is pleasant and harmless, when it is not carried too far, no one will deny; but to impress on readers or writers, as some English writers have, that they must be on the watch for "ebb and flow" in every sonnet, is ridiculous.

THE SONNET'S VOICE.

You silvery billows breaking on the beach
   Fall back in foam beneath the star-shine clear,
   The while my rhymes are murmuring in your ear
A restless lore like that the billows teach;
For on these sonnet-waves my soul would reach
   From its own depths, and rest within you, dear,
   As, through the billowy voices yearning here,
Great nature strives to find a human speech.

A sonnet is a wave of melody:
   From heaving waters of the impassioned soul
   A billow of tidal music, one and whole,
Flows in the "octave;" then returning free,
   Its ebbing surges in the "sestet" roll
Back to the deeps of Life's tumultuous sea.

                              THEODORE WATTS.

There is not space to speak critically in this place of the small army of contemporary sonneteers in England. In the anthologies mentioned will be found excellent work by the pens of Allingham, Austin, Blackie, Buchanan, De Vere, Dowden, Gosse, Graves, Hamilton, Dobson, Locker, Lang, Marston, Monkhouse, Myers, Noble, Palgrave, Patmore, Robinson, Scott, Stevenson, Symonds, Todhunter, Watts, and other well known poets. A few examples will show the high quality of some of the contemporary sonnets of England. These two first cited have fine pathos, the first having great strength in its originality of conception, the second remarkable for its symmetry and imagination. The expression of the first is simple, that of the second most artistic:—

WHEN WE ARE ALL ASLEEP.

WHEN He returns, and finds all sleeping here,
   Some old, some young, some fair, and some not fair,
Will He stoop down and whisper in each ear,
   "Awaken!" or for pity's sake forbear,
Saying, "How shall I meet their frozen stare
   Of wonder, and their eyes so woebegone?
How shall I comfort them in their despair
   If they cry out '*Too late! let us sleep on*'?"

Perchance He will not wake us up, but when
   He sees us look so happy in our rest,
Will murmur, "Poor dead women and dead men!
   Dire was their doom, and weary was their quest.
Wherefore awake them into life again?
   Let them sleep on untroubled, — it is best."
ROBERT BUCHANAN.

INEVITABLE CHANGE.

REBUKE me not! I have nor wish nor skill
   To alter one hair's breadth in all this house
   Of Love, rising with domes so luminous
And air-built galleries on life's topmost hill!
Only I know that fate, chance, years that kill,
   Change that transmutes, have aimed their darts at us;
   Envying each lovely shrine and amorous
Reared on earth's soil by man's too passionate will.

Dread thou the moment when these glittering towers,
   These adamantine walls and gates of gems,
     Shall fade like forms of sun-forsaken cloud;
When dulled by imperceptible chill hours,
   The golden spires of our Jerusalems
     Shall melt to mist and vanish in night's shroud!
J. A. SYMONDS.

This is a sonnet of sincere feeling by Mr. Watts: —

THE FIRST KISS.

If only in dreams may Man be fully blest,
  Is heav'n a dream? Is she I claspt a dream?
  Or stood she here even now where dewdrops gleam
And miles of furze shine golden down the west?
I seem to clasp her still, — still on my breast
  Her bosom beats, — I see the blue eyes beam:
  I think she kiss'd these lips, for now they seem
Scarce mine, so hallow'd of the lips they pressed!

Yon thicket's breath — can that be eglantine?
  Those birds — can they be morning's choristers?
  Can this be Earth? Can these be banks of furze?
Like burning bushes fired of God they shine!
I seem to know them, though this body of mine
  Pass'd into spirit at the touch of hers!

Andrew Lang is so well known in America, as a man who writes with enthusiasm and says things strongly and well, that one need hardly put his name under the following: —

THE ODYSSEY.

As one that for a weary space has lain
  Lulled by the song of Circe and her wine
  In gardens near the pale of Proserpine,
Where that Ægean isle forgets the main,
And only the low lutes of love complain,
  And only shadows of wan lovers pine,
  As such an one were glad to know the brine
Salt on his lips, and the large air again, —

So, gladly, from the songs of modern speech
  Men turn, and see the stars, and feel the free

Shrill wind beyond the close of heavy flowers,
  And, through the music of the languid hours,
They hear, like ocean on a western beach,
  The surge and thunder of the Odyssey.

The playful satire, underlying point and deft poise in the following are also quite characteristic of Mr. Dobson: —

DON QUIXOTE.

BEHIND thy pasteboard, on thy battered hack,
  Thy lean cheek striped with plaster to and fro,
  Thy long spear leveled at the unseen foe,
And doubtful Sancho trudging at thy back,
Thou wert a figure strange enough, good lack!
  To make wiseacredom, both high and low,
  Rub purblind eyes, and (having watched thee go)
Despatch its Dogsberrys upon thy track:

Alas, poor Knight! Alas, poor soul possest!
  Yet would to-day, when Courtesy grows chill,
And life's fine loyalties are turned to jest,
  Some fire of thine might burn within us still!
Ah! would but one might lay his lance in rest,
  And charge in earnest — were it but a mill!

There is great temptation to prolong this prelude of foreign sonnets, but we must close with Mr. Gosse's curious and musical sonnet, "Alcyone."

A SONNET IN DIALOGUE.

Phœbus. WHAT voice is this that wails above the deep?
Alcyone. A wife's, that mourns her fate and loveless
        days.
Phœbus. What love lies buried in these waterways?
Alcyone. A husband's, hurried to eternal sleep.

Phœbus. Cease, O beloved, cease to wail and weep!
Alcyone. Wherefore?
Phœbus. The waters in a fiery blaze
Proclaim the godhead of my healing rays.
Alcyone. No god can sow where fate hath stood to reap.
Phœbus. Hold, wringing hands! cease, piteous tears, to fall!
Alcyone. But grief must rain and glut the passionate sea.
Phœbus. Thou shalt forget this ocean and thy wrong,
And I will bless the dead, though past recall.
Alcyone. What can'st thou give to me or him in me?
Phœbus. A name in story and a light in song.

The literature of America is so young that the diffusion of the sonnet form through it need hardly be considered chronologically. The men who brought the sonnet to perfection and popularity in this country are either still living or have but recently passed away, so that the historical view of American sonnets is a brief one at best. It is a matter for pride that the earliest of our native writers of the sonnet, as he has long been reputed to be, was so admirable a figure as Colonel David Humphreys. He mingled both literary and patriotic ambitions, was a Yale graduate, a soldier and diplomat.

It is evident that people did not take the leisure to write many sonnets in the early days of the republic. Such things could be obtained from England, and meanwhile there was plenty of more onerous work to be done in making of laws, hewing of forests, and building of states. The sonnet being a product of leisurely culture, and generally preceded by simpler forms of verse, it is not surprising, then, that there were no prominent writers of the sonnet before the patriarchal group of poets who fathered the melodious period of our own time. In this group were the accomplished Percival, the gifted Dana, the painter Allston, the versatile Willis, the dignified Bryant. But even of these it must be noted that Dana was not a sonneteer. Many of the older poets wrote only the Shakespearean or some irregular form of sonnet, Bryant declaring that he failed to see the superior melody of the Italian form. Indeed, there are a number of prominent American poets who are not sonneteers. Emerson could not bind to so rigid and intricate a form a muse that must "aye climb for its rhyme." Poe's sonnets were few, and not noteworthy when compared with his other verse. The idea of Walt Whitman's writing a sonnet is calculated to bring a smile; and this list might be extended. So it must not be expected that a sonnet anthology will wholly represent the poets of the time nor exactly measure the poetic capacity of those who are included. The men, then, who have really been pioneers in the revival of the sonnet in our literature, are poets like Longfellow, Boker, Lowell, Bayard Taylor, and Aldrich. It would only be fair to mention with them such poets among women as Mrs. Botta, Mrs. Dorr, Mrs. Preston, Mrs. Oakes Smith, etc. But closely following these is such an array of sonnet-writers — the young and the middle-aged poets of to-day — that one would have to mention scores of names to represent the group.

It must be admitted that the sonnet in America has grown of its own vitality. Until recent years there has been little written on the subject to stimulate production; while anthologies of poetry, generally compiled by poets out of sympathy with the sonnet, have given the little poem scant recognition indeed. The only anthology of American sonnets yet published in this country appeared in 1867, and its editor then lamented the poverty of good material to choose from. It notes the promising sonnets of Aldrich, a star that seemed to have just gleamed above the horizon as the book was sent to press. But the general longing on the part of the editor is like Rowland Robinson's in the old hymn —

"Teach me some melodious sonnet."

The English collection of American sonnets made by William Sharp, and published recently (when the present compilation was about half finished), gave indication of the very respectable resources of our sonnet mines. In it the compiler stated that he believed a finer collection of sonnets could be made from the contemporary American poets than from living English ones. We acknowledge the charm of many current English sonnets, but we are tempted to adopt his generous opinion; for we believe that the living American poets are holding their own against our contemporary cousins in sonnets as well as in other forms of poetry. After perusing some of the English collections of sonnets, we fancy there is a certain generic difference between the typical contemporary English sonnet and the current American one. If one may hazard the opinion, English sonnets display most conspicuously a sedate, often deep, order of thought, occasional striking imagery, and a punctilious observance of some of the older canons of verse-making, without often attaining to as great excellence in spirited movement and melody. The choice of subjects is not so wide, it seems, as in this country, and many of the poets appear to be still walking in the shadow of the great sonneteers who are dead.

The American sonnet, on the contrary, we believe is superior in nervous energy, in originality and movement; in a wider range of thought, though it may not be so deep and introspective. It attains melody and flexible strength, and yet is often marred by trivial blemishes in versification or expression, which appear to be the result of hurry. There are, of course, suggestions of imitation in some American sonnets, but this is characteristic chiefly of the work of novices. The American sonnet at its best displays a conscious inspiration, an excuse for being; it has genuine feeling and a virility which more than atone for occasional lack of repose, profound thought, or perfectly polished lines.

As when within some great, harmonious hall,
   With light and flowers and rich devices hung,
   We wait to hear the heavenly concord wrung
From voice and strings, with bird-like rise and fall,
Obedient to some potent master's call:
   So in this silence, ere a song is sung,
   We wait some mystic power to move among
The poets, as a breeze, to bend them all.

Rapt, chastened faces wait the low command,
   And fingers touch the harps of fourteen strings
     With nerves a-tremble for the mystic sign.
Spirit of Poesy! Take thou the wand —
   And swift up to the starry arches wings
     The music of thy symphony divine.

REPRESENTATIVE SONNETS.

REPRESENTATIVE SONNETS.

FAITH'S VISTA.

When from the vaulted wonder of the sky
   The curtain of the light is drawn aside,
   And I behold the stars in all their wide
Significance and glorious mystery,
Assured that those more distant orbs are suns
   Round which innumerable worlds revolve,
   My faith grows strong, my day-born doubts dissolve,
And death, that dread annulment which life shuns,

Or fain would shun, becomes to life the way,
   The thoroughfare to greater worlds on high,
The bridge from star to star. Seek how we may,
   There is no other road across the sky;
And, looking up, I hear star-voices say:
   "You could not reach us if you did not die."

                                  Henry Abbey.

RENUNCIATION.

Nay, friend, farewell! for if I loved you less,
  It might be I should strive to hold you fast
  In bonds of friendship you had long o'erpast,
And play the tyrant where I hoped to bless.
Yet, since my love still pleads, I fain would press
  Once more your hand e'en while I seem to cast
  It coldly from me with these words at last, —
I may not keep and you may not possess!

Sweet friend, believe me, it is better so, —
  To part while love finds yet no cause for grief
    In slowly-waning faith, lest haply you
    Should one day find some flaw in me you knew
Not of, and I through tears should watch you go,
  Knowing your soul in mine had lost belief.
Oscar Fay Adams.

FADING BARRIERS.

If I have ever told you all my heart
  Was yours, and perfect was the love it bore,
  Believe it not! For in the time past o'er
I, like some world-wide traveler, would start
And gaze astonished where the mountains part,
  Thinking of mountain peaks beyond no more,
  As dimly climbing from the heaven's blue shore
On loftier heights the splendor falls athwart.

So while I dream all perfect is the bliss
  Which years have added to my soul in thine,
    And say, here must be the eternal bound,
Lo, in my heart some thought of thee doth kiss
  Into clear light that undetermined line
    Which hovers on the heaven of love profound.
John Albee.

RECREATION IN LOVE.

That thou art high above me I have found
   Full oft; when all alone my heavy brain
   Turns from itself to thee, my thoughts regain
A place so far beyond their usual bound
I know they climb of other stairs the round
   Than those which their aspiring flights restrain
   In this dull house of clay. Come, not in vain
Thy height shall raise me from this lifeless ground.

Let me from thine my lampless way rewin;
   Usurp this empty-falling tenement
     With ruin underset, o'erhung by night;
Replenish it with all that once has been,
   When all it had or wished thy presence lent,
     And love trimmed fresh the intellectual light.

John Albee.

KEATS'S LOVE-LETTERS.

Rest, hunted spirit! Canst thou never sleep?
   Ah, when the ghouls and vampires of the Press
   Vex all thy tender soul in wantonness,
Canst thou know aught of peace, but still must weep!
What! shall thy heart's rich blood, poured out so deep,
   Be made a merchandise without redress,
   Nor any voice the world's base deed confess
Which prints and sells a poet's love so cheap?

My curse upon this prying, prurient age!
   And curst the eyes not closed in angry shame!
     For him whom English air and critic pen
Twice baffled ere his splendid, youthful gage
   Had measured half the heaven of love and fame,
     This shameless book has murdered once again!

John Albee.

THOREAU.

Who nearer Nature's life would truly come
  Must nearer come to him of whom I speak:
He all kinds knew, — the vocal and the dumb;
  Masterful in genius was he and unique,
Patient, sagacious, tender, frolicsome.
  This Concord Pan would oft his whistle take,
And forth from wood and fen, field, hill, and lake,
  Trooping around him in their several guise,

The shy inhabitants their haunts forsake;
  Then he, like Æsop, man would satirize,
Hold up the image wild to clearest view
  Of undiscerning manhood's puzzled eyes,
And mocking say, "Lo! mirrors here for you:
  Be true as these if ye would be more wise."

A. Bronson Alcott.

TO MRS. ALCOTT.

Mean are all titles of nobility,
  And kings poor spendthrifts while I do compare
The wealth she daily lavishes on me
  Of love, the noble kingdom that I share:
Is it the jealous year, for emphasis,
  Sheds beauteous sunshine and refreshing dews?
My maiden's mouth doth softlier court and kiss,
  Tint springtime's virgin cheek with rosier hues.

Fly faster o'er my page, impassioned quill,
  Signing this note of mine with tenderer touch!
Say I no measure find to mete my will,
  Say that I love, but cannot tell how much;
Let time and trouble the full story tell:
  I cannot love thee more, I know I love thee well.

A. Bronson Alcott.

TO L. M. A.

WHEN I remember with what buoyant heart,
   Midst war's alarms and woes of civil strife,
   In youthful eagerness thou didst depart,
At peril of thy safety, peace, and life,
   To nurse the wounded soldier, swathe the dead, —
   How piercèd soon by fever's poisoned dart,
And brought unconscious home, with 'wildered head, —
   Thou ever since, mid languor and dull pain,

To conquer fortune, cherish kindred dear,
   Hast with grave studies vexed a sprightly brain,
In myriad households kindled love and cheer;
   Ne'er from thyself by Fame's loud trump beguiled,
Sounding in this and the farther hemisphere, —
   I press thee to my heart as Duty's faithful child.
                                      A. BRONSON ALCOTT.

READ AT EMERSON'S FUNERAL.

HIS harp is silent; shall successors rise,
   Touching with venturous hand the trembling string,
Kindle glad raptures, visions of surprise,
   And wake to ecstasy each slumbering thing?
Shall life and thought flash new in wondering eyes,
As when the seer transcendant, sweet and wise,
   World-wide his native melodies did sing,
Flushed with fair hopes and ancient memories?

Ah no: that matchless lyre shall silent lie;
   None hath the vanished minstrel's wondrous skill
   To touch that instrument with art and will,
With him winged Poesy doth droop and die;
   While our dull age, left voiceless, must lament
   The bard high Heaven had for its service sent.
                                      A. BRONSON ALCOTT.

A CHILD SHALL LEAD THEM.

Thou Child-Soul, sister of the Loving Ones
  Whom Dante saw in circling, choral dance
  Above the stars; thou who in charmèd trance
Dost bind these earthly to those heavenly zones,
So that Love's spell all lower life attones
  To that far song; behold thy ministrants —
  All things that live — in loving train advance,
Thee following. Even as the Sea, that moans

With wildness, followeth the moon's white dream,
  His rage suppressed, — so, by thy heavenly mood
  The fiercer beasts that in the jungle brood
Assuagèd are: and thou, sweet maid, shalt even
Thy triumph join unto the pomp supreme —
God's Kingdom come on Earth as 't is in Heaven.

Henry Mills Alden.

SLEEP.

When to soft Sleep we give ourselves away,
  And in a dream as in a fairy bark
  Drift on and on through the enchanted dark
To purple daybreak, little thought we pay
To that sweet, bitter world we know by day.
  We are clean quit of it, as is a lark
  So high in heaven no human eye may mark
The thin swift pinion cleaving through the gray.

Till we awake ill fate can do no ill,
  The resting heart shall not take up again
    The heavy load that yet must make it bleed;
For this brief space the loud world's voice is still,
  No faintest echo of it brings us pain.
    How will it be when we shall sleep indeed?

Thomas Bailey Aldrich.

MIRACLES.

SICK of myself and all that keeps the light
  Of the blue skies away from me and mine,
  I climb this ledge, and by this wind-swept pine,
Lingering, watch the coming of the night.
'T is ever a new wonder to my sight.
  Men look to God for some mysterious sign,
  For other stars than those that nightly shine,
For some unnatural symbol of His might : —

Wouldst see a miracle as grand as those
  The prophets wrought of old in Palestine?
Come watch with me the shaft of fire that glows
  In yonder west; the fair, frail palaces,
The fading alps and archipelagoes,
  And great cloud-continents of sunset-seas.
THOMAS BAILEY ALDRICH.

FREDERICKSBURG.

THE increasing moonlight drifts across my bed,
  And on the churchyard by the road, I know
  It falls as white and noiselessly as snow. . .
'T was such a night two weary summers fled;
The stars, as now, were waning overhead.
  Listen! Again the shrill-lipped bugles blow
  Where the swift currents of the river flow
Past Fredericksburg; far off the heavens are red

With sudden conflagration: on yon height,
  Linstock in hand, the gunners hold their breath:
A signal-rocket pierces the dense night,
  Flings its spent stars upon the town beneath!
Hark! — the artillery massing on the right;
  Hark! — the black squadrons wheeling down to
    Death!
THOMAS BAILEY ALDRICH.

THREE FLOWERS.

Herewith I send you three pressed withered flowers:
   This one was white, with golden star; this, blue
     As Capri's cave; that, purple and shot through
With sunset-orange. Where the Duomo towers
In diamond air, and under hanging bowers
   The Arno glides, this faded violet grew
     On Landor's grave; from Landor's heart it drew
Its magic azure in the long spring hours.

Within the shadow of the Pyramid
   Of Caius Cestius was the daisy found,
     White as the soul of Keats in Paradise.
The pansy, — there were hundreds of them, hid
   In the thick grass that folded Shelley's mound,
     Guarding his ashes with most lovely eyes.
Thomas Bailey Aldrich.

ENGLAND.

While men pay reverence to mighty things,
   They must revere thee, thou blue-cinctured isle
     Of England, — not to-day, but this long while,
In front of nations, Mother of great kings,
Soldiers, and poets. Round thee the sea flings
   His steel-bright arm, and shields thee from the guile
     And hurt of France. Secure, with august smile,
Thou sittest, and the East its tribute brings.

Some say thy old-time power is on the wane,
   Thy moon of grandeur, filled, contracts at length, —
     They see it darkening down from less to less.
Let but a hostile hand make threat again,
   And they shall see thee in thy ancient strength,
     Each iron sinew quivering, lioness!
Thomas Bailey Aldrich.

"EVEN THIS WILL PASS AWAY."

TOUCHED with the delicate green of early May,
   Or later, when the rose unveils her face,
   The world hangs glittering in star-strown space,
Fresh as a jewel found but yesterday.
And yet 't is very old; what tongue may say
   How old it is? Race follows upon race,
   Forgetting and forgotten; in their place
Sink tower and temple; nothing long may stay.

We build on tombs, and live our day, and die;
   From out our dust new towers and temples start;
   Our very name becomes a mystery.
What cities no man ever heard of lie
   Under the glacier in the mountain's heart,
   In violet glooms beneath the moaning sea!
                THOMAS BAILEY ALDRICH.

ON THE DEATH OF COLERIDGE.

AND thou art gone, most loved, most honored friend!
No, nevermore thy gentle voice shall blend
With air of earth its pure ideal tones,
Binding in one, as with harmonious zones,
The heart and intellect. And I no more
   Shall with thee gaze on that unfathomed deep,
The human soul; as when, pushed off the shore,
   Thy mystic bark would through the darkness sweep,
Itself the while so bright! For oft we seemed
   As on some starless sea, — all dark above,
   All dark below, — yet, onward as we drove,
To plough up light that ever round us streamed.
   But he who mourns is not as one bereft
   Of all he loved: thy living truths are left.
                WASHINGTON ALLSTON.

PENITENCE.

LIFE is too short, dear love, for unkind feeling,
  Too short for harsh reproach, or bitter tone;
  For us should be but gentle words alone:
If I have wronged you, dear, here let me kneeling
Low at your side — in penitence appealing —
  Seek pardon for a fault I had not known,
  Save that my love for you so strong had grown
It passed the bounds of reason's wise concealing.

Dear love, by all our past of untold gladness,
  By every loving word and fond caress
  Which filled our lives with such sweet happiness,
Forgive, forget that one brief hour of madness;
  Then may you know the highest joy of living, —
  The God-like peace, the sweetness of forgiving.
JENNIE P. ARNOLD.

CONFESSION.

THOU art the friend and comrade, Poesy,
  For whom I suffer all things, still content
  If not in vain for thee my light is spent, —
The share of heavenly light that fell on me.
Thou art my meat, my drink, my liberty;
  Thou art my garb, thou art my tenement,
  Wherein I hide all night from floods unpent,
From lightnings, winds, and scourgings of the sea.

Oh, thou art strong and lovely as the light, —
  Yea, as the light of morning, strong and sweet!
Thou art the lover perfect in my sight,
  Attending all my steps with eager feet;
The form, the image in my dreams at night,
  The morning glory that I rise to greet.
OBADIAH C. AURINGER.

ON THE BRIDGE AT GLENN'S.

A REMINISCENCE OF COOPER.

BLANK shadow here. The heights on either hand
   Sparkle with lamps. Around me foams the bold,
   Loud Hudson, — swiftly into darkness rolled.
These vanish all, and Memory takes her stand
In that wild cave among that famous band,
   Girt round by unseen terrors manifold,
   Revealed in that enchanting fiction old,
Blown hence through many an alien tongue and land.

I see the haughty Uncas, and the wise,
   Grim Sagamore; hear Hawkeye's cheery call;
The singer's strains, of sacred sounds compact;
And then I hear the holy hymn arise
   From the sweet Sisters' lips; and, borne through all,
The plunge and tremble of the cataract.
O. C. AURINGER.

EMERSON — CARLYLE.

ONE stood upon the morning hills and saw
   The heavens revealed in symbol and in sign;
   He read their mystic meanings, line by line,
And taught in light the reign of rhythmic law.
One in the twilight valleys, pierced with awe,
   Beheld wan Hope amid great darkness shine, —
   Saw gloom and glory blent without design,
And cried against a world of blot and flaw.

Sunrise and sunset poise the perfect day:
   One was the prince of morning fair and free,
And one the lord of darkness was, and they
   Made day and night one round of harmony,
For they were kings and brothers, and their sway
   One law, — one new, divine philosophy.
O. C. AURINGER.

DEUS IMMANENS.

I SOMETIMES wonder that the human mind,
   In searching for creation's hidden things,
   Should miss that high intelligence that springs
From that which is not seen, but is divined.
Does knowing much of nature make us blind
   To nature's better self? The Greek could see
   A conscious life in every stream and tree, —
Some nymph or god. Our broader faith should find

A life divine, whose fine pulsations roll
   In endless surges through the secret veins
   Of earth and sky, which hidden still remains
Save to the instinct of the reverent soul;
   Should know that everything, from lowest sod
   To farthest star, thrills with the life of God.

T. R. BACON.

ATLANTIS.

As one who hears beside a quiet shore,
   When seas are stilled and winds and waves are spent,
   Faint murmurs of that vanished continent
Whose storied plains reach out on ocean's floor,
O'er which the dark, pulsating waters pour,
   With sound of bells by the swaying flood impent,
   Tolling, now lone and low, now full and blent,
Then lost again amid the surfy roar, —

So through the silent spaces of the dark,
When lulls the world-hum on the muffled blast,
   There strays a tender chord of some far strain
   From time when love was sweet and hope not vain;
And pulses throb, and with dear longing mark
The distant echoes of a buried past.

CHAMBERS BAIRD.

AFTER MANY YEARS.

OLD Age! I harbor thee a welcome guest:
   Thou mad'st me sage, if aught I am, and skilled
   To learn life's broadest arts. No more I build
Vain temples by forgetful Fame unblest,
Nor madly brave some luring phantom-quest.
   I count no fretting hopes yet unfulfilled;
   But know, with passionate youth's wild tremor stilled,
The lulling cadences of pulseless rest.

The tide of time flows on, still as a dream,
   Its margin crowned with calm and presage-spanned.
The years enrich me, as a silt-fraught stream,
Laden with opulent spoil from many a field,
   Gilds with its golden hoard some mellow strand.
Ah, would this lustrum might full fruitage yield!
CHAMBERS BAIRD.

LAND AHEAD.

'T IS wrought in heirlooms of our country's lore
   That when before his venturous vessel's deck
   The fancied land faded in cloudy fleck,
The patience of Columbus yet once more
With daring promise of a glittering store
   Contrived the clamorous sailors' wrath to check
   Till doubted isles drew nearer at his beck,
And flight of birds foretold the wished-for shore.

When mutinous thoughts the murmuring cry upraise,
   "To gird life's sea there lies no shining strand,"
   And we have ruled them with constraining hand
Through dreary reckoning of shoreless days,
The poets pass us with their cheering lays,
   Like birds, the proof of undiscovered land.
MARY RUSSELL BARTLETT.

ONE AUTUMN NIGHT.

Can I forget that glorious autumn night,
  So full of joyous pain, when you and I
  Stood on the shore beneath a cloudless sky,
And watched the moon, all drenched with holy light,
Sail slowly up, and toss a veil of white
  Across the heaving sea? — when waves rode by
  And pressed broad palms upon the rocks, to try
And bear away the rough stone from our sight?

Ah, no! 't was then I spoke to you of love, —
  My secret which you long ere that had guessed;
  'Twas then I first knew passion's fiery heat
And kissed your cheek, your lips, while high above
  A great star shook, and in its burning breast,
  As in my own, a red heart beat and beat.

                    Herbert Bashford.

FEBRUARY.

The old, old wonder of the lengthening days
  Is with us once again; the winter's sun,
  Slow sinking to the west when day is done,
Each eve a little longer with us stays,
And cheers the snowy landscape with his rays:
  Nor do we notice what he has begun
  Until a month or more of days have run,
When we exclaim: "How long the light delays!"

So let some kindly deed, however slight,
  Be daily done by us, that to the waste
    Of selfishness some light it may impart, —
Mayhap not noticed till we feel the night
  Is less within our souls, and broader-spaced
    Has grown the cheerful sunshine of the heart.

                    Samuel Francis Batchelder.

OUR DEAD.

WE must be nobler for our dead, be sure
   Than for the quick. We might their living eyes
   Deceive with gloss of seeming ; but all lies
Are vain to cheat a prescience spirit-pure.
Our souls' true worth and aim, however poor,
   They see who watch us from some deathless skies
   With glance death-quickened. That no sad surprise
Sting them in seeing, be ours to secure.

Living, our loved ones make us what they dream ;
   Dead, if they see, they know us as we are.
Henceforward we must be, not merely seem.
   Bitterer woe than death it were by far
To fail their hopes who love us to redeem ;
   Loss were twice loss that thus their faith should mar.
                                ARLO BATES.

A CONSOLATION.

If, like the torch-flame which some Druid hoar
   Quenched in a sacrifice, the spirit dies
   When sense and seeing from the well-loved eyes
Fade utterly, and every empty shore
In all the desolate universe evermore
   Even to search of God himself denies
   Its shape or being, what can heart devise
Of hope or comfort for its anguish sore ?

There is no comfort save the bitter thought
   That we at least alone our sorrow bear ;
That if the soul for which we yearn is nought,
   It cannot writhe in ever-fresh despair
That we are parted ; and that death has wrought
   On us alone this hurt beyond repair.
                                ARLO BATES.

FELICES.

We count them happy who have richly known
   The sweets of life, the sunshine on the hills,
   The mosses in the valley, love that fills
The heart with tears as fragrant as thine own,
O tender moonlight lily, over-blown,
   When the inevitable season wills,
   By gentle winds beside thy native rills, —
We count them happy, yet not these alone.

There is a Crown of Thorns, Way of the Cross,
   Consuming Fire that burns the spirit pure.
By lustre of the gold set free from dross,
   By light of Heaven seen best through earth's obscure,
By the exceeding gain that waits on loss,
   Behold, we count them happy who endure.
KATHARINE LEE BATES.

THE SONGS OF THE FUTURE.

America, my mother and my queen,
   Thou living Presence, thou art something more
   Than cloud-enfolded hills or foam-lit shore,
Or steepled towns, — yet silent and unseen,
Save as thou lendest to this garment sheen
   The impress of that grace for which we pour
   Dear blood in battle; toward the Delphic door
Of the closed centuries I feel thee lean.

Young, eager, beautiful, to know thy fates.
   One fate is told. This money-maddened throng
   Moves to the twilight of its troubled day,
And high souls stand without those shadowy gates,
   Thy flame-crowned bards, no echo-voices they,
   . Whose lips shall flood the waiting world with song.
KATHARINE LEE BATES.

WAIT.

SEEMS there a hand outstretched to bar the way,
    A voice that says, "This door to you is closed;"
    Are all your plans mysteriously opposed,
Your course of progress hampered by delay?
Seems chance to you but mischance, with no ray
    Of clear good-fortune through the clouds disclosed,
    Though some appear to thrive who idly dozed
While you were up and doing with the day?

So seems it to us all. Though long delayed,
    Your time will come, so labor and be wise;
So came the Indian's, who had sought the aid
    Of a small shrub — it failed him — in surprise
He frowned — but there, in glittering veins displayed,
    Potosi's mine of silver met his eyes!

LEVI F. BAUDER.

OUR BIRTHRIGHT.

Go! read the patent of thine heritage,
    Inscribed in glowing words that flash and burn
    With pregnant import. Con it well and learn
The thrilling tale that lights the storied page.
See Faith and Valor hand-to-hand engage
    Opposing powers, and by their prowess turn
    The wild into a puissant realm, and earn
A deathless fame, bright to the latest age!

'T is thine and mine! Shall we, then, hold it light, —
    Despise our birthright as some base-born churl,
    And recreant yield it with a nerveless hand,
Or stain our scutcheon with a Judas blight?
    When traitors hiss do thou, indignant, hurl
    Thy challenge back: "It is my native land!"

SAMUEL M. BAYLIS.

WAITING FOR WINTER.

What honey in the year's last flowers can hide,
  These little yellow butterflies may know :
  With falling leaves they waver to and fro,
Or on the swinging tops of asters ride.
But I am weary of the summer's pride
  And sick September's simulated show :
  Why do the colder winds delay to blow
And bring the pleasant hours that we abide ;

To curtained alcove and sweet household talks,
  Or sweeter silence by our flickering Lars,
Returning late from Autumn evening walks
  Upon the frosty hills, while reddening Mars
Hangs low between the withered mullein stalks,
  And upward throngs the host of winter stars !

Henry A. Beers.

THE SINGER OF ONE SONG.

He sang one song and died, — no more, but that :
  A single song and carelessly complete.
  He would not bind and thresh his chance-grown wheat,
Nor bring his wild fruit to the common vat,
To store the acid rinsings, thin and flat,
  Squeezed from the press or trodden under feet.
  A few slow beads, blood-red and honey-sweet,
Oozed from the grape, which burst and spilled its fat.

But Time, who soonest drops the heaviest things
  That weight his pack, will carry diamonds long.
    So through the poets' orchestra, which weaves
One music from a thousand stops and strings,
  Pierces the note of that immortal song :
    "High over all the lonely bugle grieves."

Henry A. Beers.

THE SCARLET PIMPERNEL.

O HAVE you seen the scarlet pimpernel,
   The wild, sea-flavored blossom of the strand,
   The token flower, the pledge of sea and land,
And have you learned to heed its secret spell?
Aurora's friend, it loves the morning well,
   And you shall find it open to your hand
   The sunny morning through, — but understand
Storm clouds will close it closer than a shell.

Love is the pimpernel: then do not wait;
   Go in the morning, faithful to the hour,
Go when thy lady keeps her matin state;
   Her heart is coy, and closes like a flower.
Go in the sunlight, haste and claim love's boon,
Nor tempt the changing skies and afternoon.

IDA WHIPPLE BENHAM.

NEW YORK HARBOR.

(Written in view of the harbor of New York on the loveliest and calmest of the last days of autumn.)

Is this a painting? Are those pictured clouds
   Which on the sky so movelessly repose?
Has some rare artist fashioned forth the shrouds
   Of yonder vessel? Are these imaged shows
Of outline, figure, form, or is there life —
   Life with a thousand pulses — in the scene
   We gaze upon? Those towering banks between,
E'er tossed these billows in tumultuous strife?

Billows! there's not a wave! the waters spread
   One broad, unbroken mirror! all around
   Is hushed to silence, — silence so profound
That a bird's carol, or an arrow sped
   Into the distance, would, like larum bell,
   Jar the deep stillness and dissolve the spell!

PARK BENJAMIN.

A PORTRAIT.

In the white sweetness of her dimpled chin
   The pink points of her perfumed fingers press,
   And round her tremulous mouth's loveliness
The tears and smiles a sudden strife begin:
First one and then the other seems to win;
   And o'er her drooping eyes a golden tress
   Falls down to hide what else they might confess
Their blue-veined lids are striving to shut in.

The yellow pearls that bind her throat about
   With her pale bosom's throbbing rise and fall;
     The while her thoughts like carrier doves have fled
To that far land where armies clash and shout,
   And where, beyond love's reach, a soldier tall
     With staring eyes and broken sword lies dead.

                    JAMES BERRY BENSEL.

DAHKOTA.

Sea-like in billowy distance, far away
   The half-broke prairies stretch on every hand;
How wide the circuit of their summer day, —
   What measureless acres of primeval land,
   Treeless and birdless, by no eyesight spanned!
Looking along the horizon's endless line,
   Man seems a pigmy in these realms of space;
No segment of our planet — so divine —
   Turns up such beauty to the moon's fair face!
Here are soft grasses, flowers of tender hue,
   Palimpsests of the old and coming race,
Vistas most wonderful, and vast and new;
   And see — above — where giant lightnings play,
   From what an arch the sun pours forth the day!

                    JOEL BENTON.

AT CHAPPAQUA.[1]

His cherished woods are mute. The stream glides down
  The hill as when I knew it years ago;
The dark, pine arbor with its priestly gown
  Stands hushed, as if our grief it still would show;
The silver springs are cupless, and the flow
  Of friendly feet no more bereaves the grass,
  For he is absent who was wont to pass
Along this wooded path. His axe's blow

No more disturbs the impertinent bole or bough;
Nor moves his pen our heedless nation now,
  Which, sworn to justice, stirred the people so.
  In some far world his much-loved face must glow
With rapture still. This breeze once fanned his brow.
  This is the peaceful Mecca all men know!

JOEL BENTON.

TRANSFORMATION.

"Give me the wine of happiness," I cried,
  "The bread of life! — O ye benign, unknown,
  Immortal powers! — I crave them for my own,
I am athirst, I will not be denied
Though Hell were up in arms!" No sound replied,
  But, turning back to my rude board and lone,
  My soul, confounded, there beheld — a stone,
Pale water in a shallow cup beside!

With gushing tears, in utter hopelessness,
  I stood and gazed. Then rose a voice that spoke, —
"God gave this, too, and what He gives will bless!"
  And 'neath the hands that trembling took and broke,
Lo, truly a sweet miracle divine,
The stone turned bread, the water ruby wine!

GERTRUDE BLOEDE ("*Stuart Sterne*").

[1] The home of Horace Greeley.

SOLITUDE.

I LOVE thee, O thou Beautiful and Strong,
   Invisible comrade, mute, sweet company,
   More dear than friend or lover! But to thee
My fondest hopes, my fairest dreams, belong
Forevermore! Amid the world's gay throng
   I yearn for thy soft arms that lovingly
   Soothe all the fevered wounds once fretting me.
At thy deep heart there springs the fount of song

Whose drops shall cool my burning lips athirst,—
   At thy swift beck within my sight arise
(Their bonds of silence and dim darkness burst)
   All my beloved dead, with shining eyes,—
At thy blest hand, by starlit paths untrod,
My soul draws near unto the face of God!
           GERTRUDE BLOEDE ("*Stuart Sterne*").

SILENCE.

AY, and thee, too, who wield'st a power divine,
   Greater than loudest speech or fairest lay!
   The dead, millions on millions, own thy sway
In realms where suns to rise no more, decline.
Thine is the lover's sweetest rapture, thine
   The deepest cup of grief or joy that aye
   The lips of mortal tasted, thine — yet stay!
How may I name thee, with what sound so fine

It shall not snap thy life's frail, golden thread?
   O Solitude and Silence, bid me learn
A little of your greatness! Long are fled
   The lesser gods of life, now let me turn
To ye alone, to ye in worship come,
The accents of this faltering tongue grown dumb!
           GERTRUDE BLOEDE ("*Stuart Sterne*").

ON A THREATENED INVASION.

WHAT though the cities blaze, the ports be sealed,
  The fields untilled, the hand of labor still,
  Ay, every arm of commerce and of skill
Palsied and broken; shall we therefore yield,
Break up the sword, put by the dintless shield?
  Have we no home upon the wooded hill,
  That mocks a siege? No patriot ranks to drill?
No nobler labor in the battle-field?

Or grant us beaten. While we gather might,
  Is there no comfort in the solemn wood?
No cataracts whose angry roar shall smite
  Our hearts with courage? No eternal brood
Of thoughts begotten by the eagle's flight?
  No God to strengthen us in solitude?

GEORGE H. BOKER.

LOVE DEFENDED.

How canst thou call my modest love impure,
  Being thyself the holy source of all?
  Can ugly darkness from the fair sun fall?
Or Nature's compact be so insecure
That saucy weeds may sprout up and endure
  Where gentle flowers were sown? The brooks that crawl,
  With lazy whispers, through the lilies tall,
Or rattle o'er the pebbles, will allure
With no feigned sweetness, if their fount be sweet.
  So thou, the sun whence all my light doth flow, —
  Thou, sovereign law by which my fancies grow —
Thou, fount of every feeling, slow or fleet,
  Against thyself wouldst aim a treacherous blow,
Slaying thy honor with thy own conceit.

GEORGE H. BOKER.

TO THE MEMORY OF M. A. R.

With the mild light some unambitious star
   Illumes her pathway through the heavenly blue, —
   So unobtrusive that the careless view
Scarce notes her where her haughtier sisters are, —
So ran thy life. Perhaps, from those afar,
   Thy gentle radiance little wonder drew,
   And all their praise was for the brighter few.
Yet mortal vision is a grievous bar

To perfect judgment. Were the distance riven,
   Our eyes might find that star so faintly shone
   Because it journeyed through a higher zone,
Had more majestic sway and duties given,
   Far loftier station on the heights of Heaven,
   Was next to God, and circled round his throne.
                          GEORGE H. BOKER.

LOVE AND PHILOSOPHY.

I 'll call thy frown a headsman, passing grim,
   Walking before some wretch foredoomed to death,
   Who counts the pantings of his own hard breath;
Wondering how heart can beat, or steadfast limb
Bear its sad burden to life's awful brim.
   I'll call thy smile a priest, who slowly saith
   Soft words of comfort as the sinner strayeth
Away in thought, or sings a holy hymn,

Full of rich promise, as he walks behind
   The fatal axe with face of goodly cheer,
   And kind inclinings of his saintly ear.
So, love, thou seest, in smiles or looks unkind,
Some taste of sweet philosophy I find,
   That seasons all things in our little sphere.
                          GEORGE R. BOKER.

THE TARIFF.

RATHER, my people, let thy youths parade
   Their woolly flocks before the rising sun;
   With curds and oatcakes, when their work is done,
By frugal handmaids let the board be laid;
Let them refresh their vigor in the shade,
   Or deem their straw as down to lie upon,
   Ere the great charter which our fathers won
Be rent asunder by Hell's minion, Trade!

If jarring interests and the greed of gold, —
   The corn-rick's envy of the minèd hill,
   The steamer's grudge against the spindle's skill, —
If things so mean our country's fate can mould,
   O let me hear again the shepherds trill
Their reedy music to the drowsing fold!
                            GEORGE H. BOKER.

TO ENGLAND.

I.

LEAR and Cordelia! 't was an ancient tale
   Before thy Shakespeare gave it deathless fame:
   The times have changed, the moral is the same.
So like an outcast, dowerless and pale,
Thy daughter went; and in a foreign gale
   Spread her young banner, till its sway became
   A wonder to the nations. Days of shame
Are close upon thee: prophets raise their wail.

When the rude Cossack with an outstretched hand
   Points his long spear across the narrow sea, —
   "Lo! there is England!" when thy destiny
Storms on thy straw-crowned head, and thou dost stand
Weak, helpless, mad, a by-word in the land, —
   God grant thy daughter a Cordelia be!
     (1852.)   GEORGE H. BOKER.

TO ENGLAND.

II.

Stand, thou great bulwark of man's liberty!
  Thou rock of shelter, rising from the wave,
  Sole refuge to the overwearied brave
Who planned, arose, and battled to be free,
Fell, undeterred, then sadly turned to thee, —
  Saved the free spirit from their country's grave,
  To rise again, and animate the slave,
When God shall ripen all things. Britons, ye

Who guard the sacred outpost, not in vain
  Hold your proud peril! Freemen undefiled,
  Keep watch and ward! Let battlements be piled
Around your cliffs; fleets marshalled, till the main
Sink under them; and if your courage wane,
  Through force or fraud, look westward to your child!
    (1853.)   George H. Boker.

EASTER ADVENT.

It was a stormy night in early spring.
  Long after sunset pale, green rifts of light
  Gleamed in the west, changing to vitreous white,
And when these faded, darkness was a thing
Strangely portentous. There went whirring wing
  Low in the air of birds in furious flight, —
  Wild fowls blown from their courses in the night.
It was an eve for spectral imaging.

A sinless maiden in her chamber high
  That Easter advent midnight heard a call:
    Arise! arise! and startled from her bed
She saw a glory burst along the sky.
  It lit with flame the cross upon her wall,
    And through the splendor crimson rain was shed.
                                               John H. Boner.

THE OLD GUARD.

SUMMER is routed from her rosy plains,
   The splendid queen with colors flying fled
   Far to the south, leaving her legions dead
Upon the fields all in the dismal rains.
The minstrels of her camp most plaintive strains
   Piped as they flew. Then vandal armies spread
   About the hills their tattered tents of red
And gold and purple, and their gaudy trains

Usurped the valleys, firing as they went,
   Till halted by a cordon of grim pines
     That would not yield nor furl their banners green.
Wounded they fought and moaned, though wellnigh
     spent.
   With blood-drops trickling down their chevron vines
     They fought, and stood — the Old Guard of their
       queen.
                      JOHN H. BONER.

VITA NUOVA.

THOUGH I recall no word, no glance, no tone,
   Whereon my eager memory might repose,
   Yet, like the earth where grew the Persian rose,
I feel a higher life inspire my own ;
And since that higher life I have been near,
   Some aura, some mysterious effluence,
   Transcending all the scope of thought or sense,
Surrounds me like a rarer atmosphere ;

And dwelling now in this new element,
   The world of daily life exalted seems ;
   I walk therein as in the realm of dreams,
Following the thought that leads me on intent,
   As if a stream that wandered aimlessly
   Had heard at last the murmur of the sea.
                      ANNE LYNCH BOTTA.

LARGESS.

Go forth in life, O friend, not seeking love! —
   A mendicant that with imploring eye
   And outstretched hand asks of the passer-by
The alms his strong necessities may move.
For such poor love, to pity near allied,
   Thy generous spirit may not stoop and wait, —
   A suppliant whose prayer may be denied,
Like a spurned beggar's at a palace gate; —

But thy heart's affluence lavish, uncontrolled;
   The largess of thy love give full and free,
As monarchs in their progress scatter gold;
   And be thy heart like the exhaustless sea,
That must its wealth of cloud and dew bestow,
Though tributary streams or ebb or flow!
ANNE LYNCH BOTTA.

UNREST.

O CLOUDS and winds and streams, that go your way
   Obedient to fulfill a high behest,
   Unquestioning, without or haste or rest,
Your only law to be and to obey, —
O all ye beings of the earth and air
   That people these primeval solitudes,
   Where never doubt nor discontent intrudes, —
In your divine accordance let me share;

Lift from my soul this burden of unrest,
   Take me to your companionship, teach me
   The lesson of your rhythmic lives, to be
At one with the great All, and in my breast
   Silence this voice, that asks forever, "Why,
   And whence, and where?" — unanswerable cry!
ANNE LYNCH BOTTA.

THOMAS À KEMPIS.

(De Imitatione Christi.)

TURN with me from the city's clamorous street,
  Where throng and push passions and lusts and hate,
  And enter, through this age-browned, ivied gate,
For many summers' birds a sure retreat,
The place of perfect peace. And here, most meet
  For meditation, where no idle prate
  Of the world's ways may come, rest thee and wait.
'T is very quiet. Thus doth still Heaven entreat.

With rev'rent feet, his face so worn, so fair,
  Walks one who bears the cross, who waits the crown.
    Tumult is past. In those calm eyes I see
The image of the Master, Christ, alone,
And from those patient lips I hear one prayer:
  "*Dear Lord, dear Lord, that I may be like thee!*"

R. R. BOWKER.

EVOLUTION.

I AM the child of earth and air and sea,
  My lullaby by hoarse Silurian storms
  Was chanted; and through endless changing forms
Of plant and bird and beast unceasingly
The toiling ages wrought to fashion me.
  Lo, these large ancestors have left a breath
  Of their strong souls in mine, defying death
And doom. I grow and blossom as the tree,

And ever feel deep-delving, earthy roots
  Binding me daily to the common clay;
But with its airy impulse upward shoots
  My life into the realms of light and day.
And thou, O Sea, stern mother of my soul,
Thy tempests sing in me, thy billows roll!

HJALMAR HJORTH BOYESEN.

THE LILY.

I saw the lily pale and perfect grow
   Amid its silent sisters in the mead.
   Methought within its chilly depth to read
A maidenly severity, as though
A cool young life lay slumbering in the snow
   Of its frail substance. In that chalice white,
   Whose fairy texture shone against the light,
An unawakened pulse beat faint and slow.

And I remembered, love, thy coy disdain,
   When thou my love for thee hadst first divined;
Thy proud, shy tenderness, — too proud to feign
   That willful blindness which is yet not blind.
Then toward the sun thy lily-life I turned, —
With sudden splendor flushed its chalice burned.
                   HJALMAR HJORTH BOYESEN.

PRESCIENCE OF DEATH.

I wonder oft why God, who is so good,
   Has barred so close, so close the gates of death.
   I stand and listen with suspended breath
While night and silence round about me brood,
If then, perchance, some spirit-whisper would
   Grow audible and pierce my torpid sense.
   And oft I feel a presence, veiled intense,
That pulses softly through the solitude;

But as my soul leaps quivering to my ear
   To grasp the potent message, all takes flight,
And from the fields and woods I only hear
   The murmurous chorus of the summer night.
I am as one that's dead, — yet in his gloom
Feels faintly song of birds above his tomb.
                   HJALMAR HJORTH BOYESEN.

DIVIDED.

I CANNOT reach thee; we are far, so far
  Apart, who are so dear!
                   Love, be it so;
  Else we might press so close we should not grow.
One doth deny even this so sweet a bar
For fear our souls' true shape should suffer mar.
  Ah, surface-sundered, yet do we not know
  A hidden union in the deeps below?
An intertwining where the strong roots are?

Wise husbandmen plant thus, sweetheart, — a space
  Between the trees; but after, soon or late,
    High in the sunny air their spreading boughs
Reach forth and meet. In some celestial place,
  When we two are grown tall and fair and straight,
    We shall clasp hands again — if God allows.
                  JULIA BOYNTON.

TO RICHARD HENRY STODDARD.

SITTING alone, within this dusky glow,
  Where shadows wavering in the fitful flame
  Cheat me with likeness, yet are not the same
As those we watched together, days ago,
My heart is full of memories that throw
  Their light upon a time before your name
  Meant what it means to-day, or I could claim
The well-beloved friend that now I know.

A lonely child beside the lonely sea,
  I found your footprints, followed where they led;
  And thus unconsciously was born and bred
The love — and simple art — of song in me;
  Which now — of all its sweet the sweetest part —
  Has proved the royal road to your true heart.
                  MARY BRADLEY.

SHAKESPEARE.

Working as erst by law, not miracle,
  By genius God doth lift a common soul
  To some still spot where it may glimpse the goal;
Bidding it on the mountain heights to dwell,
Yet not so far apart but it may tell
  To toilers in the plain below the whole
  Of the vision. Master, still the organ-roll
Of thy deep music vibrates, and its spell

Aids the uplift that stirs our grosser clay
  To rise and seek the heights. O soul God set
  A little lower than his white angels, yet
A round for man to climb the starward way
  Thou art. One palm with angels' long since met,
The other warm in man's grasp still doth stay.
                        ALICE WILLIAMS BROTHERTON.

A STAR-EYED DAISY.

Ensigns of empires flaunt thy flanking wall,
  Grim ancient warders guard thy storied gate,
  Loud Babeled centuries at thy bastions wait
On Spanish, French, and English seneschal.
Rich yellow folds of Castile's haughty state,
  Fair Fleur de Lys from proud Parisian hall,
  St. George's Cross triumphant o'er them all,
Recall long years of fierce and bloody hate.

But now the star-eyed daisy lifts its form
  From crevice, chink, and crumbling parapet,
Without one stain of battle's crimson storm
  On snowy leaf with golden petal set:
    Bright banneret which Nature kindly rears
    To deck with light the mould of bitter years.
                        WALLACE BRUCE.

OCTOBER.

Ay, thou art welcome, heaven's delicious breath,
  When woods begin to wear the crimson leaf,
  And suns grow meek, and the meek suns grow brief,
And the year smiles as it draws near its death.
Wind of the sunny South! O, still delay
  In the gay woods and in the golden air,
  Like to a good old age released from care,
Journeying, in long serenity, away.

In such a bright, late quiet, would that I
  Might wear out life like thee, 'mid bowers and brooks,
  And, dearer yet, the sunshine of kind looks,
And music of kind voices ever nigh;
  And when my last sand twinkled in the glass,
  Pass silently from men, as thou dost pass.
                    WILLIAM CULLEN BRYANT.

TO COLE, THE PAINTER, DEPARTING FOR EUROPE.

Thine eyes shall see the light of distant skies;
  Yet, Cole! thy heart shall bear to Europe's strand
  A living image of our own bright land,
Such as upon thy glorious canvas lies;
Lone lakes, savannas where the bison roves,—
  Rocks rich with summer garlands, solemn streams,—
  Skies where the desert eagle wheels and screams,—
Spring bloom and autumn blaze of boundless groves.

Fair scenes shall greet thee where thou goest,— fair,
  But different,— everywhere the trace of men;
  Paths, homes, graves, ruins, from the lowest glen
To where life shrinks from the fierce Alpine air:
  Gaze on them, till the tears shall dim thy sight,
  But keep that earlier, wilder image bright.
                    WILLIAM CULLEN BRYANT.

MUTATION.

They talk of short-lived pleasure — be it so —
  Pain dies as quickly: stern, hard-featured pain
Expires, and lets her weary prisoner go.
  The fiercest agonies have shortest reign;
  And after dreams of horror, comes again
The welcome morning with its rays of peace.
  Oblivion, softly wiping out the stain,
Makes the strong secret pangs of shame to cease:
Remorse is virtue's root; its fair increase
  Are fruits of innocence and blessedness:
Thus joy, o'erborne and bound, doth still release
    His young limbs from the chains that round him press.
Weep not that the world changes — did it keep
A stable, changeless state, 't were cause indeed to weep.
William Cullen Bryant.

EMERSON.

April 27, 1882.

The Keeper of the Concord Light is dead,
  And gone its shining way to Paradise;
  From that Snug Harbor of the soul he spies
A beacon-glory round his memory shed
By waves that bring to hungry mortals bread,
  Once cast upon the waters by the wise,
  Kind hand that kept the Light. His startled eyes
Gleam heavenly joy, then fill with modest dread

And turn to greet the friends of other days,
  Who lead him to his castles, late of Spain,
  Within whose halls resound his unsung lays:
The while a busy world beneath the wain,
That plucks a star from Concord's peaceful ways,
  In reverence pauses at a new-made fane.
Clarence Clough Buel.

POET AND ACTRESS.

WHEN Avon's Bard his sweetest music scored,
  A woman's vision with the numbers blent;
  Each to the other equal beauty lent
As weaving fancy robed the form adored.
O Poet, didst thou see upon the board
  Eye-filling Rosalind, whose playful bent
  Suffused thy lines? Juliet, all passion-spent?
Viola's sweet self, and Imogen's restored?

'T was thine to give the music-mated lines,
  But Heaven alone empowers the counterpart
To walk in splendor where such genius shines.
  Thrice happy we, blest heirs of dual art,
To own as mother-tongue Will Shakespeare's writ,
To live when kindling Neilson voices it.
CLARENCE CLOUGH BUEL.

A POEM IN THE PROGRAMME.

A THOUSAND fans are fretting the hot air;
  Soft swells the music of the interlude
  Above the murmurous hum of talk subdued;
But, from the noise withdrawn and from the glare,
Deep in the shadowy box your coilèd hair
  Gleams golden bright, with diamonds bedewed;
  Your head is bent; I know your dark eyes brood
On the poor sheet of paper you hold there,

That quotes my verses, and I see no more
  That bald-head Plutus by your side. The seas
    Sound in my ears; I hear the rustling pines;
Catch the low lisp of billows on the shore
  Where once I lay in Knickerbockered ease,
    And read to you those then unprinted lines.
H. C. BUNNER.

RAIN.

Dashing in big drops on the narrow pane,
   And making mournful music for the mind,
   While plays his interlude the wizard Wind,
I hear the ringing of the frequent rain:
   How doth its dreamy tone the spirit lull,
Bringing a sweet forgetfulness of pain,
While busy thought calls up the past again,
   And lingers 'mid the pure and beautiful
Visions of early childhood! Sunny faces
   Meet us with looks of love, and in the moans
   Of the faint wind we hear familiar tones,
And tread again in old familiar places!
   Such is thy power, O Rain! the heart to bless,
   Wiling the soul away from its own wretchedness!
WILLIAM HENRY BURLEIGH.

IN A LIBRARY.

A wealth of silence, that is all. The air
   Lacks life and holds no hint of tender spring,
   Of flowers wholesome-blowing, birds a-wing,
Of any creature much-alive and fair.
Perhaps you guess a murmur here and there
   Among the tomes, each book a gossip thing,
   And each in her own tongue, — yet slumbering
Seems more the bookish fashion everywhere.

And yet, could but the souls take flesh again
   That wrought these words, their hearts all passion-swirled,
   What companies would flock and fill the stage,
Resuming now their old, imperious reign,
   Knight, noble, lady, priest, the saint, and sage,
   The valor, bloom, and wisdom of a world!
RICHARD E. BURTON.

THE POET.

He's not alone an artist weak and white,
   O'erbending scented paper, toying there
   With languid fancies, fashioned deft and fair,
Mere sops to time between the day and night.
He is a poor torn soul who sees aright
   How far he fails of living out the rare
   Night-visions God vouchsafes along the air,
Until the pain burns hot, beyond his might.

The heart-beat of the universal will
   He hears, and, spite of blindness and disproof,
     Can sense amidst the jar a singing fine.
Grief-smitten that his lyre should lack the skill
   To speak it plain, he plays in paths aloof,
     And knows the trend is starward, life divine.
RICHARD E. BURTON.

AN UNPRAISED PICTURE.

I saw a picture once by Angelo, —
   "Unfinished," said the critic, "done in youth," —
   And that was all, no thought of praise, forsooth!
He was informed, and doubtless it was so.
And yet I let an hour of dreaming go
   The way of all time, touched to tears and ruth,
   Passion and joy, the prick of Conscience's tooth,
Before that careworn Christ's divine, soft glow.

The painter's yearning with an unsure hand
   Had moved me more than might his master days:
He seemed to speak like one whose Mecca land
   Is first beheld, tho' faint and far the ways;
Who may not then his shaken voice command,
   Yet trembles forth a word of prayer and praise.
RICHARD E. BURTON.

LONGING.

Oh, for a breath of spicy woodland air,
   The healing balsam of the odorous pine,
   To thrill my nerveless pulse like beaded wine!
Oh, for some sylvan Hebe to prepare
For me the nectared cups of mosses rare
   Till quickened sense shall catch the merry shine
   Of hidden wood nymph's eyes that flash on mine
'Tween waving tresses of the maidenhair!

Oh, for a day of freedom in the wood!
   To wander with head bared, with feet untamed
And cheek incarnadined with bounding blood,
   Of Nature's code and impulse unashamed.
Oh, for a day so breezy, free, and wild
The dryads haste to claim me as their child!

SARAH E. BURTON.

HOMESICKNESS.

We oft are sorrowful, yet have no word
   To tell why gloom has settled on the day
   Like clouds that blot the azure field with gray;
We know not why the singing of a bird
Touches the soul to pain as if we heard
   Within the voice another music say
   Things not translated in our human way;
We pierce ourselves with blame, yet have not erred.

Exiles we are, and when the outreaching heart
   Is quickened to sense its native atmosphere, —
When through the fair world's form the spirit part
   Reveals itself an instant, passing dear, —
When in a flower's sweet face new meanings dart,
   We mourn, shut out, for that which is so near.

MARY F. BUTTS.

O GRAVE, WHERE IS THY VICTORY.

FOR twenty years did Nature wait without,
   Besetting that storm-beaten tenement,
   Claiming her debt. From door to door she went,
Rude battering with all her hostile rout:
And we who, helpless watching, stood about
   While frail walls tottered and light bolts were bent,
   Thinking each day to see some fatal rent,
Did marvel much that house should be so stout.

But Love was there, the Lord of Life and Death,
   And held the importunate enemy at bay;
   Yet when his work was done, all peacefully,
As dawn grows day, Life yielded up his breath,
   And, led by Love Immortal, went away,
   Surrendering to a vanquished enemy.
                          WILLIAM HERBERT CARRUTH.

"WHY THIS WASTE?"

THAT eyes which pierced our inmost being through;
   That lips which pressed into a single kiss,
   It seemed, a whole eternity of bliss;
That cheeks which mantled with love's rosy hue;
That feet which wanted nothing else to do
   But run upon love's errands, this and this;
   That hands so fair they had not seemed amiss
Reached down by angels through the deeps of blue, —

That all of these so deep in earth should lie
While season after season passeth by;
   That things which are so sacred and so sweet
   The hungry roots of tree and plant should eat!
Oh for one hour to see as Thou dost see,
My God, how great the recompense must be!
                          JOHN WHITE CHADWICK.

THE HARDEST LOT.

To look upon the face of a dead friend
    Is hard; but 't is not more than we can bear
    If, haply, we can see peace written there, —
Peace after pain, and welcome so the end,
Whate'er the past, whatever death may send.
    Yea, and that face a gracious smile may wear,
    If love till death was perfect, sweet, and fair;
But there is woe from which may God defend:

To look upon our friendship lying dead,
    While we live on, and eat and drink and sleep, —
Mere bodies from which all the soul has fled, —
    And that dead thing year after year to keep
Locked in cold silence in its dreamless bed, —
    There must be hell while there is such a deep.
                            JOHN WHITE CHADWICK.

THE KING'S DIARY.
(JULY 14, 1789.)

"*Rien*," he wrote, because it chanced that day
    There was no hunt of fawn or stag or boar.
    All else was nothing to the man who wore
The crown which once the brows of Hugh Capet
Had ached beneath, eight centuries away.
    Since then what well-beloved and hated more
    Had worn it lightly, or with anguish sore,
Some strong to rule and many but to slay!

"Nothing!" And, while he wrote the senseless word,
    The tocsin rang in Paris; the human flood
    Poured onward, raging till it came where stood
The Bastile. Soon the foolish king had heard
    How prone it lay. Behold his aimless wit:
He and his kingdom were as he had writ.
                            JOHN WHITE CHADWICK.

THE DAY IS DONE.

The day has past, I never may return;
   Twelve circling years have run since first I came
   And kindled the pure truth of friendship's flame;
Alone remain these ashes in the urn, —
Vainly for light the taper may I turn, —
   Thy hand is closed, as for these years, the same,
   And for the substance nought is but the name;
No more hope, no more a ray to burn.

But once more, in the pauses of thy joy,
   Remember him who sought thee in his youth,
And, with the old reliance of the boy,
   Asked for thy treasures in the guise of truth.
The air is thick with sighs, — the shaded sun
Shows on the hillside that the day is done.

                  WILLIAM ELLERY CHANNING.

HEARTS OF ETERNITY.

Hearts of eternity, hearts of the deep!
   Proclaim from land to sea your mighty fate;
   How that for you no living comes too late,
How ye cannot in Theban labyrinth creep,
How ye great harvests from small surface reap.
   Shout, excellent band, in grand, primeval strain,
   Like midnight winds that foam along the main,
And do all things rather than pause to weep!

A human heart knows nought of littleness,
   Suspects no man, compares with no one's ways,
   Hath in one hour most glorious length of days,
A recompense, a joy, a loveliness;
   Like eaglet keen, shoots into azure far,
And always dwelling nigh is the remotest star.

                  WILLIAM ELLERY CHANNING.

THE SKILLFUL LISTENER.

The skillful listener, methinks, may hear
    The grass blades clash in sunny field together,
    The roses kissing, and the lily, whether
It laugh or sigh low in the summer's ear,
The jewel dew-bells of the mead ring clear
    When morning's nearing in the sweet June weather;
    The flocked hours winging, feather unto feather,
The last leaf wail at waning of the year.

Methinks, from these we catch a passing song,
    (The best of verities, perhaps, but seem),
    Hearing, forsooth, shy Nature, on her round,
When least she imagines it; birds, wood, and stream
    Not only, but her silences profound,
Surprised by softer footfall of our dream.
John Vance Cheney.

MUSIC.

Take of the maiden's and the mother's sigh,
    Of childhood's dream, and hope that age doth bless,
    Of roses and the south wind's tenderness,
Of fir tree's shadow, tint of sunset sky,
Of moon on meadow where the stream runs by,
    Of lover's kiss, his diffident caress,
    Of blue eyes' yellow, brown eyes' darker, tress,
Of echoes from the morning bird on high,

Of passion of all pulses of the Spring,
    Of prayer from every death-bed of the Fall,
Of joy and woe that sleep and waking bring,
    Of tremor of each blood-beat great and small;
Now pour into the empty soul each thing,
    And let His finger touch that moveth all.
John Vance Cheney.

MY PRAYER.

GRANT me, O God! the glory of gray hairs!
   To sit awhile among my friends — my peers —
   My passions all subdued, my foolish fears
Forever flown with all earth's cumbering cares!
Life's morning hours were consecrate to prayers,
   So be its evening! Penitential tears
   May fade the stains of more ambitious years,
Before fate falls upon me unawares!

Awaiting, not expecting Death, that night
   My lifelong, fondest friend shall sing or say
The grand old songs, in which we both delight,
   Until I sleep, and sleeping pass away;
Nor shall she know, though gazing on my face,
When Death usurps his sister — Slumber's — place.

                      SIMEON TUCKER CLARKE.

PENELOPE.

PENELOPE sat weaving all the day
   Her web; and I weave mine of tender thought,
   And many a quaint device by me is wrought
Of Fancy's golden threads. What will he say
When he shall come? Will he entreat and pray
   To see the legend? Will his heart be taught
   By it? Night comes and brings me naught;
I must unweave: Ulysses is away,

But when my hero shall at last have come,
   And his dear eyes have proved my colors true,
I wonder will my stammering lips be dumb,
   My heart's great love unspoken? Then must you,
Dear woven thing, help eyes and blushing cheek
To tell him all I feel, but cannot speak.

                      ELLA DIETZ CLYMER.

THE WATCH-FIRE.

My soul goes wandering in the wilderness
   All the day long; nor through the hours of light
   Can any foe my constant footing fright,
Although I fare alone and weaponless:
But when deep shadows fall and lay their stress
   Upon me, and giant creatures glare in sight,
   The panther Terror, leaping from the night,
And Pain, the lean, soft-pacing lioness, —

How guard the pilgrim then and compass him,
   And beat Abaddon from him, in the hour
When age o'ertakes him in the desert dim?
   Thy flame, O Poesy! shall fling a shower
Of guarding radiance, and the monsters grim
   Shall flee the spot protected by thy power.

TITUS MUNSON COAN.

MORNING.

I woke and heard the thrushes sing at dawn, —
   A strangely blissful burst of melody,
   A chant of rare, exultant certainty,
Fragrant, as springtime breaths, of wood and lawn.
Night's eastern curtains still were closely drawn;
   No roseate flush predicted pomps to be,
   Or spoke of morning loveliness to me,
But, for those happy birds, — the night was gone!

Darkling they sang, nor guessed what care consumes
   Man's questioning spirit; heedless of decay,
They sang of joy and dew-embalmèd blooms.
   My doubts grew still, doubts seemed so poor while they,
Sweet worshipers of light, from leafy glooms
   Poured forth transporting prophecies of day.

FLORENCE EARLE COATES.

LET ME BELIEVE.

LET me believe you, love, or let me die!
  If on your faith I may not rest secure,
  Beyond all chance of peradventure sure,
Trusting your half avowals sweet and shy,
As trusts the lark the pallid, dawn-lit sky
  Then would I rather in some grave obscure
  Repose forlorn, than, living on, endure
A question each dear transport to belie.

It is a pain to thirst and do without,
  A pain to suffer what we deem unjust,
  To win a joy and lay it in the dust;
But there's a fiercer pain,— the pain of doubt:
  From other griefs Death sets the spirit free:
  Doubt steals the light from immortality!
FLORENCE EARLE COATES.

SAPPHO.

As a wan weaver in an attic dim,
  Hopeless yet patient, so he may be fed
  With scanty store of sorrow-seasoned bread,
Heareth a blithe bird carol over him,
And sees no longer walls and rafters grim,
  But rural lanes where little feet are led
  Through springing flowers, fields with clover spread,
Clouds, swan-like, that o'er depths of azure swim,—

So when upon our earth-dulled ear new breaks
  Some fragment, Sappho, of thy skyey song,
A noble wonder in our souls awakes;
The deathless Beautiful draws strangely nigh,
  And we look up and marvel how so long
We were content to drudge for sordid joys that die.
FLORENCE EARLE COATES.

OPEN SESAME!

We strive to shield our lives as years advance
   From too close touch of others, more and more,
   Behind the guarded portals that of yore
Our childhood left wide open; covert glance
From secret loopholes when a knock doth chance,
   Not knowing if, should we unbar the door,
   Or rain or sun shall fall across the floor,
Afraid lest Pain come in Love's countenance.

This strangest lesson life must learn of all
   Brings fullest compensation. O dear love,
     The bar is down, the door stands open wide;
     I bid thee enter. See, the heart inside
   Beats as its childhood holds no record of
To hear thy footstep on the threshold fall.
                      CHARLES WASHINGTON COLEMAN.

LOCALITY.

(Crawford's Notch, New Hampshire Aug. 14, 1889.)

How still the mountains! Yet from steep to steep
   The wild winds shriek in maddest revelry,
   And laugh against the hills; to meet the sea
The impetuous torrent, like a pulse aleap,
Springs down the pass, up which the cloud-wraiths sweep
   Low through the stern rock-gates, where movelessly,
   High on the mountain watch-towers bare and free,
Great, calm, stone faces endless vigil keep.

And I, clasped by the hills storm-swept and cold,
   My pulse aleap as torrent to the strand,
Look out, like those hill-watchers, and behold
A level land, all sunshot, in the South,
   And in a tangled garden two who stand
Among the blooming roses, mouth to mouth.
                      CHARLES WASHINGTON COLEMAN.

NOT LOST.

YES, cross in rest the little, snow-white hands.
  Do you not see the lips so faintly red
    With love's last kiss ? Their sweetness has not fled,
Though now you say her sinless spirit stands
Within the pale of God's bright summer lands.
  Gather the soft hair round the dainty head,
    As in past days. Who says that she is dead,
And nevermore will heed the old commands ?

To your cold idols cling; I know she sleeps,
  That her pure soul is not by vexed winds tost
    Along the pathless altitudes of space.
This life but sows the seed from which one reaps
  The future's harvest. No, I have not lost
    The glory and the gladness of her face.

THOMAS S. COLLIER.

VENUS.

THIS is the face that shone when Greece was free,
  And, haloed by gray cloud or foaming wave,
    Thrilled coward hearts and made them strong and brave;
For love that ruled supreme, love whose degree
Was greater than the greatest kings could be,
  Glowed in the eyes whose brightness was the grave
    Of wise resolves, that should poor mortals save
From this imperial goddess of the sea.

The cool, sweet freshness of the sunlit deep
  Lay warm and tender on her cheek's soft flush,
    And made delicious her rich, fragrant breath:
Ah, how can such enchanting beauty sleep,
  Where sombre shadows fill the eternal hush
    That lies so heavy on the land of death ?

THOMAS S. COLLIER.

THE TORCH-RACE.

BRAVE racer, who hast sped the living light
   With throat outstretched and every nerve a-strain,
   Now on thy left hand labors gray-faced Pain,
And Death hangs close behind thee on the right.
Soon flag the flying feet, soon fails the sight,
   With every pulse the gaunt pursuers gain;
   And all thy splendor of strong life must wane
And set into the mystery of night.

Yet fear not, though, in falling, blindness hide
   The hand that snatches, ere it touch the sod,
   The light thy lessening grasp no more controls:
Truth's rescuer, Truth shall instantly provide.
This is the torch-race game, that noblest souls
Play on through time beneath the eyes of God.
HELEN GRAY CONE.

ON FIRST READING LANDOR'S HELLENICS.

TWO, sauntering hand in hand, one happy day,
   Along a pleasant path that neither knew,
   Came, glad and startled, on the sudden blue,
With sails unclouded, of a sunny bay,
And, hollowing toward the wave, a meadow, gray
   With honey-giving growths thick-spread as dew.
   There, goat-skin girt, with limbs like bronze in hue,
Free-bathed in sun and wind a shepherd lay,

Asleep, his reed-pipe fallen by his knee;
   And late, it seemed, a song had left his lips:
We heard but lapping ripple, prattling bee
   Above the thyme's dim purple, downy tips;
Beyond, once beat by oars of beakèd ships,
   Far outward swept the calm, the storied sea.
HELEN GRAY CONE.

HENRY WADSWORTH LONGFELLOW.

Thou wast not robbed of wonder when youth fled,
   But still the bud had promise to thine eyes,
   And beauty was not sundered from surprise,
And reverent, as reverend, was thy head.
Thy life was music, and thou mad'st it ours,
   Not thine, crude scorn of gentle household things;
   And yet thy spirit had the sea-bird's wings,
Nor rested long among the chestnut-flowers.

Spain's coast of charm, and all the North Sea's cold
   Thou knewest, and thou knewest the soul of eld,
   And dusty scroll and volume we beheld
To gold transmuted, — not to hard-wrought gold,
   But that clear shining of the eastern air,
   When Helios rising shakes the splendor of his hair.
                                  Helen Gray Cone.

ELLEN TERRY'S BEATRICE.

A wind of spring that whirls the feignèd snows
   Of blossom petals in the face and flees;
   Elusive, made of mirthful mockeries,
Yet tender with the prescience of the rose;
A strain desired, that through the memory goes,
   Too subtle-slender for the voice to seize;
   A flame dissembled, only lit to tease,
Whose touch were half a kiss, if one but knows.

She shows by Leonato's dove-like daughter
   A falcon by a prince to be possessed,
      Gay-graced with bells that ever chiming are;
In azure of the bright Sicilian water,
   A billow that has rapt into its breast
      The swayed reflection of a dancing star!
                                  Helen Gray Cone.

THE RESOLVE.

Thou intimate, malign, benumbing power
   I cannot name, since names that men have made
   For shapes of evil shine beside thy shade,
Who from the seat of mine own soul doth lower, —
Darkness itself, that doth the light devour, —
   I feel thine urgency upon me laid
   To voice despair! Thou shalt not be obeyed;
Thou art my master only for thine hour!

As some sad-eyed, wan woman that is slave
   To the swart Moor, being bid her lute to bring,
Since song of her strange land her lord doth crave,
   With lip a-tremble dares the scourge's sting,
Refusing, thy brute might so far I brave:
   I will not sing what thou wouldst have me sing!
Helen Gray Cone.

CONCERNING DEAD LOVE.

When Love is dead, who writes his epitaph?
   Who kisses his shut eyes and says, "Sleep well"?
   We do not ring for him a passing bell;
We cover him with flowers of jest and laugh,
The bitter funeral wine in silence quaff,
   And with dull heart-beats toll his secret knell.
   His grave is ours, and yet with life we strive,
Endure the years, and grind our daily task;

There is no heaven for Love that could not live;
   Earth has but mocked us with this beauteous mask.
   And when in agony our dry lips ask,
"If God deprive us, wherefore did he give?"
   There comes some dreadful question from above,
   And whispers by the grave: "Was this thing Love?"
Rose Terry Cooke.

BESIDE THE DEAD.

It must be sweet, O thou, my dead, to lie
    With hands that folded are from every task;
Sealed with the seal of the great mystery, —
    The lips that nothing answer, nothing ask.
The life-long struggle ended; ended quite
    The weariness of patience and of pain;
    And the eyes closed to open not again
On desolate dawn or dreariness of night.

It must be sweet to slumber and forget;
    To have the poor, tired heart so still at last;
Done with all yearning, done with all regret,
    Doubt, fear, hope, sorrow, all forever past;
Past all the hours, or slow of wing or fleet —
It must be sweet, it must be very sweet!

                      Ina Donna Coolbrith.

TOKENS.

Each day upon the yellow Nile, 't is said,
    Joseph, the youthful ruler, cast forth wheat,
    That haply, floating to his father's feet, —
The sad old father, who believed him dead, —
It might be sign in Egypt there was bread;
And thus the patriarch, past the desert sands
    And scant oasis fringed with thirsty green,
    Be lured toward the love that yearned unseen.
So, flung and scattered, — oh! by what dear hands!
    On the swift rushing and invisible tide,
Small tokens drift adown from far, fair lands,
    And say to us who in the desert bide,
"Are you athirst? Are there no sheaves to bind?
Beloved, here is fullness; follow on and find."

              "Susan Coolidge." (*Sarah C. Woolsey*).

TO THE KATYDID.

SHRILL oracle! proclaiming night by night
   The antique riddle man may never guess,
   But which by thy fond unforgetfulness
Thrills all the dark with music — thy delight,
Whatever Katy did, is to recite
   The act's occurrence with such ceaseless stress
   Of triple chirp as thy small powers possess,
The traveler's listening fancy to excite.

Oh! what immortal secret, strange and dear,
   Should hold thy faithful memory so long? —
     What deathless deed which thou must still withhold, —
Which autumn after autumn, year by year,
   Yea, century after century, thy song
     Reiterates, yet ever leaves untold?
                        HENRY S. CORNWELL.

LIFE AND DEATH. (I.)

O SOLEMN portal veiled in mist and cloud,
   Where all who have lived throng in, an endless line,
   Forbid to tell by backward look or sign
What destiny awaits the advancing crowd!
Bourne crossed but once, with no return allowed;
   Dumb spectral gate, terrestrial yet divine,
   Beyond whose arch all powers and fates combine,
Pledged to divulge no secrets of the shroud.

Close, close behind we step, and strive to catch
   Some whisper in the dark, some glimmering light;
Through circling whirls of thought intent to snatch
   A drifting hope, — a faith that grows to sight:
And yet assured, whatever may befall,
That must be somehow best that comes to all.
                        CHRISTOPHER PEARSE CRANCH.

LIFE AND DEATH. (VIII.)

Not for a rapture unalloyed I ask,
  Not for a recompense for all I miss;
  A banquet of the Gods in heavenly bliss,
A realm in whose warm sunshine I may bask.
Life without discipline or earnest task
  Could ill repay the unfinished work of this.
  Nay, — e'en to clasp some long-lost Beatrice
In bowers of paradise — the mortal mask

Dropped from her face now glorified and bright.
  But I would fain take up what here I left
    All crude and incomplete; would toil and strive
To regain the power of which I am bereft
  By slow decay and death, with fuller light
    To aid the larger life that may survive.

                  CHRISTOPHER PEARSE CRANCH.

OLD AGE. (III.)

This were a boon all others far excelling,
  Could we attain that faith so near yet far
  In the deep Inner-world that nought can jar
The steadfast house and home, our chosen dwelling,
Or check the immortal fountain there upwelling;
  And happy they to whom the gods unbar
  The gates of night to greet their evening star
Ere vesper chimes are changed to funeral knelling.

Ye fellow lingerers in the twilight gloom,
  Ye who with me have lived through morning's glow,
    And down life's darkening slopes have trod together,
This greeting take, this trust, — that, not to doom,
  But victory bound, our lives are pledged to know
    Another morn in Heaven's unclouded weather.

                  CHRISTOPHER PEARSE CRANCH.

THE LADY'S SONNET. TWILIGHT.

I KNOW not why I chose to seem so cold
   At parting from you, for since you are gone
   I see you still. I hear each word, each tone;
And what I hid from you I wish were told.
I, who was proud and shy, seem now too bold
   To write these lines, and yet must write to own
   I would unsay my words, now I'm alone.
From my dark window out upon the wold

I look. 'T was through yon pathway to the west
   I watched you going, while the sunset light
     Went with you, and a shadow seemed to fall
Upon my heart. And now I cannot rest
   Till I have written; for I said, "To-night
     I'll send your answer." Now I've told you all.
                CHRISTOPHER PEARSE CRANCH.

WAITING.

As little children in a darkened hall
   At Christmas-tide await the opening door,
   Eager to tread the fairy-haunted floor
Around the tree with goodly gifts for all,
Oft in the darkness to each other call, —
   Trying to guess their happiness before, —
   Or knowing elders eagerly implore
To tell what fortune unto them may fall, —

So wait we in Time's dim and narrow room,
   And, with strange fancies or another's thought,
     Try to divine before the curtain rise
The wondrous scene; forgetting that the gloom
   Must shortly flee from what the ages sought, —
     The Father's long-planned gift of Paradise.
                C. H. CRANDALL.

ADELAIDE NEILSON.

A VOICE that mocks a laughing, mountain brook,
   A smile as swift as summer swallows fly,
   And eyes that drain the beauty of the sky
To fill our hearts with but a single look!
But lack of lovely words! For if I took
   A thousand pages whereupon to try
   To draw her attributes, my pen would dry,
And I would write but " Beauty " in the book.

Yet may be found her spirit masked in flowers,
   Her genius-light in yonder steadfast star,
     Her winsome graces in the wandering stream;
While from the perfect Poet of all hours
   We hear the message, falling from afar:
     This Rosalind is worthy of my dream.
                              C. H. CRANDALL.

SAPPHO TO PHAON.

LAST night I dreamed you kissed me on the lips.
   Instead of all the wild and sweet surprise
I feel if you but touch my finger-tips
   In waking hours, I coldly met your eyes,
And heeded not your fiery words that burn
   Too late. . . . To-day you passed me with a glance:
I live — no! *starve* — upon that look, and yearn
   For all I spurned in sleep. O hard mischance
That night should heedlessly and without ruth
   Tangle anew the daylight's waste and cheat!
Waking or dreaming — which, love, is the truth?
   I may not know — yet this one thing were sweet:
That, ere forever vanishes our youth,
   My waking self thy dreaming self might meet.
                                  MARGARET CROSBY.

THE PHŒNIX.

A Sonnet for Poets.

With whirring wings that heavenward would aspire,
   The weary Phœnix seeks his fatal rest;
   Hues of the opal burn upon his breast,
Empurpled plumage tipped with golden fire.
Slowly he sinks upon the doomèd pyre,
   The waving flames leap curling to his crest;
   All beauty, joy, and hope, and love's unrest
Fuel to fan a flame that does not tire.

Gone are his years, perished his pride too late!
   In molten embers lies his guarded fame, —
When lo! they stir, and from them soars in state
   A fairer, different Phœnix, yet the same;
Death waits, a sterner and avertless fate,
   But hark! he sings and wins a deathless name.

Margaret Crosby.

TO EMMA LAZARUS.

On reading "By the Waters of Babylon."

In dead, dull days I heard a ringing cry
   Borne on the careless winds, — a nation's pain,
   A woman's sorrow in a poet's strain
Of noblest lamentation. Clear and high
It rang above our lowlands to a sky
   Of purest psalmody, till hearts are fain
   To say: "In this sweet singer once again
The powers of prophet and of psalmist lie."

Rachel of Judah! ever mournful, sad
   Must be the heart which thy lamenting hears;
Singer of Israel! ever proud and glad
   We hail a nation's hope that thus appears;
Sad mourners by the waters! ye have had
   A poet's sweetest solace for your tears.

Allen Eastman Cross.

A VISION OF NIGHT.

I saw the Spirit of the Night descend, —
　　O'er half the world outspread his pinions wide
　　Against a faint-starred sky whence day had died,
And hoveringly his silent flight suspend;
Then with mesmeric sweep of pinion bend
　　With measured motion like a pulsing tide,
　　Wind round the world his Titan arms, and ride
With his beloved through space that has no end,

To bear her onward in a blissful dream,
　　Hushing day's tumult in her surging breast,
And letting wide his star-wrought mantle stream
　　Between her and Apollo's fiery crest;
On through vast calm till smiling dawn's first beam
　　Woke the too happy world from her deep rest.

　　　　　　　　　　　　　　LULU CURRAN.

THE JERSEY PRISON SHIP.

The Prison ship, — a tomb of living men,
　　Living in death and longing but to die, —
Or, ghastlier, the rebel prison pen,
　　The foulest spot beneath the patient sky, —
Both these have proved undaunted Yankee hearts:
　　Yet, in their sad extremity forlorn,
Kind Nature solaced with her kindest arts
　　Those faithful souls by wasting torture torn;
For some Rhode Island captive, as he lay,
　　Saw in his sleep, with eager joy elate,
The level shores of Narragansett Bay,
　　And the plain landscape of his native State;
While his pale, dreaming lips did softly ope,
And murmur low her flag's dear legend, "Hope."

　　　　　　　　　　　　GEORGE WILLIAM CURTIS.

TO JULIAN M. STURTEVANT, D. D.

The eyes of night, soft closing to their rest, —
   The full-orbed moon, and Hesper, evening star,
   Driving apace his quick descending car, —
Just ere they hide behind the cloudless West
Show forth their kindly radiance at the best,
   Grow brighter to the sight, more brilliant far
   Than all their earlier zenith splendors are.
So may, O Sturtevant! the joys which blest

Thy former days grow with thy later years,
   At fourscore shine in faith, in love, in peace,
In hopes of Heaven, which banish earthly fears, —
   Virtues and happiness alike increase;
At length, when comes thy Master's last behest,
Sink gently, full-orbed, on thy Father's breast.

JULY 21, 1885.   JAMES PIERPONT DAVENPORT.

TO A. BENEDICT DAVENPORT.

So saith the Psalmist, with his eyes downcast,
   Viewing life's sorrows, as a traveler may,
   Weariedly struggling on an unknown way,
See only the rough path; each milestone past,
To him a stumbling-block, he hopes the last.
   Not so he journeys, at the close of day,
   Who sees from yonder hilltop the bright ray
Of home-lit taper. Rest, the eve's repast,
And loving welcome, close before him lie;
He mounts with joy the ascent that brings them nigh.
   Father, let not thine eyes from Heaven's light roam,
By which illumined, thy past life appears,
Not threescore ten of weary, sorrowing years,
   But seventy stepping-stones that lead toward Home.

OCTOBER 30, 1887.   JAMES PIERPONT DAVENPORT.

THE JUDGMENT OF LOVE.

If, at the general judgment of the dead,
   I should see Justice standing stern and high
   And looking down at me with awful eye,
And hear her say, "Thou goest unpardonèd!"
I should not weep, nor cry, nor bow my head,
   But straight to doom I'd go most loftily.
   But oh, if on that day I should descry
Not Justice, but my Mother's face instead,

And find her look of mild compassion gone,
   Oh, what a cry should pierce the silence then!
But it can not be thought! Yet such an one.
Is Love; the Lover is the Judge of men.
And they whom not the eyes of Justice move
   Shall feel the terrors of the eyes of Love.
                    WILLIAM C. DAVENPORT.

BEECHER.

Beecher! I will not any longer say
   That thou wert bold, or eloquent, or wise.
   These are become the words of men whose eyes
Are blind to all thou soughtest to display.
They think to prove their vision in this way;
   But all the judgments of their mood are lies,
   Because they cannot in this temper rise
That Truth to know whose light exceeds the day.

But never be it so among us here,
   Nor of such error could our souls partake
Who knew thee for a spiritual Seer, —
   A man inspired for the people's sake, —
A servant of the Christ, divinely led
From life to Life, nor dead but to the dead.
                    WILLIAM C. DAVENPORT.

SPAIN.

HARK! sack-clothed nun, pressing the cloister stone!
  For Freedom, like some meadow-cheering thrush,
  Under thy grating in the morning's flush,
Carols of gladsome things to thee unknown.
Lusty and tall thy childhood's mates have grown;
  They run where breezes blow and fountains gush,
  While thou dost hide where bat-like terrors rush,
Number a rosary, or kiss a bone.

Quit the foul relics of thy mouldy cell,
  Break the long vigil of thy sunless brow;
The green hills lying yonder ever tell
  More than these tottering walls can utter now;
  And Freedom breathes on them who take her vow
A kindlier benison than convent bell.

RICHARD EDWIN DAY.

THE POET'S ART.

CALL it not art; that sad, laborious name,
  O gentle poet, does thy warblings wrong.
  When at still eve the nightingales prolong
Delicious melody, who would not blame
The cold, mechanic term for that which came,
  Born of sweet throats, a gushing stream of song?
So from thy soul pours forth, oh, free and strong,
Thine own deep music on the air of fame.

Thy art is Nature's; thou dost only hear
  The whispered secrets of her woods and skies,
And then repeat them to the common ear,
  That cannot catch her finer harmonies:
Thou art her voice, and unto her so dear
  Her inmost heart is open to thine eyes.

CHARLES T. DAZEY.

STORM-MUSIC.

List ! through dusk silence, warningly there steal
   The first low notes of airy violins :
   With one shrill chord the symphony begins,
While oft the thunder's diapason peal
Rolls through the flame-lit sky, — God's chariot wheel.
   And hark ! what trumpets blow from yon black cloud !
   While the strong trees, in sudden terror bowed,
Seem from the tempest fleeing, then reveal

The horror of their anguish by deep moans
And wailings keen, far-tossing, to and fro,
   Their tangled branches, when the angry Wind
   Wreaks all his mighty passion unconfined,
Then leaves them shattered, like brave men laid low
By War's hot breath, to die 'mid battle groans.
Charles T. Dazey.

NIGHT ON THE RIVER.

O restless throng, massed on the shovel prow
   That eats the moonlit reaches of the river,
   Ye feel them, too, those mysteries that quiver
Through deeps of tenderness on high, below,
Shooting in stars, glancing through eyes that glow
   Yellow, red, green, among the barks, and shiver
   The north with splendors from a boundless Giver
And seam the dark with lamps that come and go.

For hushed are hoof-stamp, babble, and the sharp
   Jangle of bells, and songs uncouth are still ;
O'erhead resounds the vast Æolian harp
   Built for the god of storms by human will,
The Bridge whose twin colossi with their warp
   Frame for the dawn's white feet a curving sill.
Charles De Kay.

THE CITY TRANSFIGURED.

There lurks a deadly beauty in the air;
   Down the long wedge of street the fronts are gray
With silvery grayness, rich and warm and rare.
   Mark, in the shadows! there is that to-day
   Of liquid loveliness outpoured on all
That gilds the landscape with immortal ray,
   And makes the driest factory roof and wall
Palettes whereon the subtlest colors play.

   I know such visions, ah, too well; they mean
That woful storm shall mar to-morrow's face;
   That once again the gods have envious been,
And what they loved to raise will now debase;
   That nothing lasts; that such unearthly sheen
Is but the sleuth-hound's music on the trace.

Charles De Kay.

BE THOU MY SUN.

Be thou my sun, and rise on every morn
   To find a worshiper like him who knows
   Darkness for months among the polar snows,
And hurries, trembling, and with gloom outworn,
To that high hill where first the pallor grows
   Before the blush of sunrise. Have no scorn
   Though we of thy sweet graces are forlorn
Nor hoard thy love. She lives who love bestows.

   Yes, like the sun pour down a generous flood
     Of love unselfish, yes, though unrequited;
   Still be thou grand enough to stir the blood
Of torpid women listening to thy name.
   So shall the man whose pleading thou hast slighted
Kindle with reverence at thy noble name.

Charles De Kay.

HER APPARITION.

Hush! through the sounds and through the troubled airs
  I hear the whisper of her clinging gown:
I know her weight is on the spiral stairs,
  And now I look on her lithe figure down.
See with what grace and pride without a frown
She passes men; see her beguiling hairs,
  Demure of coil, all soft and harmless brown,
Till fine gold daggers stab you unawares.

And while she rises with her princess mien,
  Behold the face wherefrom expressions look
Like a deep autumn's daylight, clear, serene,
  A glorious title-page to oh, what book!
Back, back then, cares, and in her coming drown —
My light and love and life, my cross, my crown!

Charles De Kay.

NIGHT INFLUENCE.

Self-awed with its own glory is the night.
  Yon moon looks down with passionless aken
  Upon the Union's sleepless youth, as when
The Pyramids rose new upon her sight,
Or Amos of Tekoa by her light
  Guarded his flocks, the while Jehovah's pen
  Wrote on his heart the message unto men
Whose characters divine he read aright.

The lover longs to be alone with her
  Who is the shrine where kneels his heart; and he,
Who is of Nature ardent worshiper,
  Would in her presence unattended be;
Would to her lips of inspiration list,
With midnight's starry arbor for a tryst.

Franklin E. Denton.

PRESAGE OF AUTUMN.

As early as the waning of July,
    While yet the forest leaves are darkly green,
    And ripening berries in the fields are seen,
While yet unsickled waves the wheat and rye,
And tropically burns the sun on high, —
    Some burnished eve, before the stars convene,
    Something the heart can see in the serene
Horizon says that Fall is drawing nigh.

'Tis the handwriting on the twilight's wall,
    Warning the Summer that the boundless power
    She wields is but a transitory dower,
That e'en for her await the shroud, the pall.
    Oh, sadder than the gales and solemn tints
    Of Autumn's prime are such ethereal hints!

                                 FRANKLIN E. DENTON.

THE HUMAN TIE.

    "As if life were not sacred, too."   GEORGE ELIOT.

"SPEAK tenderly! for he is dead," we say;
    "With gracious hand smooth all his roughened past,
    And fullest measure of reward forecast,
Forgetting naught that gloried his brief day."
Yet when the brother still upon the way —
    Prone with his burdens, heart-worn in the strife —
    Totters before us, how we search his life,
Censure, and sternly punish, while we may!

Oh, weary are the paths of Earth, and hard!
And living hearts alone are ours to guard.
    At least, begrudge not to the sore distraught
    The reverent silence of our pitying thought.
Life, too, is sacred, and he best forgives
Who says, "He errs, but — tenderly! he lives."

                                 MARY MAPES DODGE.

THE STARS.

They wait all day, unseen by us, unfelt;
  Patient they bide behind the day's full glare;
  And we who watched the dawn when they were there,
Thought we had seen them in the daylight melt,
While the slow sun upon the earth-line knelt.
  Because the teeming sky seemed void and bare
  When we explored it through the dazzled air,
We had no thought that there all day they dwelt.

Yet were they over us, alive and true,
In the vast shades far up above the blue, —
The brooding shades beyond our daylight ken, —
  Serene and patient in their conscious light,
  Ready to sparkle for our joy again, —
    The eternal jewels of the short-lived night.

MARY MAPES DODGE.

OVER THE WORLD.

There is a time between our night and day,
  A space between this world and the unknown,
  Where none may enter as we stand alone
Save the one other single soul that may;
Then is all perfect if the two but stay.
  It is the time when, the home-evening flown,
  And "good-nights" sped in happy household tone,
We look out from the casement ere we pray.

Into the world of darkness deep and far
We gaze — each depth with its own deepest star,
  That brightens as we turn, nor yet recedes
  When we would search it with our sorest needs, —
O holy living-ground from heaven won!
O time beyond the night when day is done!

MARY MAPES DODGE.

LIFE AND DEATH.

"The sworder by the sword shall fall," I said,
  "Nor less the dreamer in his dream shall cease."
And Life replied, "They do but seem to fade,"
  But Death was silent; to the stony peace
That on the pallid forehead lays its hand,
  And lays its head upon the marble breast,
He pointed (as if I should understand),
  And smiled, but never syllable expressed.

Still, still I gaze into his dreamless eyes,
  And gazing feel the life within me shrink;
And still I muse upon his mysteries,
  But never nigher draw unto their brink.
When we are one — and then, alas! alone —
  The meaning of his silence shall be shown.
JOHN A. DORGAN.

SILENCE.

O GOLDEN Silence, bid our souls be still,
  And on the foolish fretting of our care
  Lay thy soft touch of healing unaware!
Once, for a half hour, even in heaven the thrill
Of the clear harpings ceased the air to fill
  With soft reverberations. Thou wert there,
  And all the shining seraphs owned thee fair, —
A white, hushed Presence on the heavenly hill.

Bring us thy peace, O Silence! Song is sweet;
  Tuneful is baby laughter, and the low
    Murmur of dying winds among the trees,
And dear the music of Love's hurrying feet;
  Yet only he who knows thee learns to know
    The secret soul of loftiest harmonies.
JULIA C. R. DORR.

DARKNESS.

Come, blessed Darkness, come and bring thy balm
   For eyes grown weary of the garish Day!
   Come with thy soft slow steps, thy garments gray,
Thy veiling shadows, bearing in thy palm
The poppy-seeds of slumber, deep and calm!
   Come with thy patient stars, whose far-off ray
   Steals the hot fever of the soul away, —
Thy stillness, sweeter than a chanted psalm!

O blessed Darkness, Day indeed is fair,
   And light is dear when summer days are long,
     And one by one the harvesters go by;
But so is rest sweet and surcease from care,
   And folded palms, and hush of evensong,
     And all the unfathomed silence of the sky!
                      JULIA C. R. DORR.

MERCÉDÈS.

(JUNE 27, 1878.)

O fair young queen, who liest dead to-day
   In thy proud palace o'er the moaning sea,
   With still, white hands that never more may be
Lifted to pluck life's roses bright with May —
Little is it to you that, far away,
   Where skies you knew not bend above the free,
   Hearts touched with tender pity turn to thee,
And for thy sake a shadow dims the day!
But youth and love and womanhood are one,
   'Though across sundering seas their signals fly;
Young Love's pure kiss, the joy but just begun,
   The hope of motherhood, thy people's cry —
   O thou fair child! was it not hard to die
And leave so much beneath the summer sun?
                      JULIA C. R. DORR.

TO-MORROW.

But thou, To-morrow! Never yet was born
   In earth's dull atmosphere a thing so fair —
   Never yet tripped with footsteps light as air,
So glad a vision o'er the hills of morn!
Fresh as the radiant dawning, — all unworn
   By lightest touch of sorrow or of care,
   Thou dost the glory of the morning share
By snowy wings of hope and faith upborne!

O fair To-morrow! what our souls have missed
   Art thou not keeping for us somewhere, still?
     The buds of promise that have never blown —
The tender lips that we have never kissed —
     The song whose high, sweet strain eludes our skill
     The one white pearl that life hath never known!
                        JULIA C. R. DORR.

RESURGAMUS.

What though we sleep a thousand leagues apart,
   I by my mountains, you beside your sea?
   What though our moss-grown graves divided be
By the wide reaches of a continent's heart?
When from long slumber we at length shall start,
   Wakened to stronger life, exultant, free,
   This mortal clothed in immortality,
Where shall I find my heaven save where thou art?

Straight as a bird that hasteth to its nest,
   Glad as an eagle soaring to the light,
     Swift as the thought that bears my soul to thine
When yon lone star hangs trembling in the west,
   So straight, so glad, so swift to thee my flight,
     Led on through farthest space by love divine!
                        JULIA C. R. DORR.

MAURICE DE GUÉRIN.

(On reading " Le Centaure.")

THE old wine filled him and he saw with eyes
   Anoint of Nature fauns and dryads fair
   Unseen by others; to him maidenhair
And waxen lilacs and those buds that rise
As sudden from tall reeds at slight surprise
   Brought charmèd thoughts; and on earth everywhere
   He, like sad Jacques, found unheard music rare
As that of Syrinx to old Grecians wise.
A pagan heart, a Christian soul had he,
   He followed Christ, yet for dead Pan he longed,
   Till earth and Heaven met within his heart:
As if Theocritus in Sicily
   Had come upon the Figure crucified,
   And lost his gods in deep, Christ-given rest.

                  MAURICE FRANCIS EGAN.

OF FLOWERS.

THERE were no roses till the first child died,
   No violets, nor balmy-breathed heart's-ease,
   No heliotrope, nor buds so dear to bees,
The honey-hearted suckle, no gold-eyed
And lowly dandelion, nor, stretching wide,
   Clover and cowslip-cups, like rival seas,
   Meeting and parting, as the young spring breeze
Runs giddy races playing seek and hide.
For all flowers died when Eve left Paradise,
   And all the world was flowerless awhile,
      Until a little child was laid in earth;
Then from its grave grew violets for its eyes,
   And from its lips rose-petals for its smile,
      And so all flowers from that child's death took
         birth.

                  MAURICE FRANCIS EGAN.

THE GOOD SHEPHERD.

Shepherd, with meek brow wreathed with blossoms sweet,
  Who guard'st thy timid flock with tenderest care —
Who guid'st in sunny paths their wandering feet, —
  And the young lambs dost in thy bosom bear; —
  Who lead'st thy happy flock to pastures fair,
And by still waters at the noon of day,
  Charming with lute divine the silent air,
What time they linger on the verdant way; —

Good Shepherd! might one gentle distant strain
  Of that immortal melody sink deep
  Into my heart and pierce its careless sleep,
And melt by powerful love its sevenfold chain —
  Oh! then my soul thy voice should know, and flee
To mingle with thy flock and ever follow thee.

Elizabeth F. Ellet.

OTHER WORLDS.

I sometimes muse when my adventurous gaze
  Has roamed the starry arches of the night,
  That were I dowered with strong, angelic sight,
All would look changed in those pale, heavenly ways.
What wheeling worlds my vision would amaze!
  What chasms of gloom would fill me and affright!
  What rhythmic equipoise would rouse delight!
What moons would beam on me, what suns would blaze!

Then through my awed soul sweeps the larger thought
  Of how Creation's edict may have set
    Vast human multitudes on those far spheres,
With towering passions to which mine are naught,
  With majesties of happiness, or yet
    With agonies of unconjectured tears!

Edgar Fawcett.

BEES.

TRADITION's favoring verdict would express
   In you all duteous thrift and toil extreme,
   Against gray wintry dearth, while summers beam,
Hoarding with zeal your honeyed bounteousness.
And yet in drowsy revery I confess
   That booming now where flowery vistas gleam,
   Among these jubilant garden-paths you seem
The murmuring incarnations of idlesse!

Nay, more; you are like those pages, clad of old
By pampering lords in velvet and in gold,
   Who bore sweet amorous words, with cautious airs,
To delicate ladies in rich robes aglow,
Strolling down glades of shadowy Fontainebleau,
   Or loitering at Versailles on marble stairs!

EDGAR FAWCETT.

SLEEP'S THRESHOLD.

WHAT footstep but has wandered free and far
   Amid that Castle of Sleep whose walls were planned
   By no terrestrial craft, no human hand,
With towers that point to no recorded star?
Here sorrows, memories, and remorses are,
   Roaming the long, dim rooms or galleries grand;
   Here the lost friends our spirits yet demand
Gleam through mysterious doorways left ajar.

But of the uncounted throngs that ever win
   The halls where Slumber's dusky witcheries rule,
     Who, after wakening, may reveal aright
By what phantasmal means he entered in? —
   What porch of cloud, what vapory vestibule,
     What stairway quarried from the mines of night?

EDGAR FAWCETT.

EARTHQUAKE.

A GIANT of awful strength, he dumbly lies
  Far-prisoned among the solemn deeps of earth;
    The sinewy grandeurs of his captive girth, —
His great-thewed breast, colossally moulded thighs,
And arms thick-roped with muscle of mighty size,
  Repose in slumber where no dream gives birth
    For months, even years, to any grief or mirth;
A slumber of tranquil lips, calm-lidded eyes!

Yet sometimes to his spirit a dream will creep
  Of the old glad past when clothed in dauntless pride
    He walked the world, unchained by tyrannous powers;
And then, while he tosses restlessly in sleep,
  Dark, terrible graves for living shapes yawn wide,
    Or a city shrieks among her tottering towers!
                            EDGAR FAWCETT.

VICTOR HUGO DEAD.

WHEN such a spirit away from earth has fled,
  With all his power of deed and of desire,
    When now no more the anointed lips respire,
And low at last has drooped the imperial head,
Nature, with whose large liberty was wed
  So many a melody that moved his lyre,
    Hath fitly bidden her lightning's wings of fire
Pierce the dark sea to tell us he is dead!

And yet with loftier love for his renown,
  O Nature, let thy stars his vigil light,
    Thy winds the music of his requiem stir!
Then lift him in thine arms and lay him down
  Sublimely where the cloisters of the night
    Shall be his archangelic sepulchre!
                            EDGAR FAWCETT.

LONGFELLOW IN WESTMINSTER ABBEY.

Erelong I paced those cloisteral aisles, erelong
  I moved where pale memorial shapes convene,
    Where poet, warrior, statesman, king or queen
In one great elegy of sculpture throng,
When suddenly, with heart-beats glad and strong,
  I saw the face of that lost friend serene
    Who robed Hiawatha and Evangeline
In such benign simplicity of song!

Then, swiftly as light mists on morning leas,
  All history, legend, England, backward drawn,
    Vanished like vision to incorporate air.
And in one sweet colonial home o'er seas
  I saw the lamp shine out across the lawn,
    I heard the old clock ticking on the stair!
Edgar Fawcett.

TRANSFORMATION.

Once in an English woodland, where awoke
  Breezes that made the dark leaves pulse and shine,
I walked at twilight, willing to invoke
  All moods of revery, mirthful or malign,
When gradually on my vision broke
  A mighty and moss-hung tree that lay supine,
Leveled by some dead tempest's cruel stroke,
  And clasped by coils of ivy serpentine. . . .

If truth now tricked herself in fancy's cloak,
  If some brief elfin madness now was mine,
Or yet if actual voices faintly spoke,
  Wandering the dusk, there stays no certain sign;
But "I was Merlin," said the bearded oak,
  And "I was Vivien," said the snaky vine.
Edgar Fawcett.

THE SNOW.

Between thy frozen eyelids, in swift grace,
  Touched with the form and splendor of the spheres,
  As white as angel's thoughts, thy gelid tears,
O mourning Nature, down thy bosom trace
Their way, and fold thee in a white embrace.
  Oh, soft as footsteps of retreating years
  That vibrate only in the soul's quick ears,
Oh, pure as kisses on an infant's face!

Thus may my days fall — white, and pure, and still —
  Upon the world's cold forehead, lending so
More grace to her bleak brows which throb and thrill
  With inward fevers; noiseless as the snow,
Oh, white and noiseless, may they drift, and fold
Dark spaces of the earth with grace untold.
                        Lillian Blanche Fearing.

A VOLUME OF DANTE.

I lie unread, alone. None heedeth me.
  Day after day the cobwebs are unswept
  From my dim covers. I have lain and slept
In dust and darkness for a century.
An old forgotten volume, I. Yet see!
  Such mighty words within my heart are kept
  That, reading once, great Ariosto wept
In vain despair so impotent to be.

And once, with pensive eyes and drooping head,
  Musing, Vittoria Colonna came,
    And touched my leaves with dreamy finger-tips,
Lifted me up half absently, and read;
    Then kissed the page with sudden tender lips,
  And sighed, and murmured one beloved name.
                        Caroline Wilder Fellowes.

NOT STRAND BUT SEA.

Upon the storm-swept beach brown broken weeds
   Lay scattered far abroad, and as I saw
   The wild disordered strand, "Behold the law,"
I cried, " of my sad mind and her dread needs."
But as I wandered there those fruitless seeds
   Were trampled by my feet, while quiet lay
   My spirit on the waves and joined their play
Round a far rock where safe the sea-bird breeds;

And then I knew, not like the strand forlorn
   But like the sea my soul her color drew
From heaven, and all the splendors of the morn
   And greater glories that with ripeness grew
   Were hers, and hers the calm that evening knew,
And every grace that out of heaven is born.
        ANNIE ADAMS FIELDS (*Mrs. James T. Fields*).

CACTUS.[1]

I know an isle, clasped in the sea's strong arms,
   Sport of his rage, and sharer of his dreams;
   A barren spot to alien eyes it seems,
But for its own it wears unfading charms.
From Spring's first kiss to Autumn's last caress,
   Gayly its moorlands bloom from strand to strand,
   And many a favored nook by west winds fanned
Holds flowers unmatched for tint and loveliness.
But most I mind me of a lonesome shore,
   For countless gulls a harbor and freehold,
   Where like some shipwrecked buccaneer of old,
Cast on the sands, condemned to roam no more,
   In spiny armature secure and bold,
   The Cactus lies at length, and guards its gold.
        EMILY SHAW FORMAN.

---

[1] *Opuntia vulgaris* reaches its farthest northern limit at Nantucket.

GOLDEN ROD.

A PATIENT, pensive silence fills the wood,
  Broken by muffled droppings, sad as tears;
  On the far hills a purple haze appears,
That veils and yet reveals their mournful mood;
Soft mists along the lowlands creep, and brood
  On lake and river. Through the hush one hears
  The tuneless drone of insects, lulling fears
And hopes alike. A sense, half understood,

Of something dear that was and is no more,
  Stirs in the heart. "Summer is gone," we say;
  But see, as dreamily she went her way,
She dropped the golden sceptre that she bore;
  Ah, precious symbol of her gracious sway,
Bright incarnation of the smile she wore!

EMILY SHAW FORMAN.

THE CARDINAL FLOWER.

No purer joy the glad midsummer holds
  For those who love to seek in secret nooks
  Of wood or mead, or by the marge of brooks,
The hidden treasures she for love unfolds,
Than on a morn when skies are perfect blue,
  And clouds are far and fleecy, loitering slow,
  To follow some wild streamlet's wayward flow,
And spy afar, O flower of matchless hue,

Thy wondrous brightness flashing through the green,
  As if a flock of red-birds stooped to drink
  In airy flutter at the brooklet's brink,
Or, as a troop of Indian girls half seen,
  Half hid, were wading in the crystal stream,
  While through the leaves their scarlet 'broideries gleam.

EMILY SHAW FORMAN.

THE SEA'S VOICE.

I.

AROUND the rocky headlands, far and near,
   The wakened ocean murmured with dull tongue,
   Till all the coast's mysterious caverns rung
With the waves' voice, barbaric, hoarse, and drear.
Within this distant valley, with rapt ear,
   I listened, thrilled, as though a spirit sung,
   Or some gray god, as when the world was young,
Moaned to his fellow, mad with rage or fear.
Thus in the dark, ere the first dawn, methought,
   The sea's deep roar and sullen surge and shock
     Broke the long silence of eternity,
And echoed from the summits where God wrought,
   Building the world, and ploughing the steep rock
     With ploughs of ice-hills harnessed to the sea.
WILLIAM PRESCOTT FOSTER.

II.

THE sea is never quiet: east and west
   The nations hear it, like the voice of fate;
   Within vast shores its strife makes desolate,
Still murmuring mid storms that to its breast
Return, as eagles screaming to their nest.
   Is it the voice of worlds and isles that wait
While old earth crumbles to eternal rest,
   Or some hoar monster calling to his mate?

O ye, that hear it moan about the shore,
   Be still and listen! that loud voice hath sung,
   Where mountains rise, where desert sands are blown;
And when man's voice is dumb, forevermore
   'T will murmur on its craggy shores among,
   Singing of gods and nations overthrown.
WILLIAM PRESCOTT FOSTER.

IN NOVEMBER.

From my hill-circled home, this eve, I heard
    The tempest singing on the windy height —
    The first wild storm of winter in its flight
Seaward — as though some mighty Arctic bird
Had left its snowy nest, and on the firred,
    Steep mountain summit paused one boisterous night
    To fill the valleys with its fierce delight.
Ah me, I thought, how every pine is stirred,

Till all its deep storm-music is unbound;
    How every waving bough gives forth its roar,
    And the firs shout, as though some harper hoar
Laid his great hand upon the hills around,
And drew a loud hymn forth, a voice to sound
    Far, far away, beyond the world's dull shore.

                             William Prescott Foster.

THE VISION OF ABRAHAM LINCOLN.

April 14, 1865.

Dreaming, he woke, our martyr President,
    And still the vision lingered in his mind,
    (Problem at once and prophecy combined) —
A flying bark with all her canvas bent:
Joy-bringing herald of some great event
    Oft when the wavering scale of war inclined
    To Freedom's side; now how to be divined
Uncertain, since rebellion's force was spent.
So, of the omen heedful, as of Fate,
    Lincoln with curious eye the horizon scanned:
At morn, with hopes of port and peace elate;
    At night, like Palinurus — in his hand
The broken tiller of the Ship of State —
    Flung on the margin of the Promised Land.

                             Wendell P. Garrison.

POST-MERIDIAN.

I. AFTERNOON.

When in thy glass thou studiest thy face,
   Not long, nor yet not seldom, half repelled
   And half attracted; when thou hast beheld
Of Time's slow ravages the crumbling trace,
(Deciphered now with many an interspace
     The characters erewhile that Beauty spelled),
   And in thy throat a choking fear hath swelled
Of Love, grown cold, eluding thy embrace:

Could'st thou but read my gaze of tenderness —
   Affection fused with pity — precious tears
Would bring relief to thy unjust distress;
   Thy visage, even as it to me appears,
Would seem to thee transfigured; thou would'st bless
   Me, who am also, Dearest! scarred with years.
                    Wendell P. Garrison.

II. EVENING.

Age cannot wither her whom not gray hairs
   Nor furrowed cheeks have made the thrall of Time;
   For Spring lies hidden under Winter's rime,
And violets know the victory is theirs.
Even so the corn of Egypt, unawares,
   Proud Nilus shelters with engulfing slime;
   So Etna's hardening crust a more sublime
Volley of pent-up fires at last prepares.
O face yet fair, if paler, and serene
   With sense of duty done without complaint!
O venerable crown! — a living green,
   Strength to the weak, and courage to the faint —
Thy bleaching locks, thy wrinkles, have but been
   Fresh beads upon the rosary of a saint!
                    Wendell P. Garrison.

FREEDOM OF THE MIND.

(Written in Prison.)

High walls and huge the BODY may confine,
    And iron grates obstruct the prisoner's gaze,
And massive bolts may baffle his design,
    And vigilant keepers watch his devious ways;
Yet scorns th' immortal MIND this base control!
    No chains can bind it, and no cell enclose:
Swifter than light, it flies from pole to pole,
    And, in a flash, from earth to heaven it goes!
It leaps from mount to mount — from vale to vale
    It wanders, plucking honeyed fruits and flowers;
It visits home, to hear the fireside tale,
    Or in sweet converse pass the joyous hours:
'T is up before the sun, roaming afar,
And, in its watches, wearies every star!

                      WILLIAM LLOYD GARRISON.

THE SILENT LIFE.

Happy the man who has the poet's heart,
    E'en though he lack the poet's golden tongue!
    Happy is he who having never sung
And hopeless e'er to sing though but small part
Of those fair visions that before him start
    Still lives within a world forever young,
    Still walks high fancies, noble thoughts among,
And feels the influence which the planets dart.

His life is fed from pure unfailing springs;
    And silent flows, a stranger to unrest,
    Like some deep stream that finds its voiceless way
Amid the timorous haunts of all wild things,
    And their unconscious beauty day by day
Mirrors within the quiet of its breast.

                            LEWIS E. GATES.

PISA.

On the Lung' Arno, in each stately street,
   The silence is a hunger and craves food
   Like Ugolino cowering o'er his brood.
Sad Pisa! in thy garments obsolete
Still grand, the sceptre fallen at thy feet,
   An impuissant queen of solitude,
   Thine inconsolable gaze speaks widowhood
Fixed on the river, voiceless and deplete.

A trance more lonely — lo! not many rods
   From the shrunk Arno, a more slumberous air,
   A dream of heaven in marbles rich and rare!
Oppressed with sleep the Campanile nods;
   But in the Campo Santo's hush of breath,
   Orcagna's pathos paints, not Sleep but Death!
                               WILLIAM GIBSON.

LAND AND SEA.

Look where the sea, with swift, resistless tide
   Breaks on the sandy beach and rock-bound shore,
   Awhile with plaintive murmur, then a roar
Like that of cagèd beasts, their food denied;
And see with what calm strength and sovran pride
   The rocks, unshaken and triumphant, soar
   Above the battling waves, that more and more
Seek to encompass them on every side.

I am the ocean, thou, my Love, the land,
   That spurns the humble suitor at her feet
   And lifts her queenly head where she may meet
Such homage as the sun and stars command.
   The land shall yield at last unto the sea,
   And sooner, Love, or later, thou to me!
       · JOSEPH B. GILDER ("*Randall Blackshaw*").

THE CELESTIAL PASSION.

O WHITE and midnight skies! O starry bath!
    Wash me in thy pure, heavenly, crystal flood;
Cleanse me, ye stars! from earthly soil and scath,
    Let not one taint remain in spirit or blood!
Receive my soul, ye burning, awful deeps!
    Touch and baptize me with the mighty power
That in ye thrills, while the dark planet sleeps, —
    Make me all yours for one blest, secret hour.
O glittering host! O high celestial choir!
    Silence each tone that with thy music jars —
Fill me, even as an urn, with thy white fire,
    Till all I am is kindred to the stars.
Make me thy child, thou infinite, holy night!
So shall my days be full of heavenly light.
                          RICHARD WATSON GILDER.

HOLY LAND.

THIS is the earth He walked on; not alone
    That Asian country keeps the sacred stain;
    'T is not alone the far Judæan plain,
Mountain and river! Lo, the sun that shone
On Him, shines now on us; when day is gone
    The moon of Galilee comes forth again
    And lights our path as his; an endless chain
Of years and sorrows makes the round world one.

The air we breathe He breathed, — the very air
    That took the mould and music of his high
And godlike speech. — Since then shall mortal dare
    With base thought front the ever-sacred sky, —
Soil with foul deed the ground whereon He laid
In holy death his pale, immortal head!
                          RICHARD WATSON GILDER.

"DAY UNTO DAY UTTERETH SPEECH."

The speech that day doth utter and the night,
   Full oft to mortal ears it hath no sound;
   Dull are our eyes to read upon the ground
What's written there and stars are hid by light.
So when the dark doth fall awhile our sight
   Kens the unwonted orbs that circle round,
   Then quick in sleep our human sense is bound:
Speechless for us the starry heavens and bright.

But when the day doth close there is one word
   That 's writ amid the sunset's golden embers;
And one at morn; by them our hearts are stirred:
   Splendor of Dawn, — and Evening that remembers;
These are the rhymes of God; thus, line on line,
Our souls are moved to thoughts that are divine.
Richard Watson Gilder.

ON THE LIFE-MASK OF ABRAHAM LINCOLN.

This bronze doth keep the very form and mould
   Of our great martyr's face. Yes, this is he:
   That brow all wisdom, all benignity;
That human, humorous mouth; those cheeks that hold
Like some harsh landscape all the summer's gold;
   That spirit fit for sorrow, as the sea
   For storms to beat on; the lone agony
Those silent, patient lips too well foretold.

Yes, this is he who ruled a world of men
   As might some prophet of the elder day, —
   Brooding above the tempest and the fray
With deep-eyed thought and more than mortal ken.
   A power was his beyond the touch of art
   Or armèd strength: It was his mighty heart.
Richard Watson Gilder.

WEAL AND WOE.

O HIGHEST, strongest, sweetest woman-soul!
  Thou holdest in the compass of thy grace
  All the strange fate and passion of thy race:
Of the old, primal curse thou knowest the whole:
Thine eyes, too wise, are heavy with the dole,
  The doubt, the dread of all this human maze;
  Thou in the virgin morning of thy days
Hast felt the bitter waters o'er thee roll.

Yet thou knowest, too, the terrible delight,
  The still content, and solemn ecstasy, —
Whatever sharp, sweet bliss thy kind may know.
Thy spirit is deep for pleasure as for woe —
  Deep as the rich, dark-caverned, awful sea
That the keen-winded, glimmering dawn makes white.
RICHARD WATSON GILDER.

"CALL ME NOT DEAD."

CALL me not dead when I, indeed, have gone
  Into the company of the ever-living
  High and most glorious poets! Let thanksgiving
Rather be made. Say — "He at last hath won
Rest and release, converse supreme and wise,
  Music and song and light of immortal faces:
  To-day, perhaps, wandering in starry places,
He hath met Keats and known him by his eyes.

To-morrow (who can say) Shakespeare may pass, —
  And our lost friend just catch one syllable
  Of that three-centuried wit that kept so well, —
Or Milton, — or Dante, looking on the grass
  Thinking of Beatrice, and listening still
  To chanted hymns that sound from the heavenly hill."
RICHARD WATSON GILDER.

CONFESSION.

Believe me, dear, unyielding though I be,
   Ambitions flourish only in the sun —
   In noisy daylight every race is run,
With lusty pride for all the world to see.
When darkness sinks the earth in mystery,
   When eye or ear or sight or sound is none,
   But death, a tide that waits to bear us on,
And life, a loosening anchor in the sea,

When time and space are huge about the soul,
   And ties of custom lost beyond recall,
     And courage as a garment in the flame,
Then all my spirit breaks without control,
   Then the heart opens, then the hot tears fall
     To prove me wholly woman that I am.

Dora Read Goodale.

AN ICE STORM.

All night keen winds have scourged the frosty plain;
   All night the groaning boughs have clashed and swung;
   Now chaste and clear the morning breaks along
The still, cold glory wrought by wind and rain.
What wondrous grace a fettered limb may gain!
   Earth seems a grand white flower from tempest sprung,
   In perfect poise uplifted, drooped and hung,
With petals lily-curved and pure of stain.

The ground is ridged with crystal, every tree
   Bending and swaying, cased in glittering mail,
     And fringed with icicles the swinging vine;
Winter's white radiance deepens dazzlingly;
   Now milk-white pearls, in shimmering crescents pale,
     Now flashing diamonds light her crystal shrine.

Elaine Goodale.

THE SISTINE MADONNA.

BEHOLD the Maid and Mother, doubly blest,
  In sweet amazement holding in her arms
  The wondrous Child! no timorous alarms
Stir her pure bosom, with love's weight oppressed,
But sacred awe holds her entranced: at rest,
  Within her arms he sits, as on a throne,
  Looking serenely on the world unknown
He came to save; majestic, uncaressed,

In meditation lost; and Heaven lies
In the clear orbs of those amazing eyes.
  Depth within depth; in circling amplitude,
Angels and cherubs wait on poisèd wing
To gaze upon the vision, pondering
  The holy mystery of Motherhood.

HENRY M. GOODWIN.

LOVE'S IMAGINING.

DEAR Love, I sometimes think how it would be
  If thou shouldst love me, if, on such a day,
  O day of wonder! thou shouldst come and say
I love thee, or but let me guess thy plea —
If once thine eyes should brighten suddenly,
  If once thy step should hasten or delay
  Because of me, if once thy hand should stay
A needless instant in my own! Ah, me!

From such imaginings I wake and start,
  And dull and worthless life's endeavors seem
  Before the tender beauty of my dream —
And then I whisper my impatient heart,
  "Be still, be comforted, O heart of mine,
  Thou art not all bereft, the dream is thine."

HOPESTILL GOODWIN.

APHELION.

Like the eccentric wanderer of the skies,
  By thee, my sun, repelled, from thee I sped
Across the desolate starless void that lies
  Between thee and the space where pain is dead.
And out in the half-hopeful dim beyond
  I caught the luminous warmth of one fair sun,
  Chilled and death-darkened ere it scarce begun
To shine for me. Weighted with passionate, fond
  Regret, through realms of sorrow, lone and vast,
  I coursed with lessening swiftness, turned at last,
And far, far off I saw thee shining still,
Drawing me back, with sweet unconscious will,
  Straight to thy heart. Ah love! to let me roam
  No more, forever, from that heart, my home.
                          HOMER GREENE.

WINTER BOUGHS.

How tenderly, spread to the sunset's cheer,
  Far on the hill, our quiet tree-tops fade!
  A broidery of northern sea-weed, laid
Long in a book, were scarce more fine and clear.
Untangled, on the frosty atmosphere
  The web floats darkening. Never June but's made
  For grosser worship with her builded shade:
The green domes fall, to leave this wonder here.

O ye forgetting and outliving boughs,
  With not a plume, gay in the jousts before,
Left for the archer! So, in evening's eye,
So stilled, so lifted, let your lover die,
Set in the upper calm no voices rouse,
  Stript, meek, withdrawn, against the heavenly door.
                          LOUISE IMOGEN GUINEY.

SLEEP.

O GLORIOUS tide, O hospitable tide
  On whose moon-heaving breast my head hath lain,
  Lest I, all eased of wounds and washed of stain,
Thro' holy hours, be yet unsatisfied,
Loose me betimes! for in my soul abide
  Urgings of memory, and exile's pain
  Weighs on me, as the spirit of one slain
May throb for the old strife wherein he died.

Often and evermore across the sea
  Of dark and dreams, to fatherlands of day
    O speed me! like that outworn king erewhile
From kind Phæacia shoreward borne; for me,
  Thy loving, healèd Greek, thou too shalt lay
    Beneath the olive boughs of mine own isle.
                    LOUISE IMOGEN GUINEY.

APRIL DESIRE.

WHILE in these spacious fields is my sojourn,
  Needs must I bless the blossomy outbreak
  Of earth's pent beauty, and for old love's sake
Trembling, the bees' oncoming chant discern;
Hail the rash hyacinth, the ambushed fern,
  High-bannered boughs that green defiance make,
  And watch from sheathing ice the brave Spring take
Her broad, bright river blade. Ah! then, in turn

Long-hushèd forces stir in me; I feel
  All the most sharp unrest of the young year;
Fain would my spirit, too, like idling steel
    Be snatched from its dull scabbard, for a strife
    With cold oppressions! straightway, if not here,
    In consummated freedom, ampler life.
                    LOUISE IMOGEN GUINEY.

TWOFOLD SERVICE.

CHAMPIONS of men, with brawny fist and lung,
   You righteous! with eyes oped and utterance terse,
   Whose greed of energies would fain disperse
Ere any mould be cast, or roundel sung,
Your gentle brothers still at play among
   The smirch and jangle of the Universe,
   Mere fool-blind trespassers for you to curse,
The Sabbath-breakers, the unchristened young; —

Peace! These, too, know: these are as ye employed,
Nor of laborious help and value void,
   Living; who, faithful to their fellows' need,
Fling life away for truth, art, fatherland,
Like a gold largess from a princely hand,
   Without one trading thought of heavenly meed.
                            LOUISE IMOGEN GUINEY.

AMONG THE FLAGS.

(In Doric Hall, Massachusetts State House.)

DEAR witnesses, all-luminous, eloquent,
   Stacked thickly on the tessellated floor!
   The soldier-blood stirs in me, as of yore
In sire and grandsire who to battle went:
I seem to know the shaded valley tent,
   The armed and bearded men, the thrill of war,
   Horses that prance to hear the cannon roar,
Shrill bugle-calls, and camp-fire merriment.
And as fair symbols of heroic things,
   Not void of tears mine eyes must e'en behold
      These banners lovelier as the deeper marred:
A panegyric never writ for kings
   On every tarnished staff and tattered fold;
      And by them, tranquil spirits standing guard.
                            LOUISE IMOGEN GUINEY.

HER CHOICE.

"Behold! it is a draught from Lethe's wave.
    Thy voice of weeping reacheth even that strand
    Washed by strange waters in Elysian land;
I bring the peace thy weary soul doth crave.
Drink, and from vain regret thy future save."
    She lifted deep, dark eyes wherein there lay
    The sacred sorrow of love's ended day,
Then took the chalice from the angel's hand.

Life with new love, or life with memory
    Of the old love? Her heart made instant choice;
    Like tender music rang the faithful voice:
"O sweet my love, an offering to thee!"
    And with brave smile, albeit the tears flowed fast,
    Upon the earth the priceless draught she cast.
Eliza Calvert Hall.

ONE WAY OF LOVE.

I cannot measure for thee, drop by drop,
    Thy draught of love, my hands, Dear, tremble so.
    Behold the chalice! How the bright drops glow!
And still I pour although thou bidst me stop,
Till the rich wine mounts to the goblet's top
    And the dry earth receives the overflow.
    Too generous am I? Beloved, no!
Love that doth count its gift is a weak prop

Whereon to stay a weary human heart.
    Yes, draw me closer still: perchance I may,
    Clasped in thine arms, forget the dreaded day
When thou, my love, my life, my soul's best part,
    In cold satiety will turn thee round,
    And dash the poor cup, broken, to the ground.
Eliza Calvert Hall.

IN THE DIM CHAMBER.

In the dim chamber whence but yesterday
   Passed my belovèd, filled with awe I stand;
   And haunting Loves, fluttering on every hand,
Whisper her praises who is far away;
A thousand delicate fancies glance and play
   On every object which her robes have fanned,
   And tenderest thoughts and hopes bloom and expand
In the sweet memory of her beauty's ray.

Ah! could that glass but hold the faintest trace
   Of all the loveliness once mirrored there,
   The clustering glory of the shadowy hair
That framed so well the dear young angel-face!
   But no, it shows my own face, full of care,
And my heart is her beauty's dwelling-place.

JOHN HAY.

THE POET'S MIND.

Day follows day; years perish; still mine eyes
   Are opened on the self-same round of space;
   Yon fadeless forests in their Titan grace,
And the large splendors of those opulent skies.
I watch, unwearied, the miraculous dyes
   Of dawn or sunset; the soft boughs which lace
   Round some coy Dryad in a lonely place,
Thrilled with low whispering and strange sylvan sighs:—

Weary? The poet's mind is fresh as dew,
   And oft refilled as fountains of the light.
His clear child's soul finds something sweet and new
Even in a weed's heart, the carved leaves of corn,
The spear-like grass, the silvery rime of morn,
   A cloud rose-tinged, and fleeting stars at night.

PAUL HAMILTON HAYNE.

A COMPARISON.

I THINK, ofttimes, that lives of men may be
   Likened to wandering winds that come and go,
   Not knowing whence they rise, whither they blow
O'er the vast globe, voiceful of grief or glee.
Some lives are buoyant zephyrs sporting free
   In tropic sunshine; some long winds of woe
   That shun the day, wailing with murmurs low,
Through haunted twilights, by the unresting sea;

Others are ruthless, stormful, drunk with might,
   Born of deep passion or malign desire:
   They rave 'mid thunder-peals and clouds of fire.
Wild, reckless all, save that some power unknown
Guides each blind force till life be overblown,
Lost in vague hollows of the fathomless night.

PAUL HAMILTON HAYNE.

A LONGING.

PENT in this common sphere of sensual shows,
   I pine for beauty, — beauty of fresh mien,
   And gentle utterance, and the charm serene,
Wherewith the hue of mystic dreamland glows;
I pine for lulling music, the repose
   Of low-voiced waters, in some realm between
   The perfect Aidenn, and this clouded scene
Of love's sad loss, and passion's mournful throes;

A pleasant country, girt with twilight calm,
   In whose fair heaven a moon of shadowy round
     Wades through a fading fall of sunset rain;
Where drooping lotos flowers, distilling balm,
   Dream by the drowsy streamlets Sleep hath crowned,
     And Care forgets to sigh, and Patience conquers Pain.

PAUL HAMILTON HAYNE.

WINTER SKIES.

The stars are glittering in the frosty sky,
   Numerous as pebbles on a broad sea-coast;
And o'er the vault the cloud-like galaxy
   Has marshaled its innumerable host.
Alive all heaven seems! with wondrous glow
   Tenfold refulgent every star appears,
As if some wide, celestial gale did blow,
   And thrice illume the ever-kindled spheres.
Orbs, with glad orbs rejoicing, burning, beam
   Ray-crowned, with lambent lustre in their zones,
Till o'er the blue, bespangled spaces seem
   Angels and great archangels on their thrones;
A host divine, whose eyes are sparkling gems,
And forms more bright than diamond diadems.
                            CHARLES HEAVYSEGE.

EVE.

Lone in the sunrise of primeval day,
   More lovely than the virgin world around,
   With finger pressed on lips that made no sound,
She stood and gazed. Spread out before her lay
The future — and the clouds were rolled away.
   The war of kings in empires still unfound,
   The crash of cannon that should yet resound,
She heard, and saw the great world rock and sway.

Across the crimson sky above her head
   There came a cry of children asking food;
A wail of women for the nation's dead
   Went upward to the stars. So, pale, she stood,
Then to some secret place in Eden fled,
   And wept in presage of her motherhood.
                            WILLIAM J. HENDERSON.

THE WANDERING JEW.

Amid the thunder of creation's fall,
  With fire and rain and hail across the sky,
  One stood alone with fearless, upturned eye,
And aspect that no horror could appall.
In all that wreck of matter, proud and tall,
  As one who scorned for grace or aid to cry,
  He waited moveless, as if asking why
There came for him no pealing trumpet call.

Last of his race and of the sons of men,
  He stood devoid of tremor or of fear,
And stretched his hands out to the sky, and then
  He spake in accents bold and strangely clear:
"Thou bad'st me 'Tarry till I come again;'
  Behold, Messiah, I am waiting here."

William J. Henderson.

TERRA INCOGNITA.

Ah me! that it has nearly passed away,
  The grateful mystery, the vague delight,
  Of those dim ancient days when yet there might
Be undreamed things where sombre Thule lay
In clamorous seas; or where, 'neath passing day,
  Hung blessed isles sometimes almost in sight;
  Or, later, where fair Avalon was bright,
Or shone the golden cities of Cathay.

Old ocean holds no terrors any more;
  We touch the limits of the farthest zone,
And would all Nature's fastnesses explore:
  Oh, leave some spot that Fancy calls its own —
Some far and solitary wave-worn shore,
  Where all were possible and all unknown!

George A. Hibbard.

TO DUTY.

LIGHT of dim mornings; shield from heat and cold;
   Balm for all ailments; substitute for praise;
   Comrade of those who plod in lonely ways,
(Ways that grow lonelier as the years wax old);
Tonic for fears; check to the over-bold;
   Nurse, whose calm hand its strong restriction lays,
   Kind, but resistless, on our wayward days;
Mart, where high wisdom at vast price is sold;

Gardener, whose touch bids the rose-petals fall,
   The thorns endure; surgeon, who human hearts
Searchest with probes, though the death-touch be given;
   Spell that knits friends, but yearning lovers parts;
Tyrant relentless o'er our blisses all; —
Oh, can it be, thine other name is Heaven?

                      THOMAS WENTWORTH HIGGINSON.

"SINCE CLEOPATRA DIED."

"SINCE Cleopatra died!" Long years are past,
   In Antony's fancy, since the deed was done.
   Love counts its epochs, not from sun to sun,
But by the heart throb. Mercilessly fast
Time has swept onward since she looked her last
   On life, a queen. For him the sands have run
   Whole ages through their glass, and kings have won
And lost their empires o'er earth's surface vast

Since Cleopatra died. Ah! Love and Pain
   Make their own measure of all things that be.
No clock's slow ticking marks their deathless strain;
   The life they own is not the life we see;
   Love's single moment is eternity;
Eternity a thought in Shakespeare's brain.

                      THOMAS WENTWORTH HIGGINSON.

TO THE MEMORY OF H. H.

O SOUL of fire within a woman's clay!
   Lifting with slender hands a race's wrong,
   Whose mute appeal hushed all thine early song,
And taught thy passionate heart the loftier way;
What shall thy place be, in the realms of day?
   What disembodied world can hold thee long,
   Binding that turbulent pulse with spell more strong?
Dwell'st thou, with wit and jest, where poets may?

Or with ethereal women (born of air
   And poets' dreams) dost live in ecstasy,
Teach new love-thoughts to Shakespeare's Juliet fair,
   New moods to Cleopatra? Then, may be,
The woes of Shelley's Helen thou dost share,
   Or weep with poor Rossetti's Rose Mary.
                     THOMAS WENTWORTH HIGGINSON.

THE BEST GIFT.

I.

AROUND the cradle that thy childhood bare
   Came God's own angels, with their pitying eyes,
   And gazed upon thee in their still surprise
To see beyond heaven's portal aught so fair.
They brought thee precious gifts. One gave to thee
   The gift of beauty for thy body's grace,
   Deep-smiling eyes to light a dreamy face,
And perfect limbs as young Apollo's be.

One set the crown of Genius on thy head,
   And one bestowed a heart like woman's own,
      Strong as the sea and trembling at a breath.
Last a veiled figure bent above the bed,
   And said: "I give thee everything in one.
      In heaven I am named Love; men call me Death."
                     KATHARINE HILLARD.

THE BEST GIFT.

II.

" So shalt thou never tread the weary ways
    That lead men up the dusty slopes of life,
    Nor feel the fierceness of the noonday strife,
Knowing alone the morning of thy days.
For thee the dew shall linger on the flower ;
    The light that never was on land or sea
    Shall have no momentary gleam for thee,
But brighten into love's immortal hour.

Thy beauty's grace shall never know decay,
    Nor Sorrow lay her hand upon thy heart ;
Neither shall chill mistrust thy spirit slay,
But like a star thy life shall pass away,
    Its light still shining, though itself depart,
Until all stars are lost in one eternal day."

KATHARINE HILLARD.

MOTHERHOOD.

She softly sings, and paces to and fro,
    Patient, unwearied, bearing in her arms
    The fretful, sickly child, with all his harms,
Deformed and imbecile, her love and woe.
Croons, with caressing intonation, low,
    Some sweet, old minor melody, that charms
    The ear that listens, and the sufferer calms,
And her own sorrow soothes with silver flow.
O holy tenderness of motherhood !
    Most pitiful and patient to the child,
    Foolish, unlovely, seemingly defiled
By powers of death and darkness. The All Good
    Alone so loveth and remembereth,
    And, like a tender parent, pitieth.

ABBY S. HINCKLEY.

TWO HOMES.

I HASTEN homeward, through the gathering night,
   Tow'rd the dear ones who in expectance sweet
   Await the coming of my weary feet,
With faces in the hearth-fire glowing bright,
And please my heart with many a lovely sight
   Of way-worn neighbors stepping from the street
   Through doors thrown wide and bursts of light that greet
Their entrance, painting all their paths with white;
And then I think, with a great thrill of bliss,
   That all the world, and all of life it brings,
Tell me true tales of other realms than this,
   As faithful types of spiritual things;
And so I know that home's rewarding kiss
   Insures the hope of heaven that in me springs.

                JOSIAH GILBERT HOLLAND.

(PROEM.) "SONGS IN MANY KEYS."

(WRITTEN DURING THE CIVIL WAR.)

THE piping of our slender, peaceful reeds
   Whispers uncared for while the trumpets bray;
   Song is their air; our hearts' exulting play
Beats time but to the tread of marching deeds,
Following the mighty van which Freedom leads,
   Her glorious standard flaming to the day!
   The crimsoned pavement where a hero bleeds
Breathes nobler lessons than the poet's lay.
Strong arms, broad breasts, brave hearts are better worth
   Than strains that sing the ravished echoes dumb.
   Hark! 't is the loud reverberating drum
Rolls o'er the prairied West, the rock-bound North:
The myriad-handed Future stretches forth
   Its shadowy palms. Behold, we come — we come!

                OLIVER WENDELL HOLMES.

THE DEAD SINGER.

(LONGFELLOW.)

On many a saddened hearth the evening fire
    Burns paler as the children's hour draws near, —
    That joyous hour his song made doubly dear, —
And tender memories touch the faltering choir.
He sings no more on earth; our vain desire
    Aches for the voice we loved so long to hear
    ·In Dorian flute-notes breathing soft and clear, —
The sweet contralto that could never tire.

Deafened with listening to a harsher strain,
    The Mænad's scream, the stark barbarian's cry;
    Still for those soothing, loving tones we sigh;
Oh, for our vanished Orpheus once again!
The shadowy silence hears us call in vain!
    His lips are hushed; his song shall never die.
                    OLIVER WENDELL HOLMES.

JOSEPH WARREN, M. D.

Trained in the holy art whose lifted shield
    Wards off the darts a never-slumbering foe,
    By hearth and wayside lurking, waits to throw,
Oppression taught his helpful arm to wield
The slayer's weapon: on the murderous field
    The fiery bolt he challenged laid him low,
    Seeking its noblest victim. Even so
The charter of a nation must be sealed!
The healer's brow the hero's honors crowned,
    From lowliest duty called to loftiest deed.
Living, the oak-leaf wreath his temples bound;
    Dying, the conqueror's laurel was his meed,
    Last on the broken ramparts' turf to bleed
Where Freedom's victory in defeat was found.
                    OLIVER WENDELL HOLMES.

HARVARD.

(1643 — "Veritas" — 1878.)

Truth: So the frontlet's older legend ran,
  On the brief record's opening page displayed;
  Not yet those clear-eyed scholars were afraid
Lest the fair fruit that wrought the woe of man
By far Euphrates, — where our sire began
  His search for truth, and seeking, was betrayed, —
  Might work new treason in their forest shade,
Doubling the curse that brought life's shortened span.
Nurse of the future, daughter of the past,
  That stern phylactery best becomes thee now:
  Lift to the morning star thy marble brow!
Cast thy brave truth on every warring blast!
  Stretch thy white hand to that forbidden bough,
  And let thine earliest symbol be thy last!

Oliver Wendell Holmes.

COLUMBUS.

He failed. He reached to grasp Hesperides,
  To track the footsteps of the sun that flies
  Toward some far western couch, and watch it rise, —
But fell on unknown sand-reefs, chains, disease.
He won. With splendid daring from the seas'
  Hard, niggared fist he plucked the prize,
  And gave a virgin World to Europe's eyes,
Where gold-dust choked the streams and spice the breeze.
He failed fulfillment of the task he planned,
And dropped a weary head on empty hand,
  Unconscious of the vaster deed he'd done;
But royal legacy to Ferdinand
  He left: a key to doorways gilt with sun, —
  And proudest title of "World-father" won!

George W. W. Houghton.

PAST.

THERE, as she sewed, came floating through her head
  Odd bits of poems, learned in other days
  And long forgotten in the noisier ways
Through which the fortunes of her life now led;
And looking up, she saw upon the shelf
  In dusty rank her favorite poets stand,
  All uncaressed by her fond eye or hand;
And her heart smote her, thinking how, herself,

She loved them once and found in them all good
  As well as beauty filling every need;
    But now they could not fill the emptiness
Of heart she felt even in her gayest mood.
  She wanted once no work her heart to feed,
    And to be idle once was no distress.
                      WINIFRED HOWELLS.

THE SOUL.

MY heaven-born soul! by body unconfined,
  Leave that low tenement and roam abroad;
Forestall the time, when, left each clog behind,
  Thy flight shall mount where never mortal trod.
Even now, methinks, upborne in trancèd dreams,
  The disencumbered essence tries its wings,
Sees better planets, basks in brighter beams,
  To purer sight mysterious symbols brings,
  Of unconceived, unutterable things.
Though dust returned to dust the worms devour,
  Thee can dread Death annihilate or bind?
There, King of Terrors! stops thy dreaded power;
  The bright assurgent, from all dross refined,
    High o'er the immense of space regains the world of mind.
                      DAVID HUMPHREYS.

TELLUS.

Why here on this third planet from the sun
   Fret we and smite against our prison bars?
   Why not in Saturn, Mercury, or Mars
Mourn we our sins, the things undone and done?
Where was the soul's bewildering course begun?
   In what sad land among the scattered stars
   Wrought she the ill which now forever scars
By bitter consequence each victory won?

I know not, dearest friend; yet this I see
   That thou for holier fellowships wast meant;
Through some strange blunder thou art here; and we,
   Who on the convict ship were hither sent
By judgment just, must not be named with thee,
   Whose tranquil presence shames our discontent.
                           WILLIAM R. HUNTINGTON.

GEORGE ZABRISKIE GRAY.

Friend of the open hand, the genial eye,
   The lip that faltered never, — where art thou?
   We cannot think thee idle, though the plough
Halfway the furrow thus forsaken lie.
Thou didst not loose thy grasp for lack of high
   And purposeful endeavor, for till now
   No laggard glance from under that clear brow
Fell, backwards cast. Oh, why then would'st thou die?

Thus broke the answer: "God hath other fields
   Than those ye know. His sunlight and his rain
      Fall not alone on the remembered earth;
But here as there the duteous harvest yields
   Reward to all; and I am glad again,
      Tilling the land of this my newer birth."
                           WILLIAM R. HUNTINGTON.

ELYSIAN HOURS.

Some days, in this prosaic, earnest life,
   Insentient things conspire to give us joy:
   The oft-time dross is gold without alloy;
Within, without, there is no war nor strife,
Nor sad presentiments, nor warnings rife
   Of danger for us: nor is Nature coy,
   But jubilant as any careless boy, —
She celebrates the hours with drum and fife!

For on such days, so joyous, rare, serene,
   The song of bird seems sweeter, skies more blue,
   The air ethereal, flowers more radiant gleam,
The dew more pearly, clearer meadow stream;
   Our homes are blessed, all our friends more true —
   Such days are heralds of the Life unseen.
                              MARY E. IRELAND.

SYMPATHY.

Why art thou troubled, O my cherished friend,
   Thy simple pleasures shadowed thy life through,
   Because the benefactions thou wouldst do
Are not within thy reach to give nor lend, —
No sanctuaries build, no treasure send
   To foil grim Poverty, — in thine own view
   Art helpless, useless, longing good to do,
Yet powerless? Let Friendship thee defend.

Thy tender heart turns not from humble needs,
   And while thou toilest for the household band
      Dependent on thee, blessings crown thy head
For light which thou on sombre paths hast shed;
   Had God intended thee to do great deeds
      He would have placed the means within thy hand.
                              MARY E. IRELAND.

ARIADNE'S FAREWELL.

The daughter of a king, how should I know
  That there were tinsels wearing face of gold,
  And worthless glass, which in the sunlight's hold
Could shameless answer back my diamond's glow
With cheat of kindred fire? The currents slow,
  And deep and strong and stainless which had rolled
  Through royal veins for ages, what had told
To them, that hasty heat and lie could show

As quick and warm a red as theirs?
                          Go free!
  The sun is breaking on the sea's blue shield
Its golden lances; by their gleam I see
  Thy ship's white sails. Go free, if scorn can yield
Thee freedom! Then, alone, my love and I, —
We both are royal; we know how to die.
HELEN HUNT JACKSON.

THOUGHT.

O messenger, art thou the king, or I?
  Thou dalliest outside the palace gate
  Till on thine idle armor lie the late
And heavy dews. The morn's bright scornful eye
Reminds thee; then in subtle mockery,
  Thou smilest at the window where I wait
  Who bade thee ride for life. In empty state
My days go on, while false hours prophesy

Thy quick return; at last, in sad despair,
I cease to bid thee, leave thee free as air;
  When lo, thou stand'st before me glad and fleet,
  And lay'st undreamed-of treasures at my feet.
Ah! messenger, thy royal blood to buy
I am too poor. Thou art the king, not I.
HELEN HUNT JACKSON.

EMIGRAVIT.

WITH sails full set, the ship her anchor weighs.
   Strange names shine out beneath her figure-head.
   What glad farewells with eager eyes are said!
What cheer for him who goes, and him who stays!
Fair skies, rich lands, new homes and untried days
   Some go to seek; the rest but wait instead,
   Watching the way wherein their comrades led,
Until the next stanch ship her flag doth raise.

Who knows what myriad colonies there are
   Of fairest fields, and rich, undreamed-of gains
   Thick planted in the distant shining plains
Which we call sky because they lie so far?
   Oh, write of me, not " Died in bitter pains,"
But " Emigrated to another star!"
HELEN HUNT JACKSON.

FAME.

(GARFIELD.)

How poor is all that fame can be or bring!
   Although a generation feed the pyre,
   How soon dies out the lifeless, loveless fire!
The king is dead. Hurrah! Long live the king!
The poet breathes his last. Who next will sing?
   The great man falls. Who comes to mount still
      higher?
   Oh, bitter emptiness of such desire!
Earth holds but one true good, but one true thing,
And this is it — to walk in honest ways
   And patient, and with all one's heart belong
   In love unto one's own! No death so strong
That life like this he ever conquers, slays;
   The centuries do to it no hurt, no wrong:
They are eternal resurrection days.
HELEN HUNT JACKSON.

OCTOBER.

I.

BENDING above the spicy woods which blaze,
   Arch skies so blue they flash, and hold the sun
   Immeasurably far; the waters run
Too slow, so freighted are the river-ways
With gold of elms and birches from the maze
   Of forests. Chestnuts, clicking one by one,
   Escape from satin burrs; her fringes done,
The gentian spreads them out in sunny days,

And like late revelers at dawn, the chance
   Of one sweet, last, mad hour, all things assail,
And conquering, flush and spin; while to enhance
   The spell, by sunset door, wrapped in a veil
   Of red and purple mists, the summer, pale,
Steals back alone for one more song and dance.
HELEN HUNT JACKSON.

II.

THE month of carnival of all the year,
   When Nature lets the wild earth go its way,
   And spend whole seasons on a single day.
The springtime holds her white and purple dear;
October, lavish, flaunts them far and near;
   The summer charily her reds doth lay
   Like jewels on her costliest array;
October, scornful, burns them on a bier.

The winter holds his pearls of frost in sign
   Of kingdom: whiter pearls than winter knew,
Or Empress wore, in Egypt's ancient line,
   October, feasting 'neath her dome of blue,
   Drinks at a single draught, slow filtered through
Sunshiny air, as in a tingling wine!
HELEN HUNT JACKSON.

THE VICTORY OF PATIENCE.

ARMED of the Gods! Divinest conqueror!
   What soundless hosts are thine! Nor pomp, nor state,
   Nor token, to betray where thou dost wait.
All Nature stands, for thee, ambassador;
Her forces all thy serfs, for peace or war.
   Greatest and least alike, thou rul'st their fate, —
   The avalanche chained until its century's date,
The mulberry leaf made robe for Emperor!

Shall man alone thy law deny? — refuse
   Thy healing for his blunders and his sins?
Oh, make us thine! Teach us who waits best sues;
   Who longest waits of all most surely wins.
   When Time is spent, Eternity begins.
To doubt, to chafe, to haste, doth God accuse.
HELEN HUNT JACKSON.

COMMUNION.

ONE cannot draw the bars against the friends
   And guests that crowd for entrance at his gate
   He opes, inviting, nor the simple state
Of his abode against their train defends.
But there are chambers where the lover tends
   His sacred fires; where no feet penetrate,
   Save of immortals; where, early and late,
The breath of prayer and sacrifice ascends.

In such a spot as this, as in the shrine
   Of some white temple, in a dusk made sweet
   With incense, far from outer noise and heat,
   And hollow haste of them that part and meet,
Surrounded by dim presences divine,
My soul communes eternally with thine.
LUCY W. JENNISON ("*Owen Innsley*").

IN A LETTER.

THERE came a breath out of a distant time,
  An odor of neglected gardens where
  Unnumbered roses once perfumed the air
Through summer days in childhood's happy clime.
There came the salt scent of the sea and chime
  Of waves against the beaches, or the bare
  Gaunt rocks, as to the mind, half unaware,
Recur the words of some familiar rhyme.

And as above the gardens and the sea
  The moon arises, and her silver light
    Touches the landscape with a deeper grace,
So o'er the misty wreaths of memory,
  Turning them into pictures clear and bright,
    Rose in a halo the beloved face.
LUCY W. JENNISON (" Owen Innsley").

"WHOM HE LOVETH, HE CHASTENETH."

EVEN as the sculptor's chisel, flake on flake,
  Scales off the marble till the beauty pent,
  Sleeping within the block's imprisonment,
Beneath the wounding strokes begins to wake —
So love, which the high gods have chosen to make
  Their sharpest instrument, has shaped and bent
  The stubborn spirit, till it yields, content,
Its few and slender graces for love's sake.

But the perfected statue proudly rears
  Its whiteness for the world to see and prize,
The past hurt buried in forgetfulness;
  While the imperfect nature, grown more wise,
Turns with its new-born good, the streaming tears
  Of pain undried, the chastening hand to bless.
LUCY W. JENNISON (" Owen Innsley").

SEPARATION.

ALONG the Eastern shore the low waves creep,
   Making a ceaseless music on the sand, —
   A song that gulls and curlews understand,
The lullaby that sings the day to sleep.
A thousand miles afar, the grim pines keep
   Unending watch upon a shoreless land,
   Yet through their tops, swept by some wizard hand,
The sound of surf comes singing up the steep.

Sweet, thou canst hear the tidal litany;
   I, mid the pines land-wearied, may but dream
   Of the far shore; but though the distance seem
Between us fixed, impassable, to me
   Cometh thy soul's voice, chanting love's old theme,
And mine doth answer, as the pines the sea.
            SOPHIA JEWETT ("*Ellen Burroughs*").

NOBLESSE OBLIGE.

WHAT is diviner than the peace of foes!
   He conquers not who does not conquer hate,
   Or thinks the shining wheels of heaven wait
On his forgiving. Dimmer the laurel grows
On brows that darken; and war-won repose
   Is but a truce when heroes abdicate
   To Huns — unfabling those of elder date
Whose every corse a fiercer warrior rose.

O ye that saved the land! Ah yes, and ye
   That bless its saving! Neither need forget
      The price our destiny did of both demand —
Toil, want, wounds, prison, and the lonely sea
   Of tears at home. Oh, look on these. And yet —
      Before the human fail you — quick! your hand!
            ROBERT UNDERWOOD JOHNSON.

AMIEL.

("Le Journal Intime.")

A FEW there are who to the troubled soul
   Can lay the ear with that physician-art
   Which by a whispered accent in the heart
Follows the lurking treason that hath stole
Into the citadel; — a few whose scroll
   Of warning bears our safety — is a chart
   Of our unsounded seas, and doth impart
Courage to hold the spirit to its goal.

Of such is Amiel, lonely as a saint, —
   Or as an eagle dwelling on peaks, in shade
     Of clouds, which now he cleaves for one wide look
At the green earth, now for a circle faint
   Nearer the sun. Once more has truth betrayed
     Secrets to sorrow not in the sibyl's book.
                         ROBERT UNDERWOOD JOHNSON.

ST. MARTIN'S SUMMER.

AFTER the summer's fierce and thirsty glare,
   After the falling leaves and falling rain,
   When harsh winds beat the fields of ripened grain
And autumn's pennons from the branches flare,
There comes a stilly season, soft and fair,
   When clouds are lifted, winds are hushed again, —
   A phantom Summer hovering without pain
In the veiled radiance of the quiet air;

When, folding down the line of level seas,
   A silver mist at noonday faintly broods,
And like becalmèd ships the yellow trees
   Stand islanded in windless solitudes,
Each leaf unstirred and parching for the breeze
   That hides and lingers northward in the woods.
                                  EDITH JONES.

PARADISE REGAINED.

THE circling hills of woods and clouds snow-white
   Held in the golden hour of even-tide,
   The lake by which I walked, and seemed to hide
From view a world yet lovelier, whose light,
Streamed up behind their heights and made them glow,
   As wrapped in purest flame, and flung on high
   Bright flakes of glory 'gainst the pale blue sky
Which bridged with paths of light the lake below.

I felt sweet music that I could not hear,
   I saw a poem that I could not read.
   "What place is this," I cried! Lo, at my need,
Two lovers passed, — *'T was Paradise!* for clear
   I saw it shining in his happy eyes,
   I heard it murmured in her low replies.
MARIA W. JONES.

GEORGE ELIOT.

SHE lies in that fair land where violets spring,
   And on her grave may sweetest flowers have birth!
   The future pilgrims to that hallowed earth
Will wonder not that they are listening,
As in a dream, to voices whispering
   The well-known words of wisdom, hope, or mirth,
   That lifted life to shining heights of worth —
Now sighing in their ears from Memory's string.

The wind comes journeying from Avon's springs;
   Lingers a moment where memorials tell
   The name of him who left us "Christabel";
Then with the gathered sweetness of its wings
   It murmurs on and now a vigil keeps
   Beside the grave where Shakespeare's sister sleeps.
WILLIAM L. KEESE.

WHAT IS MY LADY LIKE?

WHAT is my lady like? thou fain wouldst know.
   A rosy chaplet of fresh apple-bloom,
Bound with blue ribbon, lying on the snow.
   What is my lady like? The violet gloom
Of evening, with deep orange light below.
   She's like the noonday smell of a pine wood;
   She's like the sounding of a stormy flood;
She's like a mountain-top high in the skies,
   To which the day its earliest light doth lend;
   She's like a pleasant path without an end;
Like a strange secret, and a sweet surprise;
   Like a sharp axe of doom, wreathed with blush-roses.
   A casket full of gems whose key one loses;
Like a hard saying, wonderful and wise.
                    FRANCES ANNE KEMBLE.

A SEA GRAVE.

YEA, rock him gently in thine arms, O Deep!
   No nobler heart was ever hushed to rest
   Upon the chill, soft pillow of thy breast —
No truer eyes didst thou e'er kiss to sleep.
While o'er his couch the wrathful billows leap,
   And mighty winds roar from the darkened west,
   Still may his head on thy cool weeds be pressed,
Far down where thou dost endless silence keep.

Oh, when, slow moving through thy spaces dim
   Some scaly monster seeks its coral cave,
And pausing o'er the sleeper, stares with grim
   Dull eyes a moment downwards through the wave,
Then let thy pale green shadows curtain him,
   And swaying sea-flowers hide his lonely grave.
                    JAMES B. KENYON.

CLEOPATRA TO ANTONY.

Go from me now; I will no longer feel
   Your burning kisses on my fevered lips;
   You shalt not hold one moment e'en the tips
Of my shut fingers, though you cry and kneel.
My face aches and my tired senses reel;
   Through all my veins a drowsy poison slips;
   My sight grows dim with gradual eclipse,
For slumber on mine eyes has set his seal.

Get hence; I will no more to-night; the bars
   Of love are placed against you now: go while
I hate you not, my Roman; the sick stars
   Wax faint and pallid in the dawn's red smile,
Look I am quenched in sleep, as nenuphars
   Are quenched in the broad bosom of the Nile.
                    JAMES B. KENYON.

ROMEO TO JULIET.

LOVE, touch my mouth with kisses as with fire;
   Lean hard against my breast, that I may feel
   From thy warm heart its influence subtly steal
Through all my veins; with overmuch desire
My spirit fainteth, and my lips suspire
   Swiftly with heavy breathings; round me reel
   The shadows of the dark, and downward wheel
The dim, far stars from heaven; draw me nigher

Unto thy bosom, love, for all my sense
   Of earth and time fleets from me.... Dayward flows
The stream of night, and into yon immense
   Blue void the slow moon fails; hold me more close,
Lest from thine arms my spirit hasten hence
   Going that viewless way no mortal knows.
                    JAMES B. KENYON.

"HE OPENED NOT HIS MOUTH."

EACH counts his lot most grievous; his distress
   Sorer than other's; each is prone to harp
   Upon his many trials (though he carp
At his poor neighbor's fretting none the less);
For all his wrongs there seemeth small redress;
   No other's ills were ever quite so sharp;
   Misfortunes all his plans do thwart and warp;
No loss his loss can match; no sorrows press

Like his! Ah! eighteen hundred years ago
   The pangs and penalties of all mankind
   Through all the groaning centuries behind
   And all the wrestling centuries to come
One Man endured, bound thrice ten years with woe,
   Yet from the Manger to the Cross was dumb!

HARRIET MCEWEN KIMBALL.

TO JOHN GREENLEAF WHITTIER.

BUT for thy gracious words, revered of men,
   Scarce had I ventured on from year to year
   To seek the great world's much-engrossèd ear
With the small rhythmic whispers of my pen.
And now to silence oft withdrawing when
   Thy songs so full and sweet, so strong and clear,
   And those of others, nobly sung, I hear,
I ask, Why do I aught but listen? Then

Myself makes answer, Who hath given thee
   This voice within that thou art fain to still?
Though few and scarcely heard thy notes may be,
   Seek not, nor yet withhold. Trust makes amends
For Trust that waits unquestioning God's will,
   Hearing His words above the words of friends.

HARRIET MCEWEN KIMBALL.

WAR CONTRASTS.

BULGARIAN.

A STRANGER lingered by Mahala's well,
   What time rude war across Bulgarian plains
Swept wildly, and the shock of battle fell
   On Russian breasts that feared nor death nor pains.
The cooling cup he took from peasant's hands,
   And when his thirst was slaked, he proudly said,
' See ! thou poor tiller of these pillaged lands !
I give thee gold ! '
                 The farmer bowed his head:
Tears dimmed his eyes ; upon his sun-browned face
   There fell a holy and a tender calm :
He gently spurned the money from his palm,
And said, with exquisite and pious grace,
   ' Nor gold nor silver from thee will I take !
I serve the water for the Lord Christ's sake.'
                                   EDWARD KING.

TURK.

ONE weary night the baleful Crescent shone
   On shameful massacres of wounded men.
The Turk was deaf alike to prayer and groan
   Of dying Russian in the Balkan glen.
The swart stern Kurd from Asiatic hill,
   The fell Circassian with his reeking blade,
The ragged bandit — all of blood their fill
   Drank fiercely, while in savage pomp arrayed,
From field to field the grim commanders strode,
   And ordered conflagration, and the sack
   Of burning villages, or o'er the track
Of dim past murders with rejoicing rode.
   The Cross of Christ each infidel defiled,
   And, in his frenzy, thought Mahomet smiled.
                                   EDWARD KING.

WILLIAM CULLEN BRYANT.

Room for our Poet in the immortal choir!
   His soul is passing; as the morning breaks,
   He to the dawn of perfect day awakes:
The Master Bards await him with desire —
Present his singing-robes, his golden lyre,
   And the vast portal with their welcome quakes!
   Now have they crowned him, — he their joy partakes
Kindled to new life by seraphic fire.

The day is breaking over sea and land;
The Sun may shine forth, but a light more grand
   — That heightened, and yet softened Nature's face —
Has disappeared: in shadow now we stand,
   Bereaved, while gazing upward to the place
   That presence late illumed, its path to trace.
June 12, 1878.   Elizabeth C. Kinney.

NIGHT.

Night and its dews come silently to earth,
   Like kindred mourners to the grave of Day;
   The stars look on with pale and throbbing ray,
   As if through tears to watch them on their way:
O holy Night! what thoughts awake to birth,
   That slumber in the day, amid its din
   And restless strife for gain, — its glare and sin!
   But Night! care-soothing Night! — O, I would win

Thy crown of peace, and wear it on my brow;
   Here at thy starry throne I bend my knee,
   All weak and humbled. I look up to thee,
And bless thee for the joy thou giv'st me now, —
   A joy so hushed and deep, I tremble, lest
   Dream-like, it fade away within my breast!
                                       Albert Laighton.

IN WEIMAR.

In shimmering haze the landscape lay concealed,
   And village spires from darkened roofs arose
   And scarlet poppies blazed and burned in rows
Of ribboned splendor all across the field
Of ripened rye; and maidens leant upon
   Their rakes, or tossed the half-dried hay,
   As by the Ilm we strayed this summer day
In Weimar's Park, where Goethe, Schiller, on

This same soft turf once trod. Dear peaceful sky!
   We turned from thee and into darkness went,
Where side by side the Poets' ashes lie
   In princely tomb, nor light from heaven is lent;
And on the sheenless, faded laurel crown
With reverent hands, we laid fresh roses down.
                      EMMA TAYLOR LAMBORN.

KARNAC.

Karnac, thy columns grand, in the moon's pale light,
   Have left upon my heart and soul and brain
Distinctest pictures; closing eyes and sight
   I stand again on Egypt's sand. The reign
Of Hatison, the glorious Queen, is here.
   She raised with filial love this obelisk gray
Whose pale, pink lotus-blossoms shine as clear
   As when these storied sculptures first saw day.

The din of Arab strife is stilled; and slain
   The headless sphinxes lie, crouching and dumb.
   Remembered perfumes to my senses come
Of lentil blooms that carpet Thebes' great plain,
   And Memnon's voice, silent through ages long,
   Speaks as I muse and bids me write this song.
                      EMMA TAYLOR LAMBORN.

OUTLOOK.

Not to be conquered by these headlong days,
   But to stand free: to keep the mind at brood
   On life's deep meaning, nature's altitude
Of loveliness, and time's mysterious ways;
At every thought and deed to clear the haze
   Out of our eyes, considering only this,
   What man, what life, what love, what beauty is,
This is to live, and win the final praise.

Though strifes, ill fortune, and harsh human need
   Beat down the soul, at moments blind and dumb
   With agony; yet, patience — there shall come
   Many great voices from life's outer sea,
Hours of strange triumph, and, when few men heed,
   Murmurs and glimpses of eternity.
ARCHIBALD LAMPMAN.

A PRAYER.

Oh earth, oh dewy mother, breathe on us
   Something of all thy beauty and thy might,
   Us that are part of day, but most of night,
Not strong like thee, but ever burdened thus
With glooms and cares, things pale and dolorous
   Whose gladdest moments are not wholly bright;
   Something of all thy freshness and thy light
Oh earth, oh mighty mother, breathe on us.

Oh mother, who wast long before our day,
   And after us full many an age shalt be,
Careworn and blind, we wander from thy way:
   Born of thy strength, yet weak and halt are we.
Grant us, oh mother, therefore, us who pray,
   Some little of thy light and majesty.
ARCHIBALD LAMPMAN.

KNOWLEDGE.

WHAT is more large than knowledge and more sweet?
   Knowledge of thoughts and deeds, of rights and wrongs,
   Of passions and of beauties and of songs;
Knowledge of life; to feel its great heart beat
Through all the soul upon her crystal seat;
   To see, to feel, and evermore to know;
   To till the old world's wisdom till it grow
A garden for the wandering of our feet?

Oh for a life of leisure and broad hours,
   To think and dream, to put away small things,
     This world's perpetual leaguer of dull naughts;
To wander like the bee among the flowers
   Till old age finds us weary, feet and wings
     Grown heavy with the gold of many thoughts.
                         ARCHIBALD LAMPMAN.

THE RAILWAY STATION.

THE darkness brings no quiet here, the light
   No waking: ever on my blinded brain
   The flare of lights, the rush, and cry, and strain,
The engine's scream, the hiss and thunder smite:
I see the hurrying crowds, the clasp, the flight,
   Faces that touch, eyes that are dim with pain:
   I see the hoarse wheels turn, and the great train
Move laboring out into the boundless night.

So many souls within its dim recesses,
   So many bright, so many mournful eyes:
Mine eyes that watch grow fixed with dreams and guesses;
   What threads of life, what hidden histories,
What sweet or passionate dreams and dark distresses,
   What unknown thoughts, what various agonies!
                         ARCHIBALD LAMPMAN.

MIDSUMMER NIGHT.

Mother of balms and soothings manifold,
    Quiet-breathed night whose brooding hours are seven,
    To whom the voices of all rest are given,
And those few stars whose scattered names are told,
Far off beyond the westward hills outrolled,
    Darker than thou, more still, more dreamy even,
    The golden moon leans in the dusky heaven,
And under her one star — a point of gold:

And all go slowly lingering toward the west,
As we go down forgetfully to our rest,
    Weary of daytime, tired of noise and light:
Ah, it was time that thou shouldst come; for we
Were sore athirst, and had great need of thee,
    Thou sweet physician, balmy-bosomed night.

Archibald Lampman.

THE MOCKING BIRD.

Superb and sole upon a plumèd spray
    That o'er the general leafage boldly grew,
    He summ'd the woods in song; or typic drew
The watch of hungry hawks, the lone dismay
Of languid doves when long their lovers stray
    And all birds' passion-plays that sprinkle dew
    At morn in brake or bosky avenue.
Whate'er birds did or dreamed, this bird could say.

Then down he shot, bounced airily along
The sward, twitched in a grasshopper, made song
    Midflight, perched, prinked, and to his art again.
    Sweet Science, this large riddle read me plain:
How may the death of that dull insect be
The life of yon trim Shakespeare on the tree?

Sidney Lanier.

ACKNOWLEDGMENT.

Now at thy soft, recalling voice I rise
   Where thought is lord o'er Time's complete estate,
Like as a dove from out the gray sedge flies
   To tree-tops green where coos his heavenly mate.
From these clear coverts high and cool I see
   How every time with every time is knit,
And each to all is mortised cunningly,
   And none is sole or whole, yet all are fit.
Thus if this Age but as a comma show
   'Twixt weightier clauses of large-worded years,
My calmer soul scorns not the mark: I know
   This crooked print Time's complex sentence clears.
   Yet more I learn while, Friend! I sit by thee;
Who sees all time sees all eternity.

                                SIDNEY LANIER.

IN ABSENCE.

LET no man say, *He at his lady's feet*
   Lays worship that to heaven alone belongs;
Yea, swings the incense that for God is meet
   In flippant censers of light lover's songs.
Who says it, knows not God, nor love, nor thee;
   For love is large as is yon heavenly dome:
In love's great blue, each passion is full free
   To fly his favorite flight and build his home.
Did e'er a lark, with sky-ward pointing beak
   Stab by mischance a level-flying dove?
Wife-love flies level, his dear mate to seek:
   God-love darts straight into the skies above.
Crossing the windage of each other's wings
But speeds them both upon their journeyings.

                                SIDNEY LANIER.

LAUS MARIÆ.

Across the brook of Time man leaping goes
  On stepping-stones of epochs, that uprise
  Fixed, memorable, midst broad shallow flows
    Of neutrals, kill-times, sleeps, indifferencies.
So mixt each morn and night rise salient heaps:
  Some cross with but a zig-zag, jaded pace
  From meal to meal; some with convulsive leaps
    Shake the green tussocks of malign disgrace:
And some advance by system and deep art
  O'er vantages of wealth, place, learning, tact:
But thou within thyself, dear manifold heart,
  Dost bind all epochs in one dainty Fact.
Oh, sweet, my pretty sum of history,
  I leapt the breadth of Time in loving thee!
Sidney Lanier.

THE HARLEQUIN OF DREAMS.

Swift, through some trap mine eyes have never found,
  Dim-panelled in the painted scene of Sleep,
  Thou giant Harlequin of Dreams, dost leap
Upon my spirit's stage. Then Sight and Sound,
Then Space and Time, then Language, Mete and Bound,
  And all familiar Forms that firmly keep
  Man's reason in the road, change faces, peep
Betwixt the legs and mock the daily round.

Yet thou canst more than mock; sometimes my tears
  At midnight break through bounden lids — a sign
    Thou hast a heart: and oft my little leaven
Of dream-taught wisdom works me better years.
  In one night witch, saint, trickster, fool divine,
    I think thou 'rt Jester at the Court of Heaven.
Sidney Lanier.

THE WOOD-THRUSH.

WHAT is it you are whispering, solemn woods?
   What hide and hint ye, slopes of sombre green,
   Whose dark reflections blur the crimson sheen
Of the lake's mirror, whereon sunset broods,
Trance-like and tender? Speechless, conscious moods
   Are yours, ye purple mountain shapes, that lean
   Out of Day's dying glory. What may mean
This stillness through whose veil no thought intrudes

With Earth-shod feet? Can any voice unfold
   The tremulous secret of an hour like this,
   So burdened with unutterable bliss?
Oh, hush! oh, hear the soul of Twilight sing!
One poet knows this mystery. Everything
The landscape dreamed of has the woodthrush told!
LUCY LARCOM.

IN ABSENCE.

MY love for thee is like a wingèd seed
   Blown from the heart of thy rare beauty's flower,
   And deftly guided by some breezy power
To fall and rest where I should never heed
In deepest caves of memory. There, indeed,
   With virtue rife of many a sunny hour, —
   Even making cold neglect and darkness dower
Its roots with life, swiftly began to breed,

Till now wide-spreading tendrils it outspreads
   Like circling arms, to prison its own prison,
Fretting the walls with blooms by myriads,
   And blazoning in my brain full summer season:
Thy face, whose dearness presence had not taught,
In absence multiplies and fills all thought.
GEORGE PARSONS LATHROP.

IMMANENT IMPERFECTION.

O WHOLESOME Death, thy sombre funeral car
   Looms ever dimly on the lengthening way
   Of life; while, lengthening still in sad array,
My deeds that go in long procession are
As mourners of the man they helped to mar.
   I see it all in dreams such as waylay
   The wandering fancy, when the solid day
Has sunk in smoldering ruins and night's star,

Aloft there, with its steady point of light
   Mastering the eye, has wrapt the brain in sleep.
Ah, when I die, and planets take their flight
   Above my grave, still let the spirit keep
Sometimes its vigil of divine remorse,
   'Midst pity, praise, or blame heaped on my corse!
                    GEORGE PARSONS LATHROP.

IN ATHENS.

'MID thirty centuries of dust and mould
   We grope with hopeful heart and eager eye,
   And hail our treasure-trove if we but spy
A vase, a coin, a sentence carved of old
On Attic stone. In reverent hands we hold
   Each message from the Past, and fain would try
   Through myriad fragments dimly to descry
The living glories of the Age of Gold.

Vainest of dreams! This rifled grave contains
   Of Beauty but the crumbled outward grace.
   The spirit that gave it life, Hellenic then,
Immortal and forever young remains,
   But flits from land to land, from race to race,
   Nor tarries with degenerate, slavish men.
                    WILLIAM CRANSTON LAWTON.

A SNOW SONNET.

My ear can find no rest. The throbbing tide
   Of city commerce is at mid-day flow:
   Like pulse's beat the footsteps come and go;
Harsh rattles thrash the tremulous air aside,
And tumbling sounds like hoary breakers ride.
   " Who chid primeval waters, can He so
   Bind this wild flood with His great 'Hitherto'?"
So moaned I, fever-stricken, and so cried.

My ear awoke, and yet can find no sound!
   Another mid-day, and no mid-day rush!
But blessed Silence, deep, unbroke, profound,
   While feathered flakes my window lightly brush.
God came into His nursery and found
   The children noisy, so He whispered " Hush."

                                            NINA F. LAYARD.

THE TAMING OF THE FALCON.

The bird sits spelled upon the lithe, brown wrist
   Of yonder turbaned fowler, who hath lamed
   No feathered limb, but the winged spirit tamed
With his compelling eye. He need not twist
The silken toil, nor set the thick-limed snare;
   He lures the wanderer with his steadfast gaze,
   It shrinks, it quails, it trembles — yet obeys,
And lo! he has enslaved the thing of air.

The fixed, insistent human will is lord
   Of all the earth; — but in the awful sky,
Reigns absolute, unreached by deed or word,
   Above creation, through eternity,
Outshining the sun's shield, the lightning's sword,
   The might of Allah's unaverted eye.

                                              EMMA LAZARUS.

SYMPATHY.

Therefore I dare reveal my private woe,
  The secret blots of my imperfect heart,
  Nor strive to shrink or swell my own desert,
Nor beautify nor hide. For this I know
That even as I am thou also art.
  Thou past heroic forms unmoved shalt go,
  To pause and bide with me, to whisper low:
"Not I alone am weak, not I apart

Must suffer, struggle, conquer day by day.
  Here is my very cross by strangers borne,
  Here is my bosom-sin wherefrom I pray
  Hourly deliverance — this my rose, my thorn.
This woman my soul's need can understand,
Stretching o'er silent gulfs her sister hand."

Emma Lazarus.

VENUS OF THE LOUVRE.

Down the long hall she glistens like a star,
  The foam-born mother of Love, transfixed to stone,
  Yet none the less immortal, breathing on.
Time's brutal hand hath maimed but could not mar.
When first the enthralled enchantress from afar
  Dazzled mine eyes, I saw not her alone,
  Serenely poised on her world-worshiped throne
As when she guided once her dove-drawn car, —

But at her feet a pale, death-stricken Jew,
  Her life-adorer, sobbed farewell to love.
Here Heine wept! Here still he weeps anew,
  Nor ever shall his shadow lift or move,
While mourns one ardent heart, one poet brain,
For vanished Hellas and Hebraic pain.

Emma Lazarus.

LIFE AND ART.

Not while the fever of the blood is strong,
    The heart throbs loud, the eyes are veiled, no less
    With passion than with tears, the Muse shall bless
The poet-soul to help and soothe with song.
Not then she bids his trembling lips express
    The aching gladness, the voluptuous pain.
    Life is his poem then; flesh, sense, and brain
One full-stringed lyre attuned to happiness.

But when the dream is done, the pulses fail,
    The day's illusion with the day's sun set,
He, lonely in the twilight, sees the pale
    Divine Consoler, featured like Regret,
Enter and clasp his hand and kiss his brow.
Then his lips ope to sing — as mine do now.

                                    Emma Lazarus.

THE NEW COLOSSUS.

Not like the brazen giant of Greek fame,
    With conquering limbs astride from land to land,
    Here at our sea-washed sunset gate shall stand
A mighty woman with a torch, whose flame
Is the imprisoned lightning and her name
    Mother of Exiles. From her beacon hand
    Glows world-wide welcome; her mild eyes command
The air-bridged harbor that twin cities frame.

"Keep, ancient lands, your storied pomp," cries she
    With silent lips. "Give me your tired, your poor,
Your huddled masses yearning to breathe free,
    The wretched refuse of your teeming shore.
Send these, the homeless, tempest-tost, to me,
    I lift my lamp beside the golden door!"

                                    Emma Lazarus.

THE UNDINES' DANCE.

Upon the silver beach the undines dance
    With interlinking arms and flying hair;
    Like polished marble gleam their limbs left bare;
Upon their virgin rites pale moonbeams glance.
Softer the music! for their foam-bright feet
    Print not the moist floor where they trip their round:
    Affrighted, they will scatter at a sound,
Leap in their cool sea-chambers, nimbly fleet,

And we shall doubt that we have ever seen,
    While our same eyes behold stray wreaths of mist,
    Shot with faint colors by the moon rays kissed,
Floating snow-soft, snow-white, where these had been —
    Already, look! the wave-washed sands are bare,
    And mocking laughter ripples through the air.

                            EMMA LAZARUS.

THE SEA OF LIFE.

Floating upon a swelling wave of sound,
    We seemed to overlook an endless sea:
    Poised 'twixt clear heavens and glittering surf were we.
We drank the air in flight: we knew no bound
To the audacious ventures of desire.
    Nigh us the sun was dropping, drowned id gold
    Deep, deep below the burning billows rolled;
And all the sea sang like a smitten lyre.

Oh, the wild voices of those chanting waves!
    The human faces glimpsed beneath the tide!
Familiar eyes gazed from profound sea-caves,
    And we, exalted, were as we had died.
We knew the sea was Life, the harmonious cry
The blended discords of Humanity.

                            EMMA LAZARUS.

TO A FIREFLY.

When the tired bee is slumbering in his cell,
   Dreaming of fragrant flowers with honey filled,
   When buzzing fly and piping locust stilled
Like quiet citizens in slumber dwell,
Who is this wanderer that, late at night,
   Over the fields his little lantern swings,
   And traces, as a devious flight he wings,
His straying pathway by a flashing light?

Art thou a reveler whose tiny spark
   Lights thee o'er fields, with riotous comrades whirled,
     To spend in mad carouse the midnight hours?
Or else a watchman, winging through the dark,
   Guarding the slumbers of the insect world,
     And trying the closed petals of the flowers?
Walter Learned.

SOLACE.

What though you lie like the still pool of rain
   Silent, forgotten in some lonely place,
   Or, if remembered, in your being to trace
But the remainder of a past storm's pain;
What though the storm-drops falling fast again —
   Call we them " years " that hasten down apace —
   Smite your still breast as though they would efface
All sign of peace and leave but blot and stain.

Look! even now the reaper-beams appear
   And gather in the clouds' spare aftermath
     With glancing scythes of silver, every one.
While in the pool's still bosom, mirror-clear
   Is Heaven pictured; and a mystic path
     Strikes from its heart's clear centre to the sun.
Julie M. Lippmann.

STONE WALLS.

Along the country roadside, stone on stone,
  Past waving grainfield, and near broken stile,
  The walls stretch onward an uneven pile,
With rankling vines and lichen overgrown:
So stand they sentinel. Unchanged, alone,
  They 're left to watch the seasons' passing slow:
  The summer's sunlight or the winter's snow,
The spring-time's birdling, or the autumn's moan.

Who placed the stones now gray with many years?
  And did the rough hands tire, the sore hearts ache,
The eyes grow dim with all their weight of tears?
  Or did the work seem light for some dear sake?
Those lives are over. All their hopes and fears
  Are lost like shadows in the morning-break.
Julie M. Lippmann.

IN MEMORY OF CHARLES SUMNER.

River, that stealest with such silent pace
  Around the City of the Dead, where lies
  A friend who bore thy name, and whom these eyes
Shall see no more in his accustomed place,
Linger and fold him in thy soft embrace
  And say good-night, for now the western skies
  Are red with sunset, and gray mists arise
Like damps that gather on a dead man's face.

Good-night! good-night! as we so oft have said
  Beneath this roof at midnight, in the days
    That are no more, and shall no more return.
Thou hast but taken thy lamp and gone to bed;
  I stay a little longer, as one stays
    To cover up the embers that still burn.
Henry W. Longfellow.

IN THE CHURCHYARD AT TARRYTOWN.

Here lies the gentle humorist, who died
   In the bright Indian Summer of his fame!
   A simple stone, with but a date and name,
Marks his secluded resting-place beside
The river that he loved and glorified.
   Here in the autumn of his days he came,
   But the dry leaves of life were all aflame
With tints that brightened and were multiplied.

How sweet a life was his; how sweet a death!
   Living, to wing with mirth the weary hours,
     Or with romantic tales the heart to cheer;
Dying, to leave a memory like the breath
   Of summers full of sunshine and of showers,
     A grief and gladness in the atmosphere.
HENRY W. LONGFELLOW.

THE RIVER OF TO-MORROW.

"And thou, O River of to-morrow, flowing
   Between thy narrow adamantine walls,
   But beautiful, and white with waterfalls
And wreaths of mist, like hands the pathways showing;
I hear the trumpets of the morning blowing,
   I hear thy mighty voice, that calls and calls,
   And see, as Ossian saw in Morven's halls,
Mysterious phantoms, coming, beckoning, going!

It is the mystery of the unknown
   That fascinates us; we are children still,
     Wayward and wistful; with one hand we cling
To the familiar things we call our own,
   And with the other, resolute of will,
     Grope in the dark for what the day will bring."
HENRY W. LONGFELLOW.

GIOTTO'S TOWER.

How many lives, made beautiful and sweet
   By self-devotion and by self-restraint,
   Whose pleasure is to run without complaint
On unknown errands of the Paraclete,
Wanting the reverence of unshodden feet,
   Fail of the nimbus which the artists paint
   Around the shining forehead of the saint,
And are in their completeness incomplete!

In the old Tuscan town stands Giotto's tower,
   The lily of Florence blossoming in stone, —
     A vision, a delight, and a desire, —
The builder's perfect and centennial flower,
   That in the night of ages bloomed alone,
     But wanting still the glory of a spire.
                HENRY W. LONGFELLOW.

HOLIDAYS.

THE holiest of all holidays are those
   Kept by ourselves in silence and apart;
   The secret anniversaries of the heart,
When the full river of feeling overflows; —
The happy days unclouded to their close;
   The sudden joys that out of darkness start
   As flames from ashes; swift desires that dart
Like swallows singing down each wind that blows!

White as the gleam of a receding sail,
   White as a cloud that floats and fades in air,
     White as the whitest lily on the stream,
These tender memories are; — a Fairy Tale
   Of some enchanted land we know not where,
     But lovely as a landscape in a dream.
                HENRY W. LONGFELLOW.

POSSIBILITIES.

WHERE are the Poets, unto whom belong
   The Olympian heights; whose singing shafts were sent
   Straight to the mark, and not from bows half bent,
But with the utmost tension of the thong?
Where are the stately argosies of song,
   Whose rushing keels made music as they went
   Sailing in search of some new continent,
With all sail set and steady winds and strong?

Perhaps there lives some dreamy boy, untaught
   In schools, some graduate of the field or street,
   Who shall become a master of the art, —
And admiral sailing the high seas of thought,
   Fearless and first, and steering with his fleet
     For lands not yet laid down in any chart.
                    HENRY W. LONGFELLOW.

NATURE.

As a fond mother, when the day is o'er,
   Leads by the hand her little child to bed,
   Half willing, half reluctant to be led,
And leave his broken playthings on the floor,
Still gazing at them through the open door,
   Nor wholly reassured and comforted
   By promises of others in their stead,
Which, though more splendid, may not please him more:

So Nature deals with us, and takes away
   Our playthings one by one, and by the hand
     Leads us to rest so gently, that we go,
Scarce knowing if we wish to go or stay,
   Being too full of sleep to understand
     How far the unknown transcends the what we know.
                    HENRY W. LONGFELLOW.

AUREA MEDIOCRITAS.

To fawn and pander to our own conceit,
  In guise of search for truth or love of beauty;
To warp the Soul's growth in the wasteful heat
  Of passion for some vague, unreal duty, —
Is this life's best aim? — nay then, yield the prize
  To short-lived aims and joys that cannot bless
And blind the spirit's upward-looking eyes
  With petty dust of little meannesses!

In God's world we must live and not in one
Made up of our own dreams and whines, nor shun
  Its hopes and fears, its erring love and hate.
"Yes," saith a voice, "thy anger is half just;
Yet in that higher vision keep thy trust;
  Work in the small, inspired by the great!"

AUGUSTUS M. LORD.

LOVE IN WINTER.

"THESE rugged wintry days I scarce could bear,
  Did I not know that in the early spring,
  When wild March winds upon their errands sing,
Thou wouldst return, bursting on this still air,
Like those same winds, when, startled from their lair,
  They hunt up violets, and free swift brooks
  From icy caves, even as thy sweet looks
Bid my heart bloom, and sing, and break all care:

When drops with welcome rain the April day,
  My flowers shall find their April in thine eyes,
Save there the rain in dreamy clouds doth stay,
  As loath to fall out of those happy skies; —
Yet sure, my love, thou art most like to May,
  That comes with steady sun when April dies!"

ANNA MARIA LOWELL.

TO WHITTIER.

ON HIS SEVENTY-FIFTH BIRTHDAY.

NEW ENGLAND's poet, rich in love as years,
   Her hills and valleys praise thee, her swift brooks
Dance in thy verse ; to her grave sylvan nooks
Thy steps allure us, which the woodthrush hears
As maids their lovers', and no treason fears ;
   Through thee her Merrimacs and Agiochooks
   And many a name uncouth win gracious looks,
Sweetly familiar to both Englands' ears :

Peaceful by birthright as a virgin lake,
   The lily's anchorage, which no eyes behold
Save those of stars, yet for thy brother's sake
   That lay in bonds, thou blewst a blast as bold
As that wherewith the heart of Roland brake,
   Far heard across the New World and the Old.
                        JAMES RUSSELL LOWELL.

THE SPIRITUAL IN THE REAL.

I GRIEVE not that ripe Knowledge takes away
   The charm that Nature to my childhood wore,
For, with that insight, cometh, day by day,
   A greater bliss than wonder was before ;
The real doth not clip the poet's wings : —
   To win the secret of a weed's plain heart
Reveals some clue to spiritual things,
   And stumbling guess becomes firm-footed art :
Flowers are not flowers unto the poet's eyes,
   Their beauty thrills him by an inward sense ;
He knows that outward seemings are but lies,
   Or, at the most, but earthly shadows, whence
The soul that looks within for truth may guess
The presence of some wondrous heavenliness.
                        JAMES RUSSELL LOWELL.

THE EYE'S TREASURY.

Gold of the reddening sunset, backward thrown
  In largess on my tall paternal trees,
  Thou with false hope or fear didst never tease
His heart that hoards thee; nor is childhood flown
From him whose life no fairer boon hath known
  Than that which pleased him earliest still should please.
  And who hath incomes safe from Chance as these,
Gone in a moment, yet for life his own?

All other gold is slave of earthward laws;
  This to the deeps of ether takes its flight,
And on the topmost leaves makes glorious pause
  Of parting pathos ere it yield tonight:
So linger as from me earth's light withdraws,
  Dear touch of Nature, tremulously bright!

JAMES RUSSELL LOWELL.

TO JEFFRIES WYMAN.

The wisest man could ask no more of Fate
  Than to be simple, modest, manly, true,
  Safe from the Many, honored by the Few;
To count as naught in World, or Church or State,
But inwardly, in secret, to be great;
  To feel mysterious Nature ever new;
  To touch, if not to grasp, her endless clue,
And learn by each discovery how to wait.

He widened knowledge and escaped the praise;
  He wisely taught, because more wise to learn;
He toiled for Science, not to draw men's gaze,
  But for her love of self-denial stern,
That such a man could spring from our decays
  Fans the soul's nobler faith until it burn.

JAMES RUSSELL LOWELL.

BON VOYAGE!

Ship, blest to bear such freight across the blue,
   May stormless stars control thy horoscope;
   In keel and hull, in every spar and rope,
Be night and day to thy dear office true!
Ocean, men's path and their divider too,
   No fairer shrine of memory and hope
   To the underworld adown thy westering slope
E'er vanished, or whom such regrets pursue :

Smooth all thy surges as when Jove to Crete
   Swam with less costly burthen, and prepare
   A pathway meet for her home-coming soon
With golden undulations such as greet
   The printless summer-sandals of the moon
   And tempt the Nautilus his cruise to dare!
James Russell Lowell.

WITH AN ARMCHAIR.

About the oak that framed this chair, of old
   The seasons danced their round; delighted wings
   Brought music to its boughs; shy woodland things
Shared its broad roof, 'neath whose green glooms grown bold,
Lovers, more shy than they, their secret told;
   The resurrection of a thousand springs
   Swelled in its veins and dim imaginings
Teased them, perchance, of life more manifold.

Such shall it know when its proud arms enclose
   My Lady Goshawk, musing here at rest,
Careless of him who into Exile goes,
   Yet while his gift by those fair limbs is prest,
Through some fine sympathy of nature knows
   That, seas between us, she is still his guest.
James Russell Lowell.

TO MISS D. T.

ON HER GIVING ME A DRAWING OF LITTLE STREET ARABS.

As, cleansed of Tiber's and Oblivion's slime,
   Glow Farnesina's vaults with shapes again
   That dreamed some exiled artist from his pain
Back to his Athens and the Muse's clime,
So these world-orphaned waifs of Want and Crime
   Purged by Art's absolution from the stain
   Of the polluting city-flood regain
Ideal grace secure from taint of time.

An Attic frieze you give, a pictured song;
   For as with words the poet paints, for you
     The happy pencil at its labor sings,
Stealing his privilege, nor does him wrong,
   Beneath the false discovering the true,
     And Beauty's best in unregarded things.
JAMES RUSSELL LOWELL.

EGYPT.

THE unfailing starlight falls upon the plain
   Of Thebes; and on the warm, dark-bosomed Nile
   Its myriad lanterns tremblingly the while
Glimmer like drops from a celestial rain.
Piercing the gloom of Karnak's pillared fane,
   An obelisk, slim-rising, marks an aisle
   Of desert sand, where shattered sphinxes smile
In ancient majesty and calm disdain.

Swift wheels the round earth toward the yellow moon,
   And slowly, from the far horizon's rim,
     Thoth lifteth up his truth-emblazoned scroll;
And a lone ibis, starting from its swoon
   To feel the lotos ponds no longer dim,
     Wings o'er the temple like a parting soul!
CHARLES HENRY LÜDERS.

THE HAUNTS OF THE HALCYON.

To stand within a gently-gliding boat,
   Urged by a noiseless paddle at the stern,
   Whipping the crystal mirror of the fern
In fairy bays where water-lilies float;
To hear your reel's whir echoed by the throat
   Of a wild mocking-bird, or round some turn
   To chance upon a wood-duck's brood that churn
Swift passage toward their mother's warning note:

This is to rule a realm that never more
   May aught but restful weariness invade;
This is to live again the old days o'er,
   When nymph and dryad haunted stream and glade;
   To dream sweet idle dreams of having strayed
To Arcady, with all its golden lore.

                CHARLES HENRY LÜDERS.

MINOT'S LIGHT.

(SCITUATE, MASS.)

SPECTRE of stone! that from thy ocean bed,
   Pointest their pathway unto storm-tost men,
   Beckoning them back to safety's road again
Lest they should break upon that dangerous head
Where Ruin hides, with beauty overspread;
   Thou stand'st, O stony beacon, like some sage,
   Who 'mid the wreck of a tempestuous age
The wild and errant multitude has led,

Staying the turbulent and shifting tide
   Of rash opinion or of folly's course,
That vaunts itself with noise on every side,
   Like this mad ocean that with restless force
Strikes and forever strikes against the tower
Of Minot's monitor that mocks its power.

                ANN PARSONS LUNT.

THE PHILOSOPHERS.

"Τὸ καλόν."

THROUGHOUT the world in vain, in vain they sought
   Some solid good to fill the restless mind;
   The long-desired, but still unfound, to find,
The heart's last refuge and the goal of thought;
What in its depths the burning soul has wrought
   Of visions moulded with consuming fire,
   And all that sprang spontaneous to the lyre
In harmonies of golden words they caught;
Upon the mountain-top, where silence broods,
   They questioned of the stars; and by the shore
   Asked of its waves, and pondered all the lore
Of peopled plain, or taught in solemn woods;
   Without — within — alas, how vain the quest!
   Nor mind nor nature breathed heaven's holiest whisper — Rest.

GEORGE LUNT.

ALCYONE.

I.

AMONG the thousand, thousand spheres that roll
   Wheel within wheel, through never ending space,
   A mighty and interminable race,
Yet held by some invisible control,
And led as to a sure and shining goal,
   One star alone with still, unchanging face
   Looks out from her perpetual dwelling place,
Of these swift orbs the centre and the soul.
Beyond the moons that beam, the stars that blaze,
   Past fields of ether, crimson, violet, rose,
     The vast star-garden of eternity,
Behold! it shines with white, immaculate rays,
   The home of peace, the haven of repose,
     The lotus flower of heaven, Alcyone.

FRANCES L. MACE.

II.

It is the place where life's long dream comes true:
  On many another swift and radiant star
  Gather the flaming hosts of those who war
With powers of darkness: those stray seraphs too
Who hasten forth God's ministries to do;
  But here no sounds of eager trumpets mar
  The subtler spell which calls the soul from far,
Its wasted springs of gladness to renew.

It is the morning land of the Ideal,
  Where smiles, transfigured to the raptured sight,
    The joy whose flitting semblance now we see;
Where we shall know, as visible and real,
  Our life's deep aspiration, old yet new,
    In the sky-splendor of Alcyone.

                        Frances L. Mace.

III.

What lies beyond we ask not. In that hour
  When first our feet that shore of beauty press,
  It is enough of heaven, its sweet success,
To find our own. Not yet we crave the dower
Of grander action and sublimer power;
  We are content that life's long loneliness
  Finds in love's welcoming its rich redress,
And hopes, deep hidden, burst in perfect flower.

Wait for me there, O loved of many days!
  Though with warm beams some beckoning planet
    glows,
  Its dawning triumphs keep, to share with me:
For soon, far winging through the starry maze,
  Past fields of ether, crimson, violet, rose,
    I follow, follow to Alcyone!

                        Frances L. Mace.

ST. CECILIA.

When St. Cecilia, soul of song and fire,
   Heard angels sing the numbers that had lain
   Unutterable within her fervid brain,
Heart-sick with hopeless, passionate desire,
In fragments at her feet she dashed the lyre!
   Broken it could no longer mock her pain,
   Nor voice so ill the sweet, ideal strain
Which rang melodious from the heavenly choir.

O sad saint! was it not enough to know
   Such music lived, though still beyond thy reach?
And wiser far, with tender touch and slow,
   Thy instrument's mute helplessness to teach?
Content if ever from its strings should flow
   Some syllables of that celestial speech!

                            FRANCES L. MACE.

THE CRICKET.

The twilight is the morning of his day.
   While Sleep drops seaward from the fading shore,
   With purpling sail and dip of silver oar,
He cheers the shadowed time with roundelay,
Until the dark east softens into gray.
   Now as the noisy hours are coming — hark!
   His song dies gently — it is getting dark —
His night, with its one star, is on the way.

Faintly the light breaks over the blowing oats —
   Sleep, little brother, sleep: I am astir.
Lead thou the starlit nights with merry notes,
And I will lead the clamoring day with rhyme:
   We worship Song, and servants are of her —
I in the bright hours, thou in shadow-time.

                            CHARLES EDWIN MARKHAM.

LOVE'S VIGIL.

Love will outwatch the stars,. and light the skies
   When the last star falls, and the silent dark devours;
   God's warrior, he will watch the allotted hours,
And conquer with the look of his sad eyes :
He shakes the kingdom of darkness with his sighs,
   His breathèd sighs, while all the Infernal Powers
   Tremble and pale upon their central towers,
Lest, haply, his bright universe arise.

All will be well if he have strength to wait,
   Till his lost Pleiad, white and silver-shod,
Regains her place among the mourning Seven :
Then all the worlds will know that Love is Fate —
That somehow he is sweeter even than Heaven —
   That in the abyss of being he is God.
                             CHARLES EDWIN MARKHAM.

IN HIGH SIERRAS.

I stray with Ariel and Caliban :
   I know the gusty ridge of pines — I know
   Where the jay's nest swings in wilding dell below :
I climb where fallen cedars darkly span
Bright streams, where, in a valley under ban,
   The west winds set a thousand bells ablow —
   High places, where I hear in the morning glow
The eerie music blown from pipes o' Pan.

Arcadian sounds swoon in upon the air :
   A satyr steps — a wood-god's dewy notes
   Come faintly from the vales of blowing oats ;
   Ho, there ! what white thing in the vista crost?
Ha ! will I come on Dian unaware,
   Look on her fearful beauty and be lost !
                             CHARLES EDWIN MARKHAM.

THE PINES' THOUGHT.

WITHIN the shadow of ourselves we stand.
   And see a thousand brilliancies unfold
   Where autumn woods, in gorgeous ruin, hold
One late, last revel. Upon every hand
Riot of color, death in pomp and state,
   Decay magnificent, inconstant blaze, —
   We have no part or splendor in these days.
They shall be changed, — we are inviolate;

Their voices shall be hushed on every hill,
   Their lights be quenched — all color fade and die,
And when they stand like spectres gaunt and still,
   With naked boughs against the far, cold sky,
Lo! we shall hide the flying moon from sight,
And lead the wind on many a roaring night.
                        JULIET C. MARSH.

MAY.

I SAW a child, once, that had lost its way
   In a great city: ah, dear Heaven, such eyes! —
   A far-off look in them, as if the skies
Her birthplace were. So looks to me the May.
April is winsome; June is glad and gay;
   May glides betwixt them in such wondering wise, —
   Lovely as dropped from some far Paradise,
And knowing, all the while, herself astray.

Or, is the fault with us? Nay, call it not
   A fault, but a sweet trouble. Is it we, —
   Catching some glimpse of our own destiny
In May's renewing touch, some yearning thought
   Of Heaven, beneath her resurrecting hand, —
   We who are aliens, lost in a strange land?
                        CAROLINE A. MASON.

JUNE.

FAIR month of roses! Who would sing her praise,
  One says, should come direct from banqueting
  On honey from Hymettus, that he bring
Fit flavor to the strain his lip essays.
As if, around these exquisite, rare days
  Of richest June, for him who fain would sing
  Her loveliness, did not such sweetness cling
As Hybla or Hymettus scarce could raise

For all their storied bees!
                       And yet, in vain,
  Poet, your verse: extol her as you will,
  One perfect rose her praises shall distill
More than all song, though Sappho lead the strain.
  Forbear, then; since, for any tribute fit,
  Her own rare lips alone can utter it.
                            CAROLINE A. MASON.

"THAT LASS O' LOWRIE'S."

LIKE those grand heights of far-off northern lands
  (With desolation at their skirts), which bare
  Their brows to radiance of transcendent air,
Majestic in her loneliness she stands —
Yet tender to a touch: with craving hands
  That draw a slighted baby's mouth to share
  The sweetness of her lips, in kisses rare
Of love her own defrauded life demands.

What matchless courage sets her steadfast feet
  Along their path of thorns! She, hopeless, takes
    Her pain, her love, all hopes most sweet and near,
And goes — unwitting — crowning joy to meet!
  The Joan of our love! whose story makes
    Our true and tender womanhood more dear.
                                  MARIE MASON.

THE RIVAL OF THE ROSES.

(A Persian Legend.)

Once in the wave-girt garden of the world,
  The roses clustered chastely white and fair,
  Drooping embosomed on the amorous air :
When lo ! one morn, 'mid golden hair unfurled,
Stepped stately Eve upon the grass that curled
  Tenderly round her feet ; her bosom bare,
  Her limbs more white than all the roses there,
Herself God's opal from his depths empearled.

Then stirred the royal flowers with envious shame,
  To see their beauty mocked by this young queen ;
These crimson glowed, — those, the consuming flame
  Faded to paler tints of hopeless spleen !
And from that hour the roses keep the same —
  Trophies of Beauty's power in such demesne.

SUSANNA MASSEY.

OCTOBER.

Upon the dreamy upland aureoled,
  I saw the sombre artist, Autumn, stand,
  Ghostlike, against the dim and shadowy land,
Limning the hills with purple and with gold ;
And while I gazed a mighty mist uprolled,
  As at the touch of some enchanter's wand,
  And all the woods by sudden winds were fanned,
And darkness fell upon the amber wold.

Out of the frosty north, like Indian arrows,
  In never-falt'ring flight, the wild ducks flew ;
And from the windy fields the summer sparrows
  Reluctantly their feathery tribes withdrew, —
As from the heart the hopes of manhood fly,
When the sad winter of old age draws nigh.

JAMES NEWTON MATTHEWS.

DEATH — WHAT IS IT?

It is a peaceful end of all desire,
   An end of dreaming, and an end of song, —
   A happy winding-up of right and wrong,
A quiet quenching of the vital fire;
A shadow lying on a broken lyre, —
   A beggar's holiday, — a twilight long, —
   A landing-place where weary pilgrims throng,
A tranquil terminus of ways that tire.

Death is a respite from each vain regret,
   It drops the curtain, it concludes the play,
   It turns the lights out, and it leads the way,
When o'er the house-tops all the stars have set;
   Death is the epilogue to which we list,
   Just as the weary audience is dismissed.
JAMES NEWTON MATTHEWS.

EARLY MORN.

When Sleep's soft thrall with dawn of day is breaking,
   With joy I see — just lifting up my head —
   Through the broad, bounteous windows near my bed,
The first delicious glow of life awaking.
I watch the bright, unruffled ocean making
   The fair young morning blush with timid red
   To see her beauty mirrored there and spread
Far o'er the waves. I watch the tall ships taking

On flag and canvas all the colors rare
   Of her sweet beauty and her rich attire;
The violet veil that binds her golden hair,
   The chain of crimson rubies flashing fire;
Until the blue calm sky, with tender air,
   Charms the belovèd morn to come up higher.
CAROLINE MAY.

PATIENCE.

I WOULD far rather wear upon my breast
    A lily of the valley, pure and white,
    Than see upon my table bouquets bright
Of rare exotics, rich and gayly drest:
And I would rather choose, if choose I might,
    Patience, that makes the soul in quiet rest,
    Even when most it seems to be unblest,
Than all the hot-bed flowers of earth's delight.

Sweet Patience, lily Patience, who dost throw
    Through the green shades of Sorrow such a power
Of far-extending fragrance, canst thou grow
    In my heart's stubborn soil? O lovely flower!
Fain would I there enroot thee, deep and low,
    While it is softened by a rainy hour.
                                 CAROLINE MAY.

THE THUNDER CLOUD.

(MARYLAND, 1863.)

ALL hushed the farm lands with a listening air;
    Silent the straggling suburbs. In the warm,
    Paved street hoof-wakened echoes suddenly swarm.
A turn, and lo! — still, black, before you there,
As noiseless as a picture, in the square
    A thousand horse drawn up in marching form,
    And at their head, as sungleam to the storm,
A fair-faced boy with long, bright-streaming hair.

Not a breath sounded nor a trooper stirred,
    And yet you saw how fierce would leap and flash
The lightning of a thousand sabres, heard
    How all the elements would clang and clash,
    The thunder-riven valley quake and crash,
When Custer turned his head and gave the word!
                                 JAMES T. McKAY.

THE WHISPERING GALLERY.

SHE flushed and paled and, bridling, raised her head:
  "How could you know that I was in distress,
  To come so far and timely with redress?
For well and close, I thought, I kept my dread
From common scorn or pity."
                            "So?" he said,
  "I scarce can tell, and yet it seems no less
  Than that all circling winds and waters press
To bring me tidings how your life is led;

And I could hear the whisper of your name
  Around the world. If the whole earth should lie
Between us and you fled when peril came,
  I'd feel your footbeats throb, I think, and fly,
And come through sea or waste or battle-flame,
  And thank God's favor in your cause to die."

JAMES T. MCKAY.

SORROW.

So long he walked a desert bleak and bare
  No added grief could rouse him to surprise;
  And one was with him in unseemly guise,
Yet gentle-voiced, who led him from despair;
He knew her mantle hid a face most fair,
  He felt the veilèd glory of her eyes,
  And in the luxury of glad surmise
Forgot his weariness and all his care.

At length uprose a portal dark before, —
  "I lead thee to the truth; its joy is thine;"
Then light burst forth whenas she swung the door,
  And so celestially her face did shine
His heart was thrilled, and then he turned to go
Joyward reluctant, for he loved her so!

WILLIAM P. MCKENZIE.

SONNET AND ACROSTIC.

INSCRIBED TO A DESCENDANT OF ROBERT CUSHMAN.

A RECORD of God's work, what He has done,
    Unfolds in lives of those whom God has met;
    Good men of His own host, whose hearts are set
Upheld by grace till victor's crowns are won.
Still in the lapse of years, from son to son,
    Time should not make successive sons forget
    Ancestral virtues of the dead, who yet
Claim audience, inferior to none.

Upon unchanging truth the right shall stand
    Secure for all who choose the Pilgrim's way,
Heirs they are written to the Promised Land.
March, pilgrims, on, nor swerve to either hand, —
    Angels your servitors, by night, by day,
Near, they escort you to the blessèd strand.
                           JOHN H. MELLISH.

DECORATION DAY.

WITH acclamation and with trumpet tone,
    With prayer and praise, and with triumphal state
    Of warlike columns, and the moving weight
Of men, whose firmness never overthrown,
Proved itself steadfast; which did add to fate
    Speed, vision, certainty, and ever grown
    More terrible as more enduring shone
A fire of retribution and swift hate,

All visibly advancing — with these we keep
    Unsullied in our breast and pure and white
The spirit of gratitude that may not sleep, —
    A nation's safeguard against shame and blight, —
Since sacred memories and the tears men weep
    Alone can keep a nation at its height.
                           LANGDON ELWYN MITCHELL.

LOVE DEATHLESS.

When I do hear the changeful trumpet blow,
  The gay, glad fife, or the repining lute ;
When I do see clear rivers smoothly flow
  Reflecting heaven in this action mute ;
Or if across the green of evening skies
  A sombre mass of scarlet leaves I see,
Or through her cloudy hair the golden eyes
  Of evening gaze — straight do I think of thee !
Yea, straight art thou in all thy radiance brought
  More visible before me than the scene :
Yet of thee in my mind there was no thought,
  No more than if thou hadst not ever been :
If thus, unseen, thy shadow doth me move,
Can I then vouch the very death of love !

Langdon Elwyn Mitchell.

NATURAL NUPTIALS.

Lo, as sweet instruments of music play
  In diverse tones the self-same melody ;
Or as earth's green and the clear blue of day
  Compose that heaven of colors that we see :
Even thus when youth and love do celebrate
  On earth their natural nuptials, should it be,
Two hearts being melted by the fire of fate
  Into a strangely sweet conformity ;
The priest superfluous, and precaution vain,
  A blushing joy hath married them with sighs,
Their lips in meeting murmured an amen,
  And marriage contracts read they in their eyes ;
And if it is not thus, what then ? — Love 's lame,
Being bound to earth and being tied to shame !

Langdon Elwyn Mitchell.

WITH A COPY OF SHELLEY.

BEHOLD I send thee to the heights of song,
  My brother! Let thine eyes awake as clear
  As morning dew, within whose glowing sphere
Is mirrored half a world; and listen long,
Till in thine ears, famished to keenness, throng
  The bugles of the soul, till far and near
  Silence grows populous, and wind and mere
Are phantom-choked with voices. Then be strong —

Then halt not till thou seest the beacons flare
  Souls mad for truth have lit from peak to peak.
Haste on to breathe the intoxicating air —
  Wine to the brave and poison to the weak —
Far in the blue where angels' feet have trod,
Where earth is one with heaven and man with God.

HARRIET MONROE.

TO POVERTY.

COME, link thine arm in mine, good Poverty,
  Penniless yeoman in the tattered gear!
  Let's jog adown the brazen world and steer
For ports where toil is aristocracy!
Utopia laughs not at our sackcloth. See!
  Here's fair Sir Lackland and right many a peer,
  With doublets threadbare as our own, full near,
Would vow us love and hospitality!

Our gold's laid up in sunsets safe from thieves;
  And all our current silver's in the stars.
We've naught to lose save honest hearts, who steals
Shall get more treasure than he knows or feels.
  Here's sweetest roots from out our scrip, good Sirs,
And waters clear and couches in the leaves.

HARRISON S. MORRIS.

A GREEK PANEL.

AN Attic girl with garlands on her hair
   Holding aloft a light-touched instrument;
  And, at her side, a youth with cheeks round-bent,
Blowing melodious reeds with mellow air;
And, slow of foot, a timbrel-beating pair
   Whose rounded mouths with Panic hymns are rent:
  Thereafter Bacchic women, wine o'erspent,
And Mœnads, loose of robe and ankle bare.

Behold! as if a dream could learn delay,
   Or Beauty's prelude keep eternal march:
With carven joy, down carven forest arch,
   This troop treads, ever fluting time away —
Blows out beneath the leaves of marble larch
   The marble music of a golden day.
HARRISON S. MORRIS.

HOMER.

A BROW of stone and sunken eyes of stone,
   And lips apart for uttering Ilion's woes;
   And multitudes of hair a sea-wind blows
Behind him like a ragged sail outblown:
His face uppropped with giant arms on knees
   At gaze among old sunless vasts of thought,
   Behold him statued, where the clouds are caught
Along Olympus, brooding over Greece!

The blue Ægean waves are at his feet,
   And cities shut in craggy cavities;
   Yet his eternal stare goes over-seas
To towers leaguer'd with a warrior fleet.
   Deep in his ruined eyes that Troy arose,
   Yet builded where his roaring rhythm flows.
HARRISON S. MORRIS.

FRIENDS.

That which is noblest in the noblest men
    Make comrade of, and hold it dear to thee.
    Put forth thy hand; invite it eagerly; —
Give it the freedom of a citizen
To come and go with thee — and come again.
    Put down thy passion — up thy charity;
    Grant much to waywardness; thyself be free
From waywardness : — but still within thy ken

The times and seasons keep of utmost need,
    Which make the noblest stoop, the tallest bend.
Then let thy unused means thy comrade feed,
    Thy garrison his weaker camp defend.
The good mend not by chiding. Silence lies
Reprovingly within the true friend's eyes.
                              James Herbert Morse.

SENSE.

Less high, my thought, fly sweetly near the ground!
    This soil is dear, this rude, vine-trellised rock,
    These small delights, which please and do not mock,
This healthy child of mine, whose little round
Of happiness is rich and sweet and sound.
    The senses have their part; oft they unlock
    Into the mysteries the gates that block
The way to finer reason more profound.

This outward is most nicely intertwined
    With the elusive, subtle inner sense;
They root alike in one soil where they find
    One source, one method, and one providence.
Divide me not, O thought, from what is mine:
Let me be earthy, as I am divine.
                              James Herbert Morse.

H. W. LONGFELLOW.

(MARCH 24, 1882.)

SWEET Poesy, most shy and gentle maid,
   Hiding alone, far off, by English rills, —
   How didst thou flee our windswept, sunny hills
Till he, pursuing long in bosky glade,
His gentle spell on thy sweet wildness laid!
   Now by our rivers how thy woodnote thrills,
   How the far echo each deep valley fills,
Since thy dear feet came hither unafraid!
Mourn for him now — our eldest son of song —
   Eldest but one, and dearest in thy sight,
That made the new world echo of thee long, —
   Mourn with those thousand " voices of the night "
That rose and fell along the rocky shore —
Whose solemn music he shall hear no more!
JAMES HERBERT MORSE.

IMMORTALITY.

AND will the spirit falter and its fire
   Burn low and slow, and die, when we grow old?
   The brain be silent, and the heart be cold,
And love be old and cold, and all desire
Be quenched, that now higher and higher,
   Immortal fire, through dungeon keep and hold,
   Turret and spire of this proud life, is rolled —
Shall this grow old and cold and then expire?

Oh let the dream live on, the mortal die, —
   The vision thrive, the costly form decay, —
   The beauty old and cold all pass away,
The spirit higher and higher, in fire uprolled,
Wrap tower and spire and battlement on high
And earth and sky, so that it ne'er grow old!
JAMES HERBERT MORSE.

THE LAST GOOD-BYE.

How shall we know it is the last good-bye?
    The skies will not be darkened in that hour,
    No sudden blight will fall on leaf or flower,
No single bird will hush its careless cry,
And you will hold my hands, and smile or sigh
    Just as before. Perchance the sudden tears
    In your dear eyes will answer to my fears;
But there will come no voice of prophecy:

No voice to whisper, "Now, and not again,
    Space for last words, last kisses, and last prayer,
    For all the wild, unmitigated pain
Of those who, parting, clasp hands with despair."
"Who knows?" we say, but doubt and fear remain,
    Would any *choose* to part thus unaware?

LOUISE CHANDLER MOULTON.

A CRY.

O WANDERER in unknown lands, what cheer?
    How dost thou fare on thy mysterious way?
    What strange light breaks upon thy distant day,
Yet leaves me lonely in the darkness here?
O bide no longer in that far-off sphere,
    Though all Heaven's cohorts should thy footsteps stay.
    Break through their splendid, militant array,
And answer to my call, O dead and dear!

I shall not fear thee, howsoe'er thou come.
    Thy coldness will not chill, though Death is cold —
    A touch and I shall know thee, or a breath;
Speak the old, well-known language, or be dumb;
    Only come back! Be near me as of old,
    So thou and I shall triumph over Death!

LOUISE CHANDLER MOULTON.

SISTER SORROW.

I FOUND her walking in a lonely place,
  Where shadows lingered and the light was low ;
  She trod a devious path with footsteps slow,
And by the waning light I scanned her face,
And in its pensive loveliness beheld the trace
  Old tears had left, and woes of long ago :
  Then knew she I was kin to her, and so
Stretched forth her chill, soft hand with welcoming grace.

Now I walk with her through her realm of shade —
  I hear gay music sound, and laughter ring,
    And voices call me that I knew of old,
But of their mocking mirth I am afraid ;
  Led through the dusk by her to whom I cling,
    May I not reach some Blessedness untold ?
            LOUISE CHANDLER MOULTON.

COMFORT.

COME not with wordy comfort, insincere,
  Painting my death-black loss in lighter hues.
  Talk not in threadbare phrase, as preachers use,
But clasp my hand, and mingle tear with tear.
Talk of my lost one, friends, and let me hear
  Your sobbing voices. Make my dead heart feel
  The love you bear me. You cannot conceal
This burning, thirsty desert, — but one clear,

Pure drop of love may save me from despair.
  Oh ! as these precious tears o'erflow your eyes,
    Love's shadow cools my soul, which blesses you,
As a poor flow'r, sun-withered, when the air
  Is like a furnace breath, revives and tries
    To lift its head, and bless the night for dew.
            CHARLES H. NOYES ("*Charles Quiet*").

REFLECTIONS.

Within a sluggish pool I saw a bank
   Reflected, where coarse weeds and nettles grew,
   And glowing poison-berries that I knew
Were deadly to the taste; while grasses rank
Leaned o'er the edge and of the waters drank.
   But looking deeper, I beheld the blue
   Of far-off heaven, and one stray bird that flew
Across the sky and to her nestlings sank.

So in the soul of man I saw gross weeds
   Of evil that had flourished, mirrored fair,
   But safe beyond the sins white wings of prayer,
And gleams of heavenly light in noble deeds.
   O friends! look deep in every human soul,
   And lo! God's image glorifies the whole.
                        JESSIE F. O'DONNELL.

ORPHEUS.

Each Orpheus must unto the depths descend,—
   For only thus the poet can be wise;
Must make the sad Persephone his friend,
   And buried love to second life arise;
Again his love must lose through too much love,
   Must lose his life by living life too true,
For what he sought below is passed above,
   Already done is all that he would do;
Must tune all being with his single lyre,
   Must melt all rocks free from their primal pain,
Must search all Nature with his one soul's fire,
   Must bind anew all forms in heavenly chain.
If he already sees what he must do,
Well may he shade his eyes from the far-shining view.
                        MARGARET FULLER OSSOLI.

THE LIFE, THE TRUTH, THE WAY.

O THOU great Friend to all the sons of men,
   Who once appeared in humblest guise below
Sin to rebuke, to break the captive's chain,
   To call thy brethren forth from want and woe!
Thee would I sing. Thy truth is still the light
   Which guides the nations on their groping way,
Stumbling and falling in disastrous night,
   Yet hoping ever for the perfect day.

Yes, thou art still the life; thou art the way
   The holiest know, — light, life, and way of heaven;
And they who dearest hope and deepest pray
   Toil by the truth, life, way that thou hast given;
And in thy name aspiring mortals trust
To uplift their bleeding brothers from the dust.
                              THEODORE PARKER.

THE PILGRIM'S STAR.

To me thou cam'st, the earliest lamp of light,
   When youthful day must sadly disappear, —
A star prophetic in a world of night,
   Revealing what a heaven of love was near:
And full of rapture at thy joyous sight,
   I journeyed fearless on the starlight way, —
A thousand other lights came forth on height,
   But queenliest of all still shone thy ray.

O blessed lamp of Beauty and of Love,
   How long I 've felt thy shining far away!
Now, when the morn has chased the shadows gray,
Still guided by thy memory forth I rove,
I 'll journey on till dark still lighter prove,
   And Star and Pilgrim meet where all is Day.
                              THEODORE PARKER.

TO A POET IN THE CITY.

Cherish thy Muse! for life hath little more,
   Save what we hold in common with the herd:
   O blessing of these woods! to walk unstirred
By clash of commerce and the city's roar!
What finds the scholar in those flaming walls
   But wearied people, hurrying to and fro,
   Most with too high, and many without aim,
Crowded in vans or sweltering in huge halls

To hear loud emptiness or see the show?
   Were this a life to scape the Muse's blame?
Rather than such would I the Parcæ ask,
   Folding mine arms, to stretch me on the floor
Where Agamemnon in his golden mask
   Dreams not of Argolis or Argos more.

                  Thomas William Parsons.

SLEEP.

O Sleep, good mother of enchanting dreams,
   Within thy soothing arms oh let me lie,
   What time the night-wind sings a lullaby,
And the moon kisses down with cooling gleams
Mine eyelids weary of day's sultry beams;
   Then let thy rarest visions come anigh,
   Dead hopes fulfilled in perfect radiancy,
Whose fairness all my waking pain redeems;

With Loline let me stray through jasmine bowers,
A balmy world of love whose stars are flowers,
   Where zephyrs sigh in such a tender way
   They seem to breathe the words we long to say;
And when these dreams have come, good Sleep, ah then
I pray thee do not let me wake again.

                  Samuel Minturn Peck.

MY LOVE.

" IF on the clustering curls of thy dark hair,
  And the pure arching of thy polished brow,
  We only gaze, we fondly dream that thou
Art one of those bright ministers who bear,
Along the cloudless bosom of the air,
  Sweet, solemn words, to which our spirits bow, —
  With such a holy smile thou lookest now,
And art so soft and delicately fair.

A veil of tender light is mantling o'er thee ;
  Around thy opening lips young loves are playing,
  And crowds of youths, in passionate thought delaying,
Pause, as thou movest by them, to adore thee ;
  By many a sudden blush and tear betraying
How the heart trembles when it bends before thee ! "

JAMES GATES PERCIVAL.

NIGHT.

AM I not all alone ? — The world is still
  In passionless slumber, — not a tree but feels
  The far-pervading hush, and softer steals
The misty river by. Yon broad bare hill
Looks coldly up to heaven, and all the stars
  Seem eyes deep fixed in silence, as if bound
  By some unearthly spell, — no other sound
But the owl's unfrequent moan. — Their airy cars

The winds have stationed on the mountain peaks.
Am I not all alone ? — A spirit speaks
  From the abyss of night, "Not all alone :
Nature is round thee with her banded powers,
And ancient genius haunts thee in these hours ;
  Mind and its kingdom now are all thine own."

JAMES GATES PERCIVAL.

IN ANSWER TO A SONNET.

A VISION fair you show me, that I deem
   Most worthy in a poet's heart to rise,
   As Dian lovely in the summer skies;
Reflected in your soul as in a stream,
You show me mine own image, like a dream
   Of sweet, inspiring womanhood, most wise,
   Serene and tender, that with steadfast eyes
The ideal of fair friendliness would seem.

Ah! where a sharper pang than thus to see
   Myself, high imaged in another heart?
   To see, and feel with hot, reproachful tears,
That thus I might have been, thus should I be!
   Thus will I be! Nor shall that dream depart
   Save as the moon retreats when day appears.
LILLA CABOT PERRY.

ABRAHAM LINCOLN.

STERN be the pilot in the dreadful hour
   When a great nation, like a ship at sea
   With the wroth breakers whitening at her lee,
Feels her last shudder if her Helmsman cower;
A godlike manhood be his mighty dower!
   Such and so gifted, Lincoln, may'st thou be,
   With thy high wisdom's low simplicity
And awful tenderness of voted power.

From our hot records then thy name shall stand
   On Time's calm ledger out of passionate days —
   With the pure debt of gratitude begun,
   And only paid in never-ending praise —
One of the many of a mighty Land,
   Made by God's providence the Anointed One.
JOHN JAMES PIATT.

THE RETURN.

STILL unto thee, my brightest, fairest, best,
   The wandering heart returns as the pure dove
   Seeking in vain the olive-branch of love,
Nor finding peace save in its ark of rest.
My flight has been wide, o'er the tossing wave:
   Nor bower, nor tree, nor mantling vine were there;
And like rich pearls deep in their ocean cave,
   Were hidden all things beautiful and fair.

Send me not forth again, though the fair sky
   Smile o'er the green enameling of earth;
   Bright joys again be clustered round the hearth,
And the air rife with breathing melody;
Still to its resting-place the dove would flee; —
Angel of beauty! shall it dwell with thee?

                       NORMAN PINNEY.

TO SCIENCE.

SCIENCE! true daughter of Old Time thou art!
   Who alterest all things with thy peering eyes.
Why preyest thou thus upon the poet's heart,
   Vulture whose wings are dull realities?
How should he love thee? or how deem thee wise,
   Who wouldst not leave him in his wandering
To seek for treasure in the jeweled skies,
   Albeit he soared with an undaunted wing?

Hast thou not dragged Diana from her car?
   And driven the Hamadryad from the wood
To seek a shelter in some happier star?
   Hast thou not torn the Naiad from her flood,
The Elfin from the green grass, and from me
The summer dream beneath the tamarind tree?

                       EDGAR ALLAN POE.

A LOVER'S SONNET.

HASTEN, soft wind, and when amid the gay
    She moves with eyes of calm and tender light,
    And forehead pale as foam-lit waves at night,
And voice harmonious as the warbling lay
Of birds that usher in the fragrant May,
    Whisper, soft wind, that she remains the bright
    Pure empress of this heart, whose sole delight
Is thus to muse on moments passed away;

O, whisper this and tell how little I
    Have known of joy since last I saw her face,
How the bright stars, lamps of yon changing sky,
    Woods, streams, and every secret place,
Bear witness to my truth; yes, murmur this, then die
    On those fair lips, bright opening buds of grace.

                        C. E. DA PONTE.

TO ROBERT COLLYER.

I MISS thy face, dear friend, thy voice, thy hand, —
    Thy rugged face through which the clear soul shines,
    Thy voice, now plaintive as the moan of pines
And, then, a trumpet mighty in command,
Thy honest palm whose grasp all understand.
    Though pleasant be the places where the lines
    Are fallen to me, yet my heart repines
Oft for the gardens of that goodly land

    Where our souls wandered when they haply met
With yearnings strong for man's diviner day,
    And landscapes blossomed which no tears could wet,
Till old things fit to perish passed away,
    And life to God's great harmony was set,
And Love was monarch with unhindered sway.

                        HORATIO NELSON POWERS.

THE CATHEDRAL.

(TO JAMES RUSSELL LOWELL ON HIS 70TH BIRTHDAY.)

THROUGH the Cathedral of thy finished song,
   Oh happy architect! we walk to-day, —
   The better for thy building. Far away,
The groined roof springs: thy luminous fancies throng
The great stained oriel, — trail weird hues along
   Sir Launfal in his niche, and fling a ray
   Across the choir whose haunting lyrics lay
A spell upon our souls, — so sweet — so strong!

Each pillar bears its legend, nature-wrought —
   Of Willows — Pines — June roses, — ermined Snow:
     Even rollick Satire lurks within the stall,
Now hallowed by Commemorative thought:
Heartsease and Rue upon the altar glow;
   And thou, High Priest, dost consecrate it all!

MARGARET J. PRESTON.

"CONVIVA SATUR." (HORACE.)

IF *he* could say it, turning from the board
   His creedless life had spread him, nor repine
   That in his dear Digentia, other wine
Than his should gather coolness, or the hoard
Of Sabine olives be for others stored, —
   Then surely I! The love this heart of mine
   Knew of all draughts to be the most divine,
Into life's crystal goblet hath been poured
Till it runs over. Faith, the living bread,
Hallows the table; while on every side,
   With heaping clusters have my hopes been fed;
Nor tempered appetite been once denied.
So, I am ready, when the thanks are said,
   To rise and leave the banquet, — satisfied.

MARGARET J. PRESTON.

"SIT, JESSICA."

As there she stood, that sweet, Venetian night,
  Her pure face lifted to the skies, aswim
  With stars from zenith to horizon's rim,
I think Lorenzo scarcely saw the light
Asleep upon the bank, or felt how bright
  The patines were. *She* filled the heavens for him;
  And in her low replies the cherubim
Seemed softly quiring from some holy height.

And when he drew her down and soothed her tears,
  Stirred by the minstrelsy, with passionate kiss,
Whose long, sweet iterations left her lips
  Trembling as roses tremble after sips
Of eager bees, the music of the spheres
  Held not one rhythmic rapture like to this!

MARGARET J. PRESTON.

HAWTHORNE.

HE stood apart — but as a mountain stands
  In isolate repose above the plain,
  Robed in no pride of aspect, no disdain,
Though clothed in power to steep the sunniest lands
In mystic shadow. At the mood's demands,
  Himself he clouded, till no eye could gain
  The vanished peak; no more, with sense astrain
Than trace a footprint on the surf-washed sands.

Yet, hidden within that rare, sequestered height,
  Imperially lonely, what a world
    Of splendor lay! What pathless realms untrod!
What rush and wreck of passion! What delight
    Of woodland sweets! What weird winds, phantom-whirled!
  And over all, the immaculate sky of God!

MARGARET J. PRESTON.

"PHILIP, MY KING."

(To Philip Bourke Marston.)

Thou art the same, my friend, about whose brow,
  In cradle years, a poet twined the lays
  Through which she glorified in poet's phrase
Those splendid eyes, that forced her to avow
Heart-fealty to thee, her liege, and bow
  Before thy regal looks with regal praise
  Of more enduring freshness than the bays
Which blatant crowds bind for their heroes now.

Had she prevision that above those eyes
  God meant to press his hand, the better so
    To cage the lark-like spirit? Should it soar
Too deep into the sapphire of the skies,
  We earthly listeners, standing far below,
    Must fail to catch the ethereal music more.
Margaret J. Preston.

THE SPIRIT OF NATURE.

O Earth! thou hast not any wind that blows
  Which is not music; every weed of thine,
  Pressed rightly, flows in aromatic wine;
And every humble hedge-row flower that grows,
And every little brownbird that doth sing,
  Hath something greater than itself, and bears
A living word to every living thing,
  Albeit it holds the message unawares.
All shapes and sounds have something which is not
  Of them; a spirit broods amid the grass,
Vague outlines of the everlasting thought
  Lie in the melting shadows as they pass,
And touch of an eternal presence thrills
The fringes of the sunsets and the hills.
Richard Realf.

DISCORD.

O THAT some poet, with awed lips on fire
   Of far ineffable altars, would arise,
   And with his consecrated songs baptize
Our souls in harmony, that we might acquire
Insight into the essential heart of life,
   Beating with rhythmic pulses! There is lost,
In the gross echoes of our brawling strife,
   Music more rare than that which did accost

Shakespeare's imagination when it swept
   Nearest the infinite. Our spirits are
All out of tune; our discords intercept
   The strains which, like the singing of a star,
Stream downward from the Holies, to attest,
Beyond our jarring restlessnesses, rest.
RICHARD REALF.

TELL ME SOME WAY.

OH, you who love me not, tell me some way
   Whereby I may forget you for a space;
   Nay, clean forget you and your lovely face —
Yet well I know how vain this prayer I pray.
All weathers hold you. Can I make the May
   Forbid her boughs blow white in every place?
   Or rob June of her rose that comes apace?
Cheat of their charm the elder months and gray?

Aye, were you dead, you could not be forgot;
   So sparse the bloom along the lanes would be;
   Such sweetness out the briery hedges fled;
My tears would fall that you had loved me not;
   And bitterer tears that you had gone from me;
   Living you break my heart, so would you dead!
L. WOODWORTH REESE.

MONOSYLLABLES.

MINE be the force of words that tax the tongue
   But once, to speak them full and round and clear.
   They suit the speech, or song, and suit the ear,
Like bells that give one tone when they are rung;
Or bird-notes on the air, like rain-drops flung,
   That pour their joy for all who pause to hear.
   Their short, quick chords the dull sense charm and cheer,
That tires and shrinks from words to great length strung.

Strong words of old that shot right to the brain,
   And hit the heart as soon were brief and terse.
   Who finds them now, and fits them to his sling,
Smooth stones from brooks of English are his gain,
   Which shall make strong his thought, in prose or verse,
   Wills he with scribes to write, or bards to sing.
                       WILLIAM C. RICHARDS.

TO R. W. EMERSON.

DEAR, amiable man, of soul sublime,
   How like a tower thou risest to our eyes,
   Or like a stately ship of rich emprise,
Laden with choicest freight from some far clime,
To scatter blessings in a needful time!
   Well hast thou wrought thy way through masses deep
   Of rampart evils; or through those that sleep,
Yet, when awakened charge thee with their crime.

No lack have we on our New England soil
   Of gifted spirits, to their country dear,
Who, in their noble spheres, unceasing toil;
   But in the highest walks thou hast no peer.
A Parker or a Beecher may at need
Plough the wild land, but thou must sow the seed.
                       DANIEL RICKETSON.

(Brooklawn, New Bedford, 1858.)

WHEN SHE COMES HOME.

When she comes home again! A thousand ways
   I fashion, to myself, the tenderness
   Of my glad welcome: I shall tremble — yes;
And touch her, as when first in the old days
I touched her girlish hand, nor dared upraise
   Mine eyes, such was my faint heart's sweet distress.
   Then silence: and the perfume of her dress:
The room will sway a little, and a haze

Cloy eyesight — soulsight, even — for a space:
   And tears — yes; and the ache here in the throat,
To know that I so ill deserve the place
   Her arms make for me; and the sobbing note
I stay with kisses, ere the tearful face
Again is hidden in the old embrace.

James Whitcomb Riley.

SURRENDER.

Take all of me, — I am thine own, heart — soul —
   Brain, body — all; all that I am or dream
   Is thine forever; yea, though space should teem
With thy conditions, I'd fulfill the whole —
Were to fulfill them to be loved of thee.
   Oh, love me! — were to love me but a way
To kill me — love me; so to die would be
   To live forever. Let me hear thee say

Once only, "Dear, I love thee" — then all life
   Would be one sweet remembrance, — thou its king:
Nay, thou art that already, and the strife
   Of twenty worlds could not uncrown thee. Bring,
O Time! my monarch to possess his throne
Which is my heart and for himself alone.

Amélie Rives Chanler.

MIDWINTER THAW.

How shrink the snows upon this upland field,
   Under the dove-gray dome of brooding noon!
   They shrink with soft, reluctant shocks, and soon
In sad, brown ranks the furrows lie revealed.
From radiant cisterns of the frost unsealed
   Now wakes through all the air a watery rune —
   The babble of a million brooks atune,
In fairy conduits of blue ice concealed.

Noisy with crows, the wind-break on the hill
   Counts o'er its buds for summer. In the air
Some shy foreteller prophesies with skill —
   Some voyaging ghost of bird, some effluence rare;
And the stall-wearied cattle dream their fill
   Of deep June pastures where the pools are fair.

                        Charles G. D. Roberts.

THE POTATO HARVEST.

A high bare field, brown from the plough, and borne
   Aslant from sunset; amber wastes of sky
   Washing the ridge; a clamor of crows that fly
In from the wide flats where the spent tides mourn
To yon their rocking roosts in pines wind-torn;
   A line of gray snake-fence, that zigzags by
   A pond, and cattle; from the homestead nigh
The long deep summonings of the supper horn.

Black on the ridge, against that lonely flush,
   A cart, and stoop-necked oxen; ranged beside,
   Some barrels; and the day-worn harvest folk,
Here emptying their baskets, jar the hush
   With hollow thunders; down the dusk hillside
   Lumbers the wain; and day fades out like smoke.

                        Charles G. D. Roberts.

THE COW PASTURE.

I see the harsh, wind-ridden, eastward hill,
  By the red cattle pastured, blanched with dew;
    The small, mossed hillocks where the clay gets through;
The gray webs woven on milkweed-tops at will.
The sparse, pale grasses flicker, and are still.
    The empty flats yearn seaward. All the view
  Is naked to the horizon's utmost blue;
And the bleak spaces stir me with strange thrill.

Not in perfection dwells the subtler power
  To pierce our mean content, but rather works
  Through incompletion, and the need that irks, —
Not in the flower, but effort toward the flower.
  When the want stirs, when the soul's cravings urge,
  The strong earth strengthens and the clean heavens purge.

Charles G. D. Roberts.

LOVE'S SOVEREIGNTY.

Oh Love! thy sovereignty is great indeed!
  All other queens give largess with commands.
  Wealth with her laden ships, her laden lands,
Has bribery for every mortal greed;
Pleasure drops her swift flying gifts at need,
  And Fame lets fall the shining silver sands
  Of some fair Future's hour-glass through her hands:
Bare even of hope we follow where you lead.

Oh Love! if I could paint thee, it should be
  Without the slight, sweet glamour of a smile,
    A figure stern with patience, pale with power,
Whose arms are empty and whose breast is free
  To meet the archers without fear or guile,
    Knowing she hath eternity for dower.

Fanny Ruth Robinson.

AN ORDER FOR A CAMEO.

It shall be Eve's face, Carver, gleaming white,
   Against the Eden ground of Chrysophrase,
Child faces in the morning are less bright
   And Gabriel's less serene : you know her gaze,
Unfolding from pure lids saw Adam first,
And then a glorious, cursèd earth, uncursed.
   So Memory will not darken that still smile.
Laughter was born of tears : — not Love's grand pain,
   Nor thorns, nor dying lilies, nor still rain
   Betray her to a glimpse of afterwhile.
Miriam and Sappho show the sorrow stain,
   And Mary's loving hath its selfish guile :
Eve knows not Hope's unrest, nor Fear's annoy,
And blesses with the sweet, lost dream of Joy.
                        Fanny Ruth Robinson.

THE THYME-LEAVED SANDWORT.

When first I met you, little milk-white flower,
   Hid in the grass along my lonely way,
   'T was early spring, but even then your day
Was almost done, your life had lost its power.
And yet, along your puny stalk, the dower
   Of each day's bloom, a tiny seed there lay
   Safe held within, — the flower of yesterday,
To bloom again and fill your little hour.

O blossom small, a lesson well you teach :
   What though my life no increase seems to gain,
No fair fruition yield ? Still may I reach
   Unto my highest bound, and climb amain,
And climbing bloom, so that a seed for each
   Day's flower will show I have not lived in vain.
                        Harriet H. Robinson.

THE INFINITE CURVE.

SOUL, art thou thirsty, art thou yearning, lone?
   Thou soul who hast not crossed the span between
   Two smallest of the myriad worlds, whose sheen
Reflects the light of the Eternal's throne!
Take courage, fainting heart, and claim thy own;
   Thy very hunger is a prophecy;
   Like to the endless curve in symmetry
Move thou at thy Creator's will, the known

Held fast, faith-borne through darkness unto light;
   So by thy very being's law, heaven-high,
Thou too shalt sweep the universe with might
   And find in Him to whose omniscient eye
The reaching infinite curve is all supplied,
Thy yearning self forever satisfied.

ZULEMA A. RUBLE.

ORIGINALITY.

ONCE, as I pondered o'er strange books, and sought
   From secrets of the past a knowledge new,
   Within my mind enthralled there sudden grew
The perfect germ of a stupendous thought!
No bizarre brain as yet had ever wrought
   This odd, weird wonder into shape, and few
   Could from the stores of Fancy bring to view
A whim to equal this, to me untaught!

Its radiant advent thrilled me with delight,
   But, as I dreamed, I heard a sad voice say:
     "*I who am living in a spirit home*
With the same thought that pleasures thee to-night
   Charmed grim Tiberius through a festal day
     And made tumultuous laughter roar through
       Rome!"

FRANCIS SALTUS SALTUS.

THE BAYADERE.

Near strange, weird temples, where the Ganges' tide
   Bathes domed Delhi, I watch, by spice-trees fanned,
   Her agile form in some quaint saraband;
A marvel of passionate chastity and pride!
Nude to the loins, superb, and leopard-eyed,
   With redolent roses in her jeweled hand,
   Before some haughty Rajah, mute and grand,
Her flexile torso bends, her white feet glide!

The dull kinoors throb one monotonous tune,
And, mad with motion, as in a hasheesh trance,
Her scintillant eyes in vague, ecstatic charm,
   Burn like black stars below the Orient moon,
While the suave, dreamy languor of the dance
Lulls the grim drowsy cobra on her arm!
Francis Saltus Saltus.

PILGRIM LOVE.

"As calmest waters mirror heaven the best,
   So best befit remembrances of thee;
   Calm, holy hours from earthly passion free,
Sweet twilight musing, — Sabbaths in the breast.
No stooping thought, nor any groveling care,
   The sacred whiteness of that place shall stain,
   Where far from heartless joys and rites profane,
Memory has reared for thee an altar fair.

Yet frequent visitors shall kiss the shrine,
   And ever keep its vestal lamp alight;
   All noble thoughts, all dreams divinely bright,
That waken or delight this soul of mine."
   So Love, meek pilgrim! his young vows did pay,
   With glowing eyes that must his lips gainsay.
F. B. Sanborn.

THE GENTLE HEART.

My heart, forthlooking in the purple day,
   Tell me what sweetest image thou may'st see,
   Fit to be type of thy dear love and thee?
Lo! here where sunshine keeps the wind away,
Grow two young violets, — humble lovers they, —
   With drooping face to face, and breath to breath,
   They look and kiss and love and laugh at death: —
Yon bluebird singing on the scarlet spray

Of the bloomed maple in the blithe spring air,
   While his mate answers from the wood of pines,
   And all day long their music ne'er declines;
For love their labor is and love their care.
   "These pass with day and spring," the true heart saith, —
" Forever thou wilt love and she be fair."

F. B. Sanborn.

HAMPTON BEACH.

Ah mournful Sea! yet to our eyes he wore
   The placid look of some great god at rest;
With azure arms he clasped the embracing shore,
   While gently heaved the billows of his breast:
We scarce could hear his voice, and then it seemed
   The happy murmur of a lover true,
Who in the sweetness of his sleep has dreamed
   Of kisses falling on his lips like dew.

Far off, the blue and gleaming hills above,
   The sun looked through a veil of thinnest haze,
As coy Diana, blushing at her love,
   Half hid with her own light her earnest gaze,
When on the shady Latmian slope she found
Fair-haired Endymion slumbering on the ground.

F. B. Sanborn.

THE PLANET JUPITER.

EVER at night have I looked up for thee,
 O'er thy sidereal sisterhood supreme!
Ever at night have scanned the purple sea
 For the reflection of thy quivering beam!
When the white cloud thy diamond radiance screened,
 And the Bahama breeze began to wail,
How on the plunging bows for hours I've leaned,
 And watched the gradual lifting of thy veil!

Bright planet! lustrous effluence! thou ray
 From the Eternal Source of life and light!
Gleam on the track where Truth shall lead the way
 And gild the inward as the outward night!
Shine but as now upon my dying eyes,
And Hope, from earth to thee, from thee to Heaven
  shall rise!

EPES SARGENT.

THE MYSTIC HOPE.

WHAT is this mystic, wondrous hope in me
 When not one star from out the darkness born
 Gives promise of the coming of the morn, —
When all life seems a pathless mystery
Through which the weary eyes no way can see, —
 When illness comes and life seems most forlorn,
 Still dares to laugh the last dread threat to scorn,
And proudly cries: *Death is not, shall not be?*

I wonder at myself! Tell me, O Death,
 If that thou rul'st the earth; if "dust to dust"
  Shall be the end of love and life and strife,
From what rare land is blown this living breath
 That shapes itself to whispers of strong trust
  And tells the lie — if 't is a lie — *of Life?*

MINOT J. SAVAGE.

HER EYES.

As in some deep pool, under shadowy skies,
   At foot of mighty mountains, still and brown, —
     So deep that it seems infinite, so down
I gazed into her measureless, grave eyes.
And there I saw no shallows of surprise,
   No petty thought of self or silly frown;
     But womanhood so deep that it would drown
All flattery, all meanness, and all lies!

And O such depth of tenderness was there,
   Such noble passion, such a might of love,
     And all soul-lighted like star-brilliant space.
Such eyes, and set within a face so fair!
   A man might prize, all other things above,
     To see their deeps the mirror of his face.

MINOT J. SAVAGE.

RALPH WALDO EMERSON.

BESIDE the ocean, wandering on the shore,
   I seek no measure of the infinite sea;
     Beneath the solemn stars that speak to me,
I may not care to reason out their lore;
Among the mountains, whose bright summits o'er
   The flush of morning brightens, there may be
     Only a sense of might and majesty;
And yet a thrill of infinite life they pour

Through all my being, and uplift me high
   Above my little self and weary days.
     So, in thy presence, Emerson, I hear
A sea-voice sounding 'neath a boundless sky,
   While mountainous thoughts tower o'er life's common
       ways,
     And in thy sky the stars of truth appear.

MINOT J. SAVAGE.

LOVE'S SOVEREIGNTY.

Though Love loves well all things of outward grace
  That poets praise and gentle ladies prize,
  Yet lives he not by favor of blue eyes,
Or black or brown, or aught that he may trace
In features faultless as the perfect face
  Of Art's ideal. No! his essence lies
  Deep in the heart, not in its changing dyes
On lip and cheek. He has his dwelling-place

In the life's life. As violets deck the May —
Which yet survives when these have passed away —
All lovely things are Love's; but ne'er the less
  Health, youth, and beauty, though they serve him well,
  Are but Love's ministers, his sovereign spell
Lives in his own immortal loveliness!

JOHN G. SAXE.

MNEMOSYNE.

Oft have I thought, musing, my love, on thee,
  And all the dear delights that I have known,
  Love-crowned, since first I knew thee for my own,
That, if by cruel Fate's adverse decree
(Not mine, nor thine, for that can never be),
  I ne'er should hear thy voice's dulcet tone,
  Nor kiss nor clasp thee more — not all alone —
Companioned still by sweet Mnemosyne —

To her I'd cry, "O goddess who hast power
  To bring again my darling to my sight,
And from the Past evoke each vanished hour
  That blessed the day or glorified the night,
I envy not the joys a king can boast,
Who ne'er possessed the treasure I have lost!

JOHN G. SAXE.

MIDSUMMER.

Midway about the circle of the year
   There is a single perfect day that lies
   Supremely fair, before our careless eyes.
After the spathes of floral bloom appear,
Before is found the first dead leaf and sere,
   It comes, precursor of the Autumn skies,
   And crown of Spring's endeavor. Till it dies
We do not dream the flawless day is here.

And thus, as on the way of life we speed,
   Mindful but of the joys we hope to see,
We never think, "These present hours exceed
   All that have been or that shall ever be;"
Yet somewhere on our journey we shall stay
Backward to gaze on our midsummer day.
                      Andrew B. Saxton.

THE OVERFLOWING CUP.

Into the crystal chalice of the soul
   Is falling, drop by drop, Life's blending mead.
   The pleasant waters of our childhood speed
And enter first; and Love pours in its whole
Deep flood of tenderness and gall. There roll
   The drops of sweet and bitter that proceed
   From wedded trustfulness, and hearts that bleed
For children that outrun us to the goal.

And later come the calmer joys of age —
   The restful streams of quietude that flow
Around their fading lives, whose heritage
   Is whitened locks and voice serene and low.
These added blessings round the vessel up —
Death is the overflowing of the cup.
                      Andrew B. Saxton.

POMONA.

At noon of night the goddess, silver-stoled,
   Came with light foot across the moonlit land,
   And breezes soft as blow o'er Samarcand
Stirred her free hair that glinted like clear gold;
Sweet were her smiling lips, as when of old
   Vertumnus wooed her on the grassy strand
   Of some swift Tuscan river overspanned
By sunny skies that knew no breath of cold.

So when the door of dawn grew aureate,
   And broken was the dim night's peaceful hush
    By harvesters uprisen to greet the morn,
They knew Pomona had passed by in state,
   For on the apples was a rosier blush,
    And on the grapes a richer lustre born.
CLINTON SCOLLARD.

MEMNON.

Why dost thou hail with songful lips no more
   The glorious sunshine? — Why is Memnon mute
   Whose voice was tuned as is the silvery flute
When Thebes sat queenly by the Nile's low shore?
The chained slaves sweat no longer at the oar,
   No longer shrines are raised to man and brute,
   Yet dawn by dawn the sun thou didst salute
Gives thee the greeting that it gave of yore.

What secret spell is on thee? Dost thou wait
   (Hoping and yearning through the years forlorn)
The old-time splendor and the regal state,
   The glory and the power of empire shorn?
O break the silence deep, defying fate,
   And cry again melodious to the morn!
CLINTON SCOLLARD.

WILD COREOPSIS.

A SEA of blossoms, golden as the glow
   Of morning sunlight on a wind-rocked bay,
   Beneath the breeze of this rare autumn day
Heaves in soft undulation to and fro;
Like incense, floating o'er the marsh below,
   Come fragrant odors of the late-mown hay;
   Beyond, in harmony of green and gray,
The tapering tamaracks tower in stately row.

And wading through the shimmering waves, with song
   Upon his lips, a fair-haired youth I see
     Who swinges off the saffron blossom-bells:
Back roll the years, — a melancholy throng, —
   And I behold, in sea-girt Sicily,
     Theocritus amid the asphodels.

CLINTON SCOLLARD.

THE HUMAN LOVE DIVINE.

WHEN I beneath God's radiant beams of grace
   Do quail and quiver in sin's agony,
And flee me, hiding from his holy face,
   Whose raptured love I cannot, dare not see;
Forsakes He not the child He loving wrought
   Within his heart's most wise and hallowed deeps,
But seeks me with a Father's faithful thought,
   That in a tender yearning for me weeps:

As when the sun doth shine too fiercely bright
   For my poor eyes' full-gaze to look upon,
He turns the splendor of its dazzling light
   Into a daisy smiling in the dawn,
So He his holy yearnings earthward sends
All tempered to me in my human friends.

JOHN M. SCOTT.

A MARSH MELODY.

'Mid forest trees I heard, one summer day,
  A sweetest carol from a happy bird,
  As sweet as by man's ear is often heard;
And, looking up the leafy, emerald way,
I saw upon a branch there swing and sway
  A sombre blackbird, who had often stirred
  The grasses of the marsh the sea did gird;
And though full oft familiar with his way,

I never knew that aught of song had he
  But gutturals, unmusical and harsh.
  E'en so my brother, 'mid sin's ugly marsh,
May have some pipe of holiest melody,
  Which, if I hear, my voice may help to sing,
  'Till high and higher we towards heaven wing.

JOHN M. SCOTT.

A BUTTERFLY IN WALL STREET.

Winged wanderer from clover meadows sweet,
  Where all day long beneath a smiling sky
  You drained the wild-flowers' cups of honey dry
And heard the drowsy winds their loves repeat,
What idle zephyr whispering deceit
  Has won your heart and tempted you to fly
  Unto this noisy town and vainly pry
Into the secrets of this busy street?

To me your unexpected presence brings
  A thought of fragrant pastures, buds and flowers,
  And sleepy brooks, and cattle in the fold;
Or, watching as you soar on trembling wings,
  I think for those who toil through weary hours
  You are a type of their uncertain gold.

FRANK DEMPSTER SHERMAN.

RECALL.

"Love me, or I am slain!" I cried, and meant
    Bitterly true each word. Nights, morns, slipped by,
    Moons, circling suns, yet still alive am I;
But shame to me if my best time be spent
On this perverse, blind passion! Are we sent
    Upon a planet just to mate and die,
    A man no more than some pale butterfly
That yields his day to nature's sole intent?

Or is my life but Marguerite's ox-eyed flower,
    That I should stand and pluck and throw away,
One after one, the petal of each hour
    Like a love-dreamy girl and only say,
    "Loves me," and "loves me not," and "loves me"?
        Nay!
Let the man's mind awake to manhood's power.
        EDWARD ROWLAND SILL ("*Andrew Hedbrooke*").

QUEM METUI MORITURA.

WHAT need have I to fear — so soon to die?
    Let me work on, not watch and wait in dread:
    What will it matter, when that I am dead,
That they bore hate or love that near me lie?
'T is but a life-time and the end is nigh
    At best or worst. Let me lift up my head
    And firmly, as with inner courage tread
Mine own appointed way on mandates high.

Pain could but bring from all its evil store
    The close of pain: hate's venom could but kill;
Repulse, defeat, desertion, could no more,
    Let me have lived my life, not cowered until
The unhindered and unhastened hour was here.
So soon — what is there now for me to fear?
        EDWARD ROWLAND SILL ("*Andrew Hedbrooke*").

HER EXPLANATION.

So you have wondered at me, — guessed in vain
   What the real woman is you know so well?
   I am a lost illusion.   Some strange spell
Once made your friend there with his fine disdain
Of fact, conceive me perfect.   He would fain
   (But could not) see me always as befell
   His dream to see me, plucking asphodel,
In saffron robes on some celestial plain.

All that I was he marred and flung away
   In quest of what I was not, could not be, —
   Lilith, or Helen, or Antigone.
Still he may search; but I have had my day,
   And now the Past is all the part for me
That this world's empty stage has left to play.
        EDWARD ROWLAND SILL ("*Andrew Hedbrooke*").

CHARITY, NOT JUSTICE.

OUTWEARIED with the littleness and spite,
   The falsehood and the treachery of men,
   I cried: "Give me but justice!" thinking then
I meekly craved a common boon which might
Most easily be granted; soon the light
   Of deeper truth grew on my wondering ken,
   (Escaping baneful damps of stagnant fen),
And then I saw, that in my pride bedight

I claimed from erring man the gift of Heaven —
   God's own great vested right; and I grew calm,
With folded hands, like stone, to patience given,
   And pityings of pure love-distilling balm; —
And now I wait in quiet trust to be
All known to God, — and ask of men, sweet Charity.
        ELIZABETH OAKES SMITH.

VICTOR HUGO.

"He is a mal-formed giant." — JOHN BURROUGHS.

"A MAL-FORMED giant!" Let us rather say
   That we are dwarfs who barely touch the knee
   Of this great-passioned man, who dares to free
Himself from shackles, choosing his own way
To make us pygmies feel his mighty sway: —
   And if on level with his eyes we'd be,
   We first must reach his heart, — then we may see
From such rare height the Power he doth obey.

Or say he is a mountain-peak, his head
   Upreared beyond the line of wreathèd mist,
Where lowland dwellers may sometimes be led
   O'er rocky steeps, through many a turn and twist,
To find their native valleys wide outspread,
   Into strange beauty by the ether kissed.

FLORENCE L. SNOW.

DEAR HANDS.

ROUGHENED and worn with ceaseless toil and care,
   No perfumed grace, no dainty skill had these;
   They earned for whiter hands a jeweled ease,
And kept the scars unlovely for their share.
Patient and slow, they had the will to bear
   The whole world's burdens, but no power to seize
   The flying joys of life, the gifts that please,
The gold and gems that others find so fair.
Dear hands, where bridal jewel never shone,
   Whereon no lover's kiss was ever pressed,
   Crossed in unwonted quiet on the breast;
I see, through tears, your glory newly won,
The golden circlet of life's work well done,
   Set with the shining pearl of perfect rest.

SUSAN MARR SPALDING.

A DESIRE.

LET me not lay the lightest feather's weight
   Of duty upon Love. Let not, my own,
   The breath of one reluctant kiss be blown
Between our hearts. I would not be the gate
That bars, like some inexorable fate,
   The portals of thy life; that says, " Alone
   Through me shall any joy to thee be known: "
Rather the window, fragrant early and late

With thy sweet, clinging thoughts, that grow and twine
Around me, like some bright and blooming vine:
Through which the sun shall shed his wealth on thee
   In golden showers; through which thou may'st look out
   Exulting in all beauty, without doubt,
Or fear, or shadow of regret from me.
SUSAN MARR SPALDING.

A MOTHER'S PICTURE.

SHE seemed an angel to our infant eyes!
   Once when the glorifying moon revealed
   Her who at evening by our pillow kneeled, —
Soft-voiced and golden-haired, from holy skies
Flown to her loves on wings of Paradise, —
   We looked to see the pinions half concealed.
   The Tuscan vines and olives will not yield
Her back to me who loved her in this wise,

And since have little known her, but have grown
   To see another mother tenderly
Watch over sleeping children of my own.
Perhaps the years have changed her, yet alone
   This picture lingers; still she seems to me
   The fair, young angel of my infancy.
EDMUND CLARENCE STEDMAN.

HOPE DEFERRED.

Bring no more flowers and books and precious things!
   O speak no more of our beloved Art,
Of summer haunts, — melodious wanderings
   In leafy refuge from this weary mart!
   Surely such thoughts were dear unto my heart;
Now every word a newer sadness brings!
   Thus oft some forest-bird, caged far apart
From verdurous freedom, droops his careless wings,

Nor craves for more than food from day to day;
   So long bereft of wild-wood joy and song,
   Hopeless of all he dared to hope so long,
The music born within him dies away;
   Even the song he loved becomes a pain,
   Full-freighted with a yearning all in vain.
                           EDMUND CLARENCE STEDMAN.

TO BAYARD TAYLOR.

(With a Copy of the Iliad.)

Bayard, awaken not this music strong,
   While round thy home the indolent sweet breeze
   Floats lightly as the summer breath of seas
O'er which Ulysses heard the Sirens' song!
Dreams of low-lying isles to June belong,
   And Circe holds us in her haunts of ease;
   But later, when these high ancestral trees
Are sear, and such Odyssean languors wrong

The reddening strength of the autumnal year,
   Yield to heroic words thine ear and eye:
Intent on these broad pages thou shalt hear
   The trumpet's blare, the Argive battle-cry,
And see Achilles hurl his hurtling spear,
   And mark the Trojan arrows make reply.
                           EDMUND CLARENCE STEDMAN.

INDIAN SUMMER.

FAIR, fugitive, and few autumnal days
   That hint of pleasures vanished long ago!
   Beneath the alders leaf-clogged streamlets flow;
Upon the moorland shimmer genial rays.
The distant hills are swathed in dreamy haze;
   Along the meadows faintest zephyrs blow;
   The death-tuned insects chant their dirges low,
For joy again is in the world's wide ways.

I wonder if yet in my life there be,
   Beyond this broad, waste, melancholy scene,
   And rathe October frosts that intervene, —
   Somewhere, ere settles winter chill and gray —
A season thus serene, remembering me
   Of that sweet summer long since passed away.
HENRY JEROME STOCKARD.

DO YOU REMEMBER?

Do you remember me, my glorified,
   Fair dweller in the far-off spirit-land,
   And see the life, so buoyantly we planned
Stretch out before me now so wan and wide?
Have you a care to cross the refluent tide
   Of that strange, unimagined ocean, and
   Teach my poor, longing heart to understand
That which we pondered ere you quit my side?

If you could come just for a little while,
   And should not speak — but only lift your eyes
To mine, and bend upon me the dear smile
   That I have grieved for oh, so long and deep!
And then your home resume — it would suffice! —
   I could more patient be, and silent keep.
HENRY JEROME STOCKARD.

ABRAHAM LINCOLN.

This man whose homely face you look upon,
   Was one of Nature's masterful, great men;
Born with strong arms, that unfought battles won;
   Direct of speech, and cunning with the pen.
Chosen for large designs, he had the art
   Of winning with his humor, and he went
Straight to his mark, which was the human heart;
   Wise, too, for what he could not break he bent.
Upon his back a more than Atlas-load,
   The burden of the Commonwealth, was laid;
He stooped, and rose up to it, though the road
   Shot suddenly downwards, not a whit dismayed.
Hold, warriors, councilors, kings! All now give place
To this dear benefactor of the Race.
                        RICHARD HENRY STODDARD.

TO EDMUND CLARENCE STEDMAN.

(WITH A VOLUME OF SHAKESPEARE'S SONNETS.)

Had we been living in the antique days,
   With him whose young but cunning fingers penned
   These sugared sonnets to his strange-sweet friend,
I dare be sworn we would have won the bays.
Why not? We could have twined in amorous phrase
   Sonnets like these, where love and friendship blend,
   (Or were they writ for some more private end?)
And this, we see, remembered is with praise.

Yes, there's a luck in most things, and in none
   More than in being born at the right time,
It boots not what the labor to be done,
   Or feats of arms, or arts, or building rhyme.
Not that the heavens the little can make great,
But many a man has lived an age too late!
                        RICHARD HENRY STODDARD.

TO BAYARD TAYLOR.

(ON HIS FORTIETH BIRTHDAY.)

"WHOM the gods love die young," we have been told,
   And wise of some the saying seems to be;
   Of others foolish; as it is of thee,
Who proven hast, " Whom the gods love die old."
For have not forty seasons o'er thee rolled,
   The worst propitious, — setting like the sea
   Towards the haven of prosperity,
Now full in sight, so fair the wind doth hold?

Hast thou not fame, the poet's chief desire;
   A wife, whom thou dost love, who loves thee well;
   A child in whom your differing natures blend;
And friends, troops of them, who respect, — admire?
   (How deeply one it suits not now to tell;)
   Such lives are long and have a perfect end.

                RICHARD HENRY STODDARD.

TO THE MEMORY OF KEATS.

(ON COMING INTO POSSESSION OF HIS COPY OF "THE ROGUE:
   OR GUZMAN DE ALFARACHE." LONDON, 1634.)

GREAT Father mine, deceased ere I was born,
   And in a classic land renowned of old;
Thy life was happy, but thy death forlorn,
   Buried in violets and Roman mould.
Thou hast the Laurel, Master of my soul!
   Thy name, thou saidst, was writ in water — No,
For while clouds float on high, and billows roll,
   Thy name shall worshiped be. Will mine be so?
I kiss thy words as I would kiss thy face
   And put thy book most reverently away.
Girt by thy peers, thou hast an honored place,
   Among the kingliest, — Byron, Wordsworth, Gray.
If tears will fill mine eyes, am I to blame?
"O smile away the shades, for this is fame!"

                RICHARD HENRY STODDARD.

TO MARY BRADLEY.

I SHALL behold, I hope I shall behold
  Before the rainfall of to-morrow night,
A woman loved of old who is not old,
  To whom before I was my heart was plight.
My name with hers in Fate's great book enrolled
  Shines, as it ought to, in supernal light,
    Twins, slumbering, smiling, on the arm of might,
The mystery of one being still untold.

I know this woman — no one half so well —
  Your love, as well as mine, diviner powers!
    Whose currents, shifting always, seldom vary;
For she was born beneath a gracious spell,
  Somewhere and somehow in the countless hours
    Before I Richard was or she was Mary!
RICHARD HENRY STODDARD.

LITTLE WE KNOW WHAT SECRET INFLUENCE.

LITTLE we know what secret influence
  A word, a glance, a casual tone may bring,
  That, like the wind's breath on a chorded string,
May thrill the memory, touch the inner sense,
And waken dreams that come we know not whence;
  Or like the light touch of a bird's swift wing,
  The lake's still face a moment visiting,
Leave pulsing rings, when he has vanished thence.

You looked into my eyes an instant's space,
And all the boundaries of time and place
Broke down, and far into a world beyond
  Of buried hopes and dreams my soul had sight,
Where dim desires long lost and memories fond
  Rose in a soft mirage of tender light.
WILLIAM WETMORE STORY.

AFTER LONG DAYS OF DULL PERPETUAL RAIN.

AFTER long days of dull perpetual rain,
   And from gray skies, the sun at last shines bright,
   And all the sparkling trees are glad with light,
And all the happy world laughs out again ;
The sorrow is forgotten, past the pain ;
   For Nature has no memory, feels the blight
   Of no regret, nor mars the day's delight
With idle fears and hopes and longings vain.

Ah me! it is not so with us; the ghost
   Of vanished joys pursues us everywhere;
We live as much in all that we have lost
   As what we own; no present is so fair
That the best moment's sunlight is not crossed
   By shadowy shapes of hope, and fear, and care.

WILLIAM WETMORE STORY.

POETS.

OH, there are gentle souls on earth imbued
   With love of man and nature's loveliness,
Who, like fair trees uprising 'mid a wood,
   Grow toward heaven, the while they ever bless
   With pleasing shade and liberal fruitfulness
The seeker at their feet. Warm gratitude
   Be theirs, and theirs the soft caress
Of gentlest zephyrs ; be their solitude
Made populous with angels, all sublime
   Their history, and when the woodmen come,
Transplanting them to that far sunnier clime
   Where Eden's bays will rustle welcomes home,
   Then may their lives, as some grand epic tome,
Close with a lofty hope, like an immortal rhyme.

JOHN R. TAIT.

NUBIA.

A LAND of Dreams and Sleep, — a poppied land!
   With skies of endless calm above her head,
   The drowsy warmth of summer noonday shed
Upon her hills, and silence stern and grand
Throughout her Desert's temple-burying sand.
   Before her threshold, in their ancient place,
   With closed lips and fixed, majestic face,
Noteless of Time her dumb colossi stand.

O pass them not with light, irreverent tread;
   Respect the dream that builds her fallen throne,
   And soothes her to oblivion of her woes.
Hush! for she does but sleep; she is not dead.
   Action and Toil have made the world their own,
   But she hath built an altar to Repose.
BAYARD TAYLOR.

TO A PERSIAN BOY.
IN THE BAZAAR AT SMYRNA.

THE gorgeous blossoms of that magic tree
   Beneath whose shade I sat a thousand nights,
   Breathed from their opening petals all delights
Embalmed in spice of Orient poesy,
When first, young Persian, I beheld thine eyes,
   And felt the wonder of thy beauty grow
   Within my brain, as some far planet's glow
Deepens and fills the summer evening's skies.

From under thy dark lashes shone on me
The rich voluptuous soul of Eastern land,
   Impassioned, tender, calm, serenely sad, —
Such as immortal Hafiz felt when he
   Sang by the fountain streams of Rocnabad
Or in the bowers of blissful Samarcand.
BAYARD TAYLOR.

A WEDDING SONNET.

(To T. B. A. AND L. W.)

SAD Autumn, drop thy weedy crown forlorn,
  Put off thy cloak of cloud, thy scarf of mist,
  And dress in gauzy gold and amethyst
A day benign, of sunniest influence born,
As may befit a Poet's marriage morn!
  Give buds another dream, another tryst
  To loving hearts, and print on lips unkissed
Betrothal kisses, laughing Spring to scorn!

Yet if unfriendly, thou, with sullen skies,
  Bleak rains, or moaning winds, dost menace wrong,
Here art thou foiled: a bridal sun shalt rise
  And bridal emblems unto these belong.
Round her the sunshine of her beauty lies,
  And breathes round him the springtime of his song.

BAYARD TAYLOR.

FROM THE NORTH.

ONCE more without you! — sighing, dear, once more,
  For all the sweet, accustomed ministries
  Of wife and mother: not as when the seas
That parted us my tender message bore
From the gray olives of the Cretan shore
  To those that hid the broken Phidian frieze
  Of our Athenian home, — but far degrees,
Wide plains, great forests, part us now: my door

Looks on the rushing Neva, cold and clear:
  The swelling domes in hovering splendor lie,
    Like golden bubbles, eager to be gone,
But the chill crystal of the atmosphere
  Withholds them; and along the northern sky
    The amber midnight smiles in dreams of dawn!

BAYARD TAYLOR.

TO E. C. S.

When days were long, and o'er that farm of mine,
  Green Cedarcroft, the summer breezes blew,
  And from the walnut-shadows I and you,
Dear Edmund, saw the red lawn-roses shine,
Or, following our idyllic Brandywine
  Through meadows flecked with many a flowery hue,
  To where with wild Arcadian pomp I drew
Your Bacchic march among the startled kine, —

You gave me, linked with old Mæonides,
  Your loving sonnet, — record dear and true
    Of days as dear; and now, when suns are brief
And Christmas snows are on the naked trees,
  I give you this, — a withered winter leaf,
    Yet with your blossom from one root it grew!

BAYARD TAYLOR.

BEETHOVEN.

If God speaks anywhere, in any voice,
  To us his creatures, surely here and now
  We hear Him, while the great chords seem to bow
Our heads, and all the symphony's breathless noise
Breaks over us, with challenge to our souls!
  Beethoven's music! From the mountain peaks
The strong, divine, compelling thunder rolls;
  And, "Come up higher, come!" the words it speaks,
"Out of your darkened valleys of despair;
  Behold, I lift you upon mighty wings
Into Hope's living, reconciling air!
  Breathe, and forget your life's perpetual stings, —
Dream, folded on the breast of Patience sweet,
Some pulse of pitying love for you may beat!"

CELIA THAXTER.

MOZART.

MOST beautiful among the helpers thou !
  All heaven's fresh air and sunshine at thy voice
Flood with refreshment many a weary brow,
  And sad souls thrill with courage and rejoice,
To hear God's gospel of pure gladness sound
  So sure and clear in this bewildered world,
Till the sick vapors that our sense confound
  By cheerful winds are into nothing whirled.

O matchless melody ! O perfect Art !
  O lovely, lofty voice, unfaltering !
O strong and radiant and divine Mozart,
  Among earth's benefactors crowned a king !
Loved shalt thou be while Time shall yet endure,
Spirit of health; sweet, sound and wise and pure.
CELIA THAXTER.

MODJESKA.

DEFT hands called Chopin's music from the keys.
  Silent she sat, her slender figure's poise
Flower-like and fine and full of lofty ease
  She heard her Poland's most consummate voice
From power to pathos falter, sink and change ;
  The music of her land, the wond'rous, high,
Utmost expression of its genius strange, —
  Incarnate sadness breathed in melody.
Silent and thrilled she sat, her lovely face
  Flushing and paling like a delicate rose
  Shaken by summer winds from its repose
Softly this way and that, with tender grace,
  Now touched by sun, now into shadow turned, —
  While bright with kindred fire her deep eyes burned !
CELIA THAXTER.

THE SOUNDING SEA.

As happy dwellers by the sea-side hear
   In every pause the sea's mysterious sound,
   The infinite murmur, solemn and profound,
Incessant, filling all the atmosphere,
Even so I hear you, for you do surround
   My newly waking life, and break for aye
About the viewless shores, till they resound
   With echoes of God's greatness night and day.

Refreshed and glad I feel the full flood-tide
   Fill every inlet of my waiting soul,
   Long-striving, eager hope, beyond control,
For help and strength at last is satisfied.
   And you exalt me like the sounding sea,
   With ceaseless whispers of eternity.
CELIA THAXTER.

RESPICE FINEM.

OH, not her gentle silent forces most
   Doth Nature use to purify the world;
   But raging hurricanes in tumult hurled,
And blasting winds and tempests are her boast.
With thundering whir of ebon wings, from coast
   To coast they fly, by might resistless whirled,
   Then in their central-calm betimes are furled,
And rest content; for lo ! a new-born host

Of stronger life and fresher bloom arise.
   Thus ever have the greatest eras wrought
The changes that have made our earth so wise.
   Weak, doubting heart, receive the lesson taught:
Beyond each storm of grief a blessing lies,
   Becalmed within the centre of God's thought.
JULIA H. THAYER.

HEART OF GOLD.

WHAT matter, though the world be alien cold,
   Though to the finer senses it but deign
   A cheerless answer, making light of gain
That stirs our swift divining thoughts to hold
Us thrall in some sublimer wish untold?
   What matter, so that music yield its strain
   To thrill, fair love its rapture and its pain,
And the vast future pledge its heart of gold?

Though the deft schemes of men may sink to loss,
   Though withering care may sere the edge of sense,
Though jeweled fortune fade to feathery dross,
   If but these soul-lit joys remain intense,
Freighted with longing, winged with Argos sails,
Deem not that life is barren, Heaven avails!

STEPHEN HENRY THAYER.

GREETING.

I GIVE thee greeting — thou, my wedded heart;
   Through the fair seasons of so many a year
   Thou hast bestowed thy benediction dear
On a more shadowed life than thine; thou art
A sunny clime, a light that dost impart
   Thy radiance with more than blithesome cheer;
   A golden lining, when dark clouds appear, —
To shed thy rays unconscious of the art.

Though all else fail, thy constancy will last;
   The bond that holds us thrall I may not plead,
     'T is tried and true, and needs nor verse or rhyme;
   I gaze into thy face, I hold thee fast,
     I print love's kiss on thy sweet lips and lead
        Thee forth through all the shoals and deeps of time!

STEPHEN HENRY THAYER.

BETROTHED.

Oft have I seen her when her artless art
   Would seem to tell her secret to the eye;
   Or when her breast, o'erburdened with its sigh,
Would press to breathe the language of the heart;
And yet it was her highest joy to part
   From friend, even her dearest kin, and hie
   To solitudes of Eden-thought, and lie
In wait for finer notes of love; then start

Like frightened fawn at fancied sound of voice,
   To seek a covert, where, again alone,
Secure, she 'd dream of him her plighted choice,
   Plead to herself the bliss she dare not own;
At last to end her revery in tears —
Ideals of the long-expectant years!

STEPHEN HENRY THAYER.

THE FOUNTAINS OF THE RAIN.

The merchant clouds that cruise the sultry sky,
   As soon as they have spent their freight of rain,
   Plot how the cooling thrift they may regain:
All night along the river-marsh they lie,
And at their ghostly looms swift shuttles ply,
   To weave them nets wherewith the streams to drain;
   And often in the sea they cast a seine,
And draw it, dripping, past some headland high.

Many a slender naiad, with a sigh,
   Is in their arms uptaken from her plain;
   The trembling myrmidons of dew remain
No longer than the flash of morning's eye,
Then back unto their misty fountains fly:
   This is the source and journey of the rain.

EDITH M. THOMAS.

FROST.

How small a tooth hath mined the season's heart;
   How cold a touch hath set the wood on fire,
   Until it blazes like a costly pyre
Built for some Ganges emperor, old and swart,
Soul-sped on clouds of incense! Whose the art
   That webs the streams, each morn, with silver wire,
   Delicate as the tension of a lyre?
Whose falchion pries the chestnut-bur apart?

It is the Frost; a rude and Gothic sprite,
   Who doth unbuild the summer's palaced wealth,
And puts her dear loves all to sword or flight;
Yet in the hushed, unmindful winter's night,
   The spoiler builds again with jealous stealth,
And sets a mimic garden, cold and bright.

EDITH M. THOMAS.

A SONNET ON THE SONNET.

GRANT me twice seven splendid words, O Muse,
   (Like jewel pauses on a rosary chain,
   To tell us where the *aves* start again);
Of these, in each verse, one I mean to use —
Like Theseus in the labyrinth — for clues
   To help lost Fancy striving in the brain;
   And, Muse, if thou will still so kindly deign,
Make my rhymes move by courtly twos and twos!

Oh, pardon, shades of Avon and Vaucluse,
   This rush-light burning where your lamps yet shine;
A sonnet should be like the cygnet's cruise
   On polished waters; or like smooth old wine,
Or earliest honey, garnered in May dews —
   And all be laid before some fair love's shrine!

EDITH M. THOMAS.

A REVENGE.

Lo! I will hate my enemy, yet breathe
  No curse to bring the lightning on his head,
  Or break the earth in pitfalls; I will tread
Anear his sleep and keep my wrong in sheath;
So David bent o'er Saul, couched on the heath
  In woody Ziph, and there he might have sped
  The dreaming soul to greet the unjust dead,
But left him to that fate he stooped beneath.

O Heaven, there is but one revenge full sweet —
  That thou shouldst slay him in my memory,
  Whose bitter words and ways abide with me;
Then, for all surety that we shall not meet
In the overworld, make thou my spirit's feet
  Move trackless through the blessed nebulæ!

EDITH M. THOMAS.

THE RETURN TO NATURE.

OH, Nature, take me home, and henceforth keep!
  Laugh out at me with all thy mirthful streams,
  To break the tenor of dull-hearted dreams;
From ambush in a waving thicket leap,
And startle with a song as past I creep;
  Or speed me by invisible wild — teams
  That drive through forests and rough mountain-seams,
And furrow dark the forehead of the deep.

Nay, do thou more for me, great griefless friend!
  Hurt to the core, without the gift to weep,
Back from man's world to thine I groping tend;
  Now let thy clods unkindled smoothly sweep
This cooling clod — my heart; then do thou bend,
  Uplift, and in bright calm my spirit steep.

EDITH M. THOMAS.

APHRODITE.

AND thou whose tresses like straw-colored gold,
   Above the scarlet gladiole float and shine, —
   Whose comely breasts, whose shoulders fair and fine,
Whose fathomless eyes and limbs of heavenly mould,
Thrill me with pains and pleasures manifold,
   Racy of earth, yet full of fire divine, —
   Art thou unclean as that old Paphian dream?
I know thou art not; for thou camest to me

Out of the white foam-lilies of the sea,
   Out of the salt-clear fountain's clearest stream
The embodiment of purest purity,
   As healthful as the sun's directest beam,
So life giving that up beneath thy feet,
Wherever thou goest, the grass-flowers bubble sweet!
MAURICE THOMPSON.

EROS.

A NAKED baby Love among the roses,
   Watching with laughing gray-green eyes for me,
   Who says that thou art blind? Who hides from thee?
Who is it in his foolishness supposes
That ever a bandage round thy sweet face closes
   Thicker than gauze? I know that thou canst see!
   Thy glances are more swift and far more sure
To reach their goal than any missile is,

Except that one which never yet did miss,
   Whose slightest puncture not even Death can cure,
Whose stroke divides the heart with such a bliss
   As even the strongest trembles to endure, —
Thine arrow that makes glad the saddest weather
With the keen rustle of its purple feather!
MAURICE THOMPSON.

THE DEAD POET.[1]

Is this the only tribute we should pay —
    These funeral flowers that on his bier belong?
    Himself a singer, he deserves a song;
But who has any heart to sing to-day?
Should any stranger chance to come this way,
    And view with tearless eyes this lump of earth,
    And call for witness to its living worth,
Our grief would choke the words that we would say!

Let us be silent — like our silent dead;
    Whose virtues — Truth, Faith, Honor, and the rest, —
With one loud-chanted requiem all have said:
    "Behold our chosen dwelling was his breast!"
Since tongues like these have spoken, dumb be ours:
So let us sweetly leave him with his flowers.

THEODORE TILTON.

IF LIFE WERE ALL LOVE.

"MOST men know love but as a part of life:
    They hide it in some corner of the breast,
    Even from themselves; and only when they rest, —
In the brief pauses of that daily strife
Wherewith the world might else be not so rife, —
    They draw it forth (as one draws forth a toy
    To soothe some ardent, kiss-exacting boy),
And hold it up to sister, child, or wife.

Ah me! why may not love and life be one!
    Why walk we thus alone, when by our side
    Love, like a visible God, might be our guide?
    How would the marts grow noble, and the street,
    Worn now like dungeon-floors by weary feet,
Seem like a golden court-way of the sun!"

HENRY TIMROD.

---

[1] Occasioned by the funeral of W. H. Burleigh.

ELUSIVE NATURE.

AT last, beloved Nature, I have met
   Thee face to face upon thy breezy hills,
And boldly, where thy inmost bowers were set,
   Gazed on thee naked in thy mountain rills:
When first I felt thy breath upon my brow,
   Tears of strange ecstasy gushed out like rain,
   And with a longing, passionate as vain,
I strove to clasp thee. But I know not how,
Always before me didst thou seem to glide,
And often from one sunny mountain-side
   Upon the next bright peak I saw thee kneel,
And heard thy voice upon the billowy blast, —
   But climbing, only reached that shrine to feel
The shadow of a Presence which had passed.

HENRY TIMROD.

TO ELLEN TERRY AS "BEATRICE."

"But then, that night, there was a star danced, and under it I was born." — Much Ado About Nothing, Act I, Scene Second.

WHICH was it of the whirling orbs of might
   That danced, sweet Ellen, on thy natal eve?
   What radiant planet may we now believe
In its celestial place did so rejoice —
Moved to the dulcet music of thy voice —
   And well content its fellows fair to leave
   That it thy special favor might receive
And guide thee through this mazy world aright?
Was it not Venus, handmaid of the Night,
   That lit so fair a Beatrice to this sphere?
   A Beatrice who to us has grown as dear
As e'er she was to Benedict — poor wight, —
Whose mirth, whose grace, whose beauty, like the light
   Of evening's star, shines kindlier year by year!

JAMES B. TOWNSEND.

PROVIDENCE.

WEARY with pondering many a weighty theme,
   I slept; and in the realm of vision saw
   A mighty Angel reverently updraw
The cords of earth all woven of gloom and gleam,
Wiles, woes, and many a silver-threaded stream
   Of sighs and prayers and golden bands of law,
   And ties of faith and love with many a flaw
Riven, but reunited in my dream.

These the great Angel, gathering, lifted high,
   Like mingled lines of rain and radiance, all
   In one bright, awful braid divinely blended,
That reached the beams of heaven, — a chain whereby
   This dimly-glorious, shadow-brooding ball
   And home of man hung wondrously suspended.
JOHN TOWNSEND TROWBRIDGE.

LOVE SONNET.

O FOR a castle on a woodland height!
   High mountains round, and a pure stream below,
Within, all charms that tasteful hours invite,
   Wise books of poesy and music's flow; —
A grassy lawn through which to course our steeds,
   A gothic chapel in seclusion reared,
Where we could solace find for holiest needs,
   And grow by mutual rites the more endeared:
How such captivity alone with thee
   Would lift to Paradise each passing day!
Then all revealed my patient love would be,
   And thou couldst not a full response delay;
For Truth makes holy Love's illusive dreams,
And their best promise constantly redeems.
HENRY THEODORE TUCKERMAN.

TO ONE DECEIVED.

ALL hearts are not disloyal; let thy trust
    Be deep and clear and all-confiding still;
For though Love's fruit turn on the lips to dust,
    She ne'er betrays her child to lasting ill:
Through leagues of desert must the pilgrim go
    Ere on his gaze the holy turrets rise;
Through the long sultry day the stream must flow
    Ere it can mirror twilight's purple skies.
Fall back unscathed from contact with the vain,
    Keep thy robes white, thy spirit bold and free,
And calmly launch affection's bark again,
    Hopeful of golden spoils reserved for thee.
Though lone the way as that already trod,
Cling to thine own integrity and God!
                HENRY THEODORE TUCKERMAN.

TO A DEBUTANTE.

THE music dwells upon its dying chord,
    And thou dost linger trembling at thy start
    Across the charmèd borderlands of Art.
The footlights' arc is like a flaming sword,
To frighten yet defend thee. Every word
    Has meaning more than lies within thy part —
    Thrilled with the pathos of a fainting heart,
And asking sympathy that none afford.

But wait! and when the fostering years shall bring
    Perfection to those fairest gifts of thine,
Its tributes at thy feet a world shall fling,
    And call thy calm precision fire divine.
All other hearts' emotions thou shalt waken,
While thine amidst the tempest rests unshaken.
                HENRY TYRRELL.

IDYLLS.

Creusa, in those idyll lands delaying,
   Forever hung with mellow mists of gold,
   We find but phantoms of delights long cold.
We listen to the pine and ilex swaying
Only in echo; to the players playing,
   On faint, sweet flutes, lost melodies of old.
   The beauteous heroes are but stories told;
Vain at the antique altars all our praying.

Oh, might we join, in vales unknown to story,
   On shores unsung, by Western seas sublime,
The spirit of that loveliness and glory
   Hellenic, with these hearts of fuller time,
Then to our days would sunnier joys belong
Than thrill us now in old idyllic song.

HENRY TYRRELL.

ENOCH.

I looked to find a man who walked with God,
   Like the translated patriarch of old; —
Though gladdened millions on his footstool trod,
   Yet none with Him did such sweet converse hold.
I heard the wind in low complaint go by
   That none its melodies like him could hear; —
Day unto day spoke wisdom from on high,
   Yet none like David turned a willing ear:

God walked alone, unhonored, through the earth.
   For Him no heart-built temple open stood;
The soul, forgetful of her nobler birth,
   Had hewn Him lofty shrines of stone and wood,
And left unfinished, and in ruins still,
The only Temple he delights to fill.

JONES VERY.

THY BEAUTY FADES.

Thy beauty fades, and with it too my love,
   For 't was the selfsame stalk that bore its flower;
Soft fell the rain, and breaking from above
   The sun looked out upon our nuptial hour;
And I had thought forever by thy side
   With bursting buds of hope in youth to dwell;
But one by one Time strewed thy petals wide,
   And every hope's wan look a grief can tell:

For I had thoughtless lived beneath his sway,
   Who like a tyrant dealeth with us all,
Crowning each rose, though rooted on decay,
   With charms that shall the spirit's love enthrall,
And for a season turn the soul's pure eyes
From virtue's changeless bloom, that time and death defies.

JONES VERY.

LABOR AND REST.

Thou needst not rest: the shining spheres are thine
   That roll perpetual on their silent way,
And thou dost breathe in me a voice divine,
   That tells more sure of thine eternal sway;
Thine the first starting of the early leaf,
   The gathering green, the changing autumn hue;
To thee the world's long years are but as brief
   As the fresh tints that Spring will soon renew.

Thou needest not man's little life of years,
   Save that he gather wisdom from them all;
That in thy fear he lose all other fears,
   And in thy calling heed no other call.
Then shall he be thy child to know thy care,
And in thy glorious Self the eternal Sabbath share.

JONES VERY.

THE FROST.

The frost is out, and in the open fields,
    And late within the woods, I marked his track;
The unwary flower his icy fingers feels,
    And at their touch the crispèd leaf rolls back; —
Look, how the maple o'er a sea of green
    Waves in the autumnal wind his flag of red!
First struck of all the forest's spreading screen,
    Most beauteous, too, the earliest of her dead.

Go on: thy task is kindly meant by Him
    Whose is each flower and richly covered bough;
And though the leaves hang dead on every limb,
    Still will I praise his love, that early now
Has sent before this herald of decay
To bid me heed the approach of Winter's sterner day.

                                                            Jones Very.

THE INVITATION.

Stay where thou art, thou needst not farther go,
    The flower with me is pleading at thy feet;
The clouds, the silken clouds, above me flow,
    And fresh the breezes come thy cheek to greet.
Why hasten on — hast thou a fairer home?
    Has God more richly blest the world than here
That thou in haste wouldst from thy country roam,
    Favored by every month that fills the year?

Sweet showers shall on thee here, as there, descend;
    The sun salute thy morn and gild thy eve:
Come, tarry here, for Nature is thy friend,
    And we an arbor for ourselves will weave;
And many a pilgrim, journeying on as thou,
    Will grateful bless its shade and list the wind-struck bough.

                                                            Jones Very.

LOVE'S GOLD.

Some are there spending greedy lives of toil
   To store up gains in some deep-hidden place,
   Where, profitless to them and to their race,
They let the bright gold dull, the jewel soil
Its beauty, making useless all their spoil.
   No tears shall rain upon the upturned face
   Of such dead miser, nor shall human grace
Pour Poet's praise or woman's love like oil.

Yet thou, who hidest in thy heart the gold
   Of love — a worse than miser thou! Oh, spend
Affection's coin! Let not the rust and mould
   Feed on it; let its glorious lustre lend
A glow to earth, blending it with the sky;
It buys life's bread, let no one starve and die!

HENRY C. WALSH.

LOVE AGAINST LOVE.

As unto blowing roses summer dews,
   Or morning's amber to the tree-top choirs,
So to my bosom are the beams that use
   To rain on me from eyes that love inspires.
Your love, vouchsafe it, royal-hearted few,
   And I will set no common price thereon;
Oh! I will keep as heaven its holy blue,
   Or night her diamonds, that dear treasure won.

But aught of inward faith must I forego,
   Or miss one drop from Truth's baptismal hand,
Think poorer thoughts, pray cheaper prayers, and grow
   Less worthy trust, to meet your hearts' demand?
Farewell! your wish I for your sake deny;
Rebel to love in truth to love am I.

DAVID ATWOOD WASSON.

ROYALTY.

That regal soul I reverence in whose eyes
    Suffices not all wealth the city knows
    To pay that debt which his own heart he owes;
For less than level to his bosom rise
The low crowd's heaven and stars; above their skies
    Runneth the road his daily feet have pressed,
    A loftier heaven he beareth in his breast,
And o'er the summits of achieving hies

With never a thought of merit or of meed;
    Choosing divinest labors through a pride
Of soul, that holdeth appetite to feed
    Ever on angel-herbage, nought beside;
Nor praises more himself for hero-deed
    Than stones for weight, or open seas for tide.
DAVID ATWOOD WASSON.

DEFIANCE.

Time's wonted ravage shall not touch my love.
    His wrath I challenge, his assault defy.
Rust gathered never on the blue above,
    Nor blearing film upon day's golden eye;
Earth and the heavens have gems that are eterne,
    The ruby whitens not with bleach of years;
Ever Orion and his brothers burn,
    Nor even despair itself their fading fears.

Oh! would he say, who did all truth discern,
    That you, then, stars of my heart's heaven, may die?
Or can that heart its secret quite unlearn,
    Nor be illumined when your light is nigh?
Though Time o'ercame the skies, their azure staining,
Time's lord were Love, immortal and unwaning.
DAVID ATWOOD WASSON.

"LAST NIGHT IN BLUE MY LITTLE LOVE WAS DRESSED."

LAST night in blue my little love was dressed;
   And as she walked the room in maiden grace
   I looked into her fair and smiling face,
And said that blue became my darling best.
But when this morn, a spotless, virgin vest
   And robe of white did the blue one displace,
   She seemed a pearl-tinged cloud, and I was — space!
She filled my soul as cloud-shapes fill the West.

And so it is that, changing day by day, —
   Changing her robe but not her loveliness, —
Whether the gown be blue, or white, or gray,
   I deem that one her most becoming dress,
The truth is this: In any robe or way
   I love her just the same and cannot love her less!
              CHARLES HENRY WEBB ("*John Paul*").

BY THE BROOK.

HERE were the place to lie alone all day,
   On shadowed grass beneath the sunlit trees,
   With leaves forever trembling in the breeze,
While close beside, the brook keeps up alway
The old love-murmur, wooing me to stay
   And hear the dreamy music all at ease.
The old love-murmur; such she heard, I deem,
   White Arethusa in her maiden grace,
   When, naked after the fatiguing chase,
She bathed alone in Alpheus' shady stream,
   And throwing back the wet hair from her face,
Listening a moment, half entranced did seem;
   Then frightened, from the rising God's embrace
Fled glistening, like the spirit of a dream.
              ROBERT KELLEY WEEKS.

IN THE MEADOW.

IDLE, and all in love with idleness;
    Caught in the net-work that my oak-tree weaves
    Of light and shadow with his thrilling leaves,
And charmed to hear his murmured songs no less,
On the shorn grass I lie, and let the excess
    Of summer life seem only summer play;
    Even to the farmers working far away,
Where one man lifts and strenuously heaves
A bristly haycock up to him who stands
    Unsteadily upon the swaying load,
Which, while the shuffling oxen slowly pass,
    Touched into wakefulness by voice and goad,
He shapes and smooths, and turning in his hands,
The long fork glistens like a rod of glass.

ROBERT KELLEY WEEKS.

WITH A COPY OF SHAKESPEARE.

THIS is the deep profound that imports man;
    His shoals, his rapids, all are chartered here;
    There is no joy of voyage and no fear
That is not bodied in this mighty plan.
He knew where the sweet springs of love began,
    And whence the fires of hate and horror peer,
    What wakens merriment, and how appear
The raging passions that bewitch and ban.

Herein behold how nobly souls may mount,
    How basely fall; and see as well how sweet
        The common rill of human life may run.
It is at once the ocean and the fount;
    The compass of our triumph and defeat;
        The heart of earth, the splendor of the sun.

CHARLES GOODRICH WHITING.

BAYARD TAYLOR.

I.

FOR us he wandered through strange lands and old ;
   We saw the world through him. The Arab's tent
   To him its story-telling secret lent,
And, pleased, we listened to the tales he told.
His task, beguiled with songs that shall endure,
   In manly, honest thoroughness he wrought ;
   From humble home-lays to the heights of thought
Slowly he climbed, but every step was sure.

How, with the generous pride that friendship hath,
   We, who so loved him, saw at last the crown
   Of civic honor on his brows pressed down,
Rejoiced, and knew not that the gift was death.
   And now for him, whose praise in deafened ears
   Two nations speak, we answer but with tears !
                     JOHN GREENLEAF WHITTIER.

II.

O VALE of Chester ! trod by him so oft,
   Green as thy June turf keep his memory. Let
   Nor wood, nor dell, nor storied stream forget,
Nor winds that blow round lonely Cedarcroft ;
Let the home voices greet him in the far,
   Strange land that holds him ; let the messages
   Of love pursue him o'er the chartless seas
And unmapped vastness of his unknown star !
Love's language, heard beyond the loud discourse
   Of perishable fame, in every sphere
   Itself interprets ; and its utterance here
Somewhere in God's unfolding universe
   Shall reach our traveler, softening the surprise
   Of his rapt gaze on unfamiliar skies !
                     JOHN GREENLEAF WHITTIER.

FORGIVENESS.

My heart was heavy, for its trust had been
    Abused, its kindness answered with foul wrong.
So, turning gloomily from my fellow-men,
    One summer Sabbath-day I strolled among
The green mounds of the village burial-place;
    Where, pondering how all human love and hate
    Find one sad level; and how, soon or late,
Wronged and wrong-doer, each with meekened face,
    And cold hands folded over a still heart,
Pass the green threshold of our common grave
    Whither all footsteps tend, whence none depart,
Awed for myself, and pitying my race,
    Our common sorrow like a mighty wave,
      Swept all my pride away, and trembling I forgave!
                JOHN GREENLEAF WHITTIER.

ADJUSTMENT.

I.

The tree of Faith, its bare, dry boughs must shed
    That nearer Heaven the living one may climb;
    The false must fail, though from our shores of time
The old lament be heard — "Great Pan is dead!"
That wail is Error's from his high place hurled,
    This sharp recoil is Evil undertrod,
    Our time's unrest, an angel sent of God
Troubling with life the waters of the world.

Even as they list the winds of the Spirit blow
    To turn or break our century-rusted vanes;
    Sands shift and waste, the rock alone remains
Where led of Heaven the strong tides come and go,
    And storm-clouds rent by thunderbolt and wind
    Leave, free of mist, the permanent stars behind.
                JOHN GREENLEAF WHITTIER.

II.

THEREFORE I trust, although to outward sense
   Both true and false seem threatened: I will hold
   With newer light my reverence for the old,
And calmly wait the births of Providence.
No gain is lost: the clear-eyed saints look down
   Untroubled on the wreck of schemes and creeds;
   Love yet remains, its rosary of good deeds
Counting in task-field and o'er peopled town.

Truth has charm'd life; the Inward Word survives,
   And day by day, its revelation brings;
   Faith, hope, and charity, whatsoever things,
Which cannot be shaken, stand. Still holy lives
   Reveal the Christ of whom the letter told,
   And the new Gospel verifies the old.
                    JOHN GREENLEAF WHITTIER.

FRIENDSHIP AFTER LOVE.

AFTER the fierce midsummer, all ablaze,
   Has burned itself to ashes, and expires
   In the intensity of its own fires,
There come the mellow, mild, St. Martin days,
Crowned with the calm of peace, but sad with haze.
   So, after Love has led us till he tires
   Of his own throes and torments and desires,
Comes large-eyed Friendship: with a restful gaze

He beckons us to follow; and across
   Cool, verdant vales we wander free from care.
   Is it a touch of frost within the air?
Why are we haunted with a sense of loss?
   We do not wish the pain back or the heat;
   And yet, and yet — these days are incomplete.
                    ELLA WHEELER WILCOX.

THE SADDEST HOUR.

The saddest hour of anguish and of loss
  Is not that season of supreme despair
  When we can find no least light anywhere
To gild the dread black shadow of the Cross;
Not in that luxury of sorrow when
  We sup on salt of tears, and drink the gall
  Of memories of days beyond recall —
Of lost delights that cannot come again;

But when with eyes that are no longer wet
  We look out on the great, wide world of men,
    And, smiling, lean toward a bright to-morrow,
Then backward shrink, with sudden keen regret,
  To find that we are learning to forget:
    Ah! then we face the saddest hour of sorrow.
Ella Wheeler Wilcox.

TO THE MOCKING-BIRD.

Winged mimic of the woods! thou motley fool!
  Who shall thy gay buffoonery describe?
Thine ever-ready notes of ridicule
  Pursue thy fellows still with jest and gibe:
  Wit, sophist, songster, Yorick of thy tribe,
Thou sportive satirist of Nature's school;
  To thee the palm of scoffing we ascribe,
Arch-mocker and mad Abbot of Misrule!
  For such thou art by day, — but all night long
Thou pour'st a soft, sweet, pensive, solemn strain,
  As if thou didst in this thy moonlight song
Like to the melancholy Jacques complain,
  Musing on falsehood, folly, vice, and wrong,
And sighing for thy motley coat again.
Richard Henry Wilde.

MY OPEN POLAR SEA.

I.

As those who sail in quest of quiet seas,
   Supposed to sleep about the sleeping pole,
   Eternal halcyon waves, the term and goal
Of hazard, and of hope, and hope's unease,
Deep bays, bright islands, happy haunts — as these
   Whatever chances breasting, armed in soul
   To do or suffer, so to know the whole —
Steer toward the Arctic, up the steep degrees;

Nor daunted, though a frozen continent
   Thwart them with sheer obstruction, coast along,
And seek to find somewhere the straitening rent
   That yields them grudging entrance, right or wrong;
And still they strive, on their high aim intent,
   And strive the more, the more the perils throng:

II.

So sails my soul for that pacific sea,
   The pole and vertex of her different sphere,
   Where equatorial sway and swift career
Are charmed and changed to fast tranquillity:
Beyond where storms can beat she there shall be,
   Safe locked in blissful calms through all her year;
   Unquiet hope, no more unquiet fear,
Can vex her perfect peace and fair degree:

   But she must tend her sail, and smite her oar,
And take meanwhile the buffet of the tide;
   Nor, when she hears the rending icebergs roar
Upon her, tremble, but, abashed, abide
   To enter that strait gate and dreadful door —
This portal passed, lo, havens free and wide!

                        WILLIAM C. WILKINSON.

DECORATION DAY.

Let fall the roses gently. It may be
  That in the sunlight of some fairer clime
  They shall rebloom to beauty as sublime
As this departed flower of chivalry;
And ever as the sobbing of the sea,
  Breeze-rippled, breaks to chants of lordlier rhyme,
  Silence your dirges, and, in martial time,
Let loud-lipped trumpets blazon victory!

Yield not to grief the tribute of a tear,
  But 'neath the forefront of a spacious sky
Smile all exultant, as they smiled at fear,
  Who dared to do where doing meant to die.
So best may comrades prove remembrance dear;
  So best be hallowed earth where soldiers lie.

FRANCIS HOWARD WILLIAMS.

AN EARLY APRIL MORNING.

Across thy sky the rifted clouds pursue
  Rare shapes enwrought to wonders manifold,
  And robins glance obliquely to behold
The cawing caravans that speck the blue;
Thy jewels are half a frost and half a dew,
  And o'er the earthy stretches of the wold
  A warm caress, from fingers still a-cold,
Falls like an old song in a cadence new.

Dear morning! with thy maid's hair unconfined
  By virgin fillets of a later spring,
Risen as from a rounded dream to find
  The world a-riot for a bourgeoning,
Thy eyes spill sleep and sunlight, while the wind
  Beats blood to blushes with his gusty wing.

FRANCIS HOWARD WILLIAMS.

EARTH AND NIGHT.

(Paraphrase of Walt Whitman.)

I walk beneath the tender, growing night,
   Where darkness makes a mystery of the sea,
   Chanting beatitudes, as one made free
And soaring skyward in ecstatic flight.
Upon my lips the south wind breathes delight,
   And through the slumbering trees pours melody;
   Press close, bare-bosomed joy, for I am he
With eyes anointed to diviner sight.

Still, nodding Night! that for my solace keepest
   A beauty which no touch of tempest mars;
Sad Earth! that for departed sunset weepest,
   I read a stern evangel in thy scars.
I am the lover in whose heart thou sleepest,
   O Night! that hast the largess of the stars.

Francis Howard Williams

EVENING GLOW.

Storm had been on the hills: the day had worn
   As if a sleep upon the hours had crept;
And the dark clouds that gathered at the morn
   In dull impenetrable masses slept,
And the wet leaves hung droopingly, and all
Was like the mournful aspect of a pall.
   Suddenly, on the horizon's edge, a blue
And delicate line, as of a pencil, lay,
   And, as it wider and intenser grew,
The darkness removed silently away;
   And, with the splendor of a god, broke through
The perfect glory of departing day:
   So, when his stormy pilgrimage is o'er,
Will light upon the dying Christian pour.

Nathaniel P. Willis.

ACROSTIC SONNET.

(To Emily Marshall.)

Elegance floats about thee like a dress,
    Melting the airy motion of thy form
Into one swaying grace; and loveliness,
    Like a rich tint that makes a picture warm,
Is lurking in the chestnut of thy tress,
    Enriching it, as moonlight after storm
Mingles dark shadows into gentleness.
    A beauty that bewilders like a spell
Reigns in thy eye's clear hazel, and thy brow,
    So pure in veined transparency, doth tell
How spiritually beautiful art thou, —
    A temple where angelic love might dwell.
Life in thy presence were a thing to keep,
Like a gay dreamer clinging to his sleep.

Nathaniel P. Willis.

SUNRISE.

Flame-hearted lover of the Earth — great Sun!
    Rise from thy purple couch; stretch forth thine arms
    Through morning's parted curtains; let the charms
Of waiting love — which it were death to shun —
Persuade thy clasp. Now hath the Earth begun
    To loose her robes of mist; with mock alarms
    She yields her beauty, which love's longing warms,
Forestalling the embrace thy kiss hath won.

Arise, great god of light and life, arise,
    Enfold the fond Earth in the deathless glowing
Of thy fierce love; bend from the shimmering skies
    Which burn before thee in thine onward going.
    No cheer have we and not of thy bestowing:
Thou art the joy of all hope-lifted eyes.

Robert Burns Wilson.

AT GIBRALTAR.

I.

ENGLAND, I stand on thy imperial ground,
   Not all a stranger; as thy bugles blow,
   I feel within my blood old battles flow, —
The blood whose ancient founts in thee are found.
Still surging dark against the Christian bound
   Wide Islam presses; well its peoples know
   Thy heights that watch them wandering below;
I think how Lucknow heard their gathering sound.

I turn and meet the cruel turbaned face;
   England, 't is sweet to be so much thy son!
I feel the conqueror in my blood and race;
   Last night Trafalgar awed me, and to-day
Gibraltar wakened; hark, thy evening gun
   Startles the desert over Africa!

GEORGE E. WOODBERRY.

II.

THOU art the rock of empire, set mid-seas
   Between the East and West, that God has built;
   Advance thy Roman borders where thou wilt,
While run thy armies true with his decrees.
Law, justice, liberty, — great gifts are these;
   Watch that they spread where English blood is spilt,
   Lest, mixt and sullied with his country's guilt,
The soldier's life-stream flow and Heaven displease.

Two swords there are: one naked, apt to smite,
   Thy blade of war; and, battle-storied, one
Rejoices in the sheath and hides from light.
   American I am; would wars were done!
Now westward look, my country bids Good Night, —
   Peace to the world from ports without a gun!

GEORGE E. WOODBERRY.

APPENDIX.

The following poems are often quoted as sonnets, and are indeed of that nature, yet they contain such marked irregularities of form that it may be best to allot to them a separate position from those in the body of the work. That they are of unusual interest is a sufficient reason for including them. Mr. Webster's touching poem is merely a succession of seven couplets.

THE MEMORY OF THE HEART.

If stores of dry and learned love we gain
We keep them in the memory of the brain;
Names, things and facts — whate'er we knowledge call,
There is the common ledger for them all;
And images on this cold surface traced
Make slight impressions and are soon effaced.
But we've a page more glowing and more bright
On which our friendship and our love to write;
That these may never from the soul depart,
We trust them to *the memory of the heart.*
There is no dimming — no effacement here;
Each new pulsation keeps the record clear;
Warm, golden letters all the tablet fill,
Nor lose their lustre till the heart stands still.

DANIEL WEBSTER.

LONDON, *November* 19, 1839.

Possibly the following stanza from a poem by Benjamin F. Taylor is nearer to a sonnet than the above.

THE GOSPEL OF THE OAK.

Up to the Sun, magnificently near,
  The Lord did build a California oak,

And took no sabbath in the thousandth year,
  But builded on until it bravely broke
Into that realm wherein the morning light
Walks to and fro upon the top of night!
  Around that splendid shaft no hammers rang,
  Nor giants wrought nor truant angels sang,

But gentle winds and painted birds did bear
Its corner-stones of glory through the air;
  Grand volumes green rolled up like cloudy weather,
  And birds and stars went in and out together;
When Day on errands from the Lord came down,
It stepped from Heaven to that leafy crown!
BENJAMIN F. TAYLOR.

Even Petrarca made a few exceptions and allowed a seldom sonnet to overflow into two extra lines. But at this day it seems best to give a separate post of honor to Mr. Dana's poem, which is, in spirit, a fine sonnet.

VIA SACRA.

SLOWLY along the crowded street I go,
  Marking with reverent look each passer's face;
  Seeking, and not in vain, in each to trace
That primal soul of which he is the show.
For here still move, by many eyes unseen,
  The blessed gods that erst Olympus kept;
Through every guise these lofty forms serene
  Declare the all-holding life hath never slept,
But know each thrill that in man's heart hath been
  And every tear that his sad eyes have wept.

Alas for us! the heavenly visitants, —
  We greet them still as most unwelcome guests —
Answering their smile with hateful looks askance,
  Their sacred speech with foolish, bitter jests;
But oh! what is it to imperial Jove
That this poor world refuses all his love!
CHARLES A. DANA.

Still another sonnet is inserted here for its personal interest; its form being irregular but its sentiments admirable for kindliness and modesty. It is by the late president of Yale College.

PROEM.

(To a Book of Poems, privately printed.)

As one who, strolling on some autumn day
   Through woods with summer's life no longer crowned,
Gathers the treasures fallen from many a spray,
   And shows his friends the choicest he has found;
So, little book, do I, in life's decay,
   And seeing close at hand its wintry bound,
Bid thee, with silent footsteps, go around
To those that know me best, and whispering say:

"These leaves long pressed within the book of years,
   From which the colors may not quite have fled,
Seek private audience from kindly ears,
   To tell what thoughts my summer hours once fed,
Receive them with mild silence; scorn them not;
Let him that sends them be not quite forgot."

                        THEODORE DWIGHT WOOLSEY.

These two sonnets by "Susan Coolidge," an author who is also represented in the body of the work, have one extra line each. No line seems to be without value in them, so they are given as they are, both being poems of obvious charm and power.

"LOVE ME FOR WHAT I AM."

LOVE me for what I am, Love; not for sake
   Of some imagined thing that I might be,
   Some brightness or some goodness not in me,
Born of your hope, as dawn to those who wake
Imagined morns before the morning break.
   If I, to please you, whom I fain would please,
   Reset myself like new key to old tune,
Chained thought, remodelled action, very soon
   My hand would slip from yours, and by degrees

The loving, faulty friend you hold to-day
   Would vanish and a stranger take her place, —
   A stranger with a stranger's scrutinies,
   A new regard, an unfamiliar face;
Love me for what I am, then, if you may;
But, if you cannot, — love me either way!

READJUSTMENT.

AFTER the earthquake shock or lightning dart
  Comes a recoil of silence o'er the lands,
  And then, with pulses hot and quivering hands,
Earth calls up courage to her mighty heart,
Plies every tender, compensating art,
Draws her green, flowery veil above the scar,
  Fills the shrunk hollow, smooths the riven plain,
  And with a century's tendance heals again,
The seams and gashes which her fairness mar

So we, when sudden woe like lightning sped
  Finds us and smites us in our guarded place,
  After one brief, bewildered moment's space,
By the same heavenly instinct taught and led,
  Adjust our lives to loss, make friends with pain,
  Bind all our shattered hopes and bid them bloom again.

NOTES.

ABBEY, HENRY. Born in Rondout, N. Y., 1842, he has had considerable experience in journalistic work, and is now a prosperous grain-dealer. He is a member of the Authors' Club of New York, also of the New York Produce Exchange. One of his volumes was reprinted in London. He is his own publisher. (Kingston, N. Y.)

ADAMS, OSCAR FAY. The author of *Postlaureate Idylls, Through the Year with the Poets*, etc., is a native of Worcester, Mass. He resides in Cambridge, and does general literary work. (D. Lothrop & Co.)

ALBEE, JOHN. Born in 1833, he now resides in New Castle, N. H. He has published few sonnets in his book. The first of those selected will remind one, by its wide horizon, of the natural effect in Keats's sonnet on Chapman's Homer. *Poems*. (G. P. Putnam's Sons.)

ALCOTT, AMOS BRONSON (1798–1887). The son of a farmer in Wolcott, Conn., he pursued his calling as a schoolmaster, traveled through the South, taught children's schools in Boston, and reached the culmination of his pedagogic career in the Concord Summer School of Philosophy. He is most widely known as the intimate friend and neighbor of Emerson, and as the father of Louisa M. Alcott, author of *Little Women*. *Sonnets and Canzonets*. (Roberts Bros.)

ALDEN, HENRY MILLS. The present editor of *Harper's Magazine* was born in Mt. Tabor, Vt., in 1836. He is a graduate of Williams and Andover, and is the author of the "Western Campaigns," in *Harper's History of the Civil War*. He is accredited with the authorship of *God in his World*. The one quoted is Mr. Alden's only sonnet. It appeared in *Harper's Magazine*.

ALDRICH, THOMAS BAILEY. Born in 1836, he passed much of his boyhood in Portsmouth, N. H., the scene of his *Story of a Bad Boy*. He has long been identified with the literary life of Boston. For twenty-five years his name has been familiar to the public as the author of stories, sketches, and poems, such as *Mar-*

jorie Daw, *Prudence Palfrey*, *Baby Bell*, etc. He was chosen as the successor of Mr. Howells in the editorial chair of the *Atlantic Monthly*, but resigned his position in 1890. He has given considerable attention to the sonnet, as those are aware who are familiar with his complete poetical works. (Houghton, Mifflin & Co.) Mr. Aldrich's sonnet on *Sleep* was curiously omitted from Mr. Sharp's English collection of American sonnets.

ALLSTON, WASHINGTON (1779–1843). Prominent in early American literature, and noted as a painter as well as a poet.

ARNOLD, JENNIE PORTER. Resides in Hartford, Conn., and is the widow of Henry Lyman Arnold. She has written considerably since the death of her husband.

AURINGER, OBADIAH CYRUS. He was born where he now resides, in the lovely natural region of Glens Falls, N. Y. After considerable naval service he has settled down as a retired farmer and Presbyterian minister, and is at once active in field, church, Sunday-school, and literature. *The Bridge at Glenn's*, a reminiscence of the cave celebrated by Fenimore Cooper, also *Confession*, appeared in the *Critic*; *Winter*, in the *Century*. His last volume of poems, *Scythe and Sword*, was well received. (D. Lothrop & Co.)

BACON, THOMAS RUTHERFORD. The author of various essays and other periodical literature. His sonnet *Deus Immanens* appeared in the *Atlantic Monthly*.

BAIRD, CHAMBERS. A lawyer, who resides at Ripley, Ohio. *Atlantis* appeared in *Every Other Saturday*; the other sonnet, in the *Beta Theta Pi* magazine.

BARTLETT, MARY RUSSELL. A recent graduate of Wellesley College, where her verses were highly esteemed. The sonnet appeared in the Boston *Transcript*.

BASHFORD, HERBERT. Born in Sioux City, Iowa, in 1871, he has already printed verse in various periodicals, a poem written at the age of fifteen being accepted by the *Critic*. He resides in Tacoma, Wash. The sonnet is an unpublished one.

BATCHELDER, SAMUEL FRANCIS. A Harvard student, now about twenty-one years of age. The sonnet was written while at St. Paul's School, Concord, N. H.

BATES, ARLO. Well known as a Boston journalist, a writer for the *Courier*, correspondent of the New York *Bookbuyer*, etc. *Sonnets in Shadow* is the voice of a domestic affliction. He also published *Berries of the Briar*, and *Complete Poems*. (Roberts Bros.)

BATES, KATHARINE LEE. She is attached to Wellesley College; and having printed many fugitive poems, they were collected into a volume by the alumnæ. She recently won a prize for a quatrain on the subject of poetry. *Felices* appeared in the *Independent*, and the other sonnet in the Boston *Transcript*.

BAUDER, LEVI F. A lawyer at Cleveland, Ohio; one of a literary circle, but one who has published verse but rarely.

BAYLIS, SAMUEL M. Was born in Montreal in 1855, and is now a merchant in that city. He has contributed to many Canadian literary papers, besides being an active promoter of athletics. The sonnet appeared first in *The Dominion Illustrated*.

BEERS, HENRY AUGUSTIN. Is well known as a Yale professor and a frequent contributor to current literature. He was born in 1847. A collection of his verse is entitled *The Thankless Muse*. (Houghton, Mifflin & Co.)

BENHAM, IDA WHIPPLE. The author of the pleasant fancy, *The Pimpernell*, lives at Mystic Bridge, Conn. She was born in 1849, and is now married to Elijah B. Benham. The sonnet appeared in *Outing*.

BENJAMIN, PARK (1809–1864). One of the early literary coterie in New York, he was an editor on the *American Monthly Magazine*, the *New Yorker*, etc., and wrote several satires besides a number of pleasing poems.

BENSEL, JAMES BERRY (1855–1886). A native of New York city, he was a student in Lynn, Mass., a clerk in Boston, and, following his literary bent, an author and public reader. His life is the pathetic and too familiar story of suffering and unfulfilled promise. He published a volume of poems, *In the King's Garden*. (D. Lothrop & Co.)

BENTON, JOEL. Born in 1832, and a native of Amenia, Dutchess Co., N. Y., where he resides. At once a poet, philosopher, and agriculturist, he has written some striking vagrant poems, a paper on *Emerson as a Poet*, etc. An intimate friend of Horace Greeley, he has celebrated his memory in the sonnet *At Chappaqua*, which appeared in the Chicago *America*. *Dahkota* is taken from the *Century*.

BLOEDE, MISS GERTRUDE. "Stuart Sterne" was born on August 10, 1845; a daughter of the late Dr. G. Bloede, formerly editor of the *New Yorker Democrat*, and his wife, Marie von Sallet, an authoress, descended from a prominent Silesian family. An uncle, Friedrich von Sallet, was a noted poet of Germany. She lives in Brooklyn, and is a devoted literary worker. *Angelo*, her first poem, reached thirteen editions. *Giorgio and other Poems*, *Beyond the Shadow and other Poems*, and *Piero da Castiglione* have followed, all being published by Houghton, Mifflin & Co.

BOKER, GEORGE HENRY (1823–1890). Mr. Boker was a polished man of leisure as well as a gifted man of letters. His father was president of the Girard Bank, Philadelphia. He was intensely American, and foreign aggression or national conflict brought out some of his most stirring lyrics. The sonnet *To England* was once recited at a dinner party by Daniel Webster, much to the surprise of the young poet, who was present. Mr. Boker was appointed Minister to Turkey in 1871, and to Russia in 1875. He was a great lover of the sonnet, and wrote over three hundred. Several of his dramas were put on the stage. *Plays and Poems.* (J. B. Lippincott Co.)

BONER, JOHN HENRY. Was born in Salem, N. C., 1845, and for sixteen years was employed in the Civil Service at Washington. He is now connected with the Century Co's publications. The two sonnets appeared in the *Washington Star.*

BOTTA, ANNE LYNCH. Was born in Burlington, Vt., is the wife of Professor Vincenzo L. Botta, of Columbia College, and has long been a leader in New York literary life. She has written numerous sonnets. *Poems.* (G. P. Putnam's Sons.)

BOWKER, R. R. A contemporary author and essayist, born in Salem, Mass., 1848. The sonnet appeared in the *Century.*

BOYESEN, HJALMAR HJLORTH. A native of Norway, born in 1848, he is well-known as a college professor, first at Cornell University and now at Columbia College, as well as a lecturer and writer on literary and social subjects. He is especially well-schooled in German and Scandinavian literature. Poems, *Idylls of Norway.* (Charles Scribner's Sons.)

BOYNTON, JULIA. A young poet residing at South Byron, N. Y., and author of *Lines and Interlines.* (G. P. Putnam's Sons.)

BRADLEY, MRS. MARY. Of an elder group of writers, she still lives, and writes occasionally in her Washington home. Her muse is well represented in Griswold's *Female Poets.* The sonnet, with a companion sonnet by R. H. Stoddard, appeared in the *Cosmopolitan* recently.

BROTHERTON, MRS. ALICE WILLIAMS. Is purely a poet of the West; born in Indiana, living in Cincinnati, and never having been east of the Blue Ridge. She has published two volumes of verse, *Beyond the Veil* and the *Sailing of King Olaf,* etc. (Charles H. Kerr & Co.)

BRUCE, WALLACE. Has a home in Poughkeepsie, a cottage in Florida, and is now consul at Leith, Scotland. He was chief editor of the *Lit.* at Yale, poet at the Newburg Centennial, poet at the unveiling of the Burns statue in Central Park, and on other occasions; being a favorite with Scotchmen and Grand Army veterans. Has published *Household Poems.* (Harper & Brothers.)

BRYANT, WILLIAM CULLEN (1794-1878). A patriarch in American poetry, Mr. Bryant's career as journalist, orator, translator of Homer, poet, is familiar to all. Born in the Berkshire Hills, his last act was one of public service (the oration on Mazzini in Central Park), and he rests in the cemetery at Roslyn, L. I., near his former country seat, "Cedarmere." His poems are published by D. Appleton & Co.

BUEL, CLARENCE CLOUGH. Assistant editor of the *Century* magazine, associate editor of the *Century's* War History, and a writer of thoughtful, polished prose and verse. *Emerson* appeared in the *Tribune;* *Neilson*, in the *Century*.

BUNNER, HENRY CUYLER. The editor of *Puck* and author of *Airs from Arcady* is still a young man, and one who is well known in the literary circles of New York. His poems, of which some on the subject of Death are especially interesting, are published by Scribners.

BURLEIGH, WILLIAM H. Was an early poet of New York city, a descendant of Governor Bradford, of Massachusetts, an editor, contributor, and the author of *Poems.* (Houghton, Mifflin & Co.)

BURROUGHS, ELLEN (MISS SOPHIA JEWETT). A recent graduate of an Eastern college. The sonnet appeared in *Scribner's Magazine.*

BURTON, RICHARD EUGENE. Born in Hartford, Conn., 1859; educated at Trinity and Johns Hopkins, receiving the degree of Ph. D. at the latter. He was married in London in 1889, and is a resident of Brooklyn, N. Y. His sonnets have appeared in the *Century*, etc.

BURTON, MRS. SARAH E. Has written verse for the *Transcript*, etc. She lives in New York city. *Longing* appeared in *Outing.*

BUTTS, MARY F. A native of Westerly, R. I. Her maiden name was Barber. She has been a contributor for twenty years, and is the author of the lines, *Build a little fence of trust*, etc. In 1888, she published *Cockle Shells and Silver Bells.* (Charles A. Wenborne.)

CARRUTH, WILLIAM HERBERT. Born at Ossawatomie, Kansas, in 1859; a graduate of the State University, in which he is now Professor of German Language and Literature. He received the degree of M. A. at Harvard in 1889. He is a joint author of the *History of Municipal Suffrage in Kansas*, and co-editor of *Sunflowers*, — poems of his university. His birthplace recalls Mr. Stedman's poem, and he has himself written a sonnet on John Brown.

CHADWICK, JOHN WHITE. Born in Marblehead, Mass., 1840,

a graduate of Harvard, where he was Phi Beta Kappa poet in 1885. He has been pastor of the Second Unitarian Congregation of Brooklyn since 1864, and·is a popular lecturer as well as a poet. His poems have reached a number of editions. *A Book of Poems.* (Roberts Brothers.)

CHANNING, WILLIAM ELLERY. Born in 1818; a nephew of W. E. Channing, the late Unitarian divine. He married a sister of Margaret Fuller, and now resides in Concord, Mass. His volumes of poems appeared in 1843, 1847, 1858, 1872, and he has published *Essays from the Dial*, *Conversations in Rome*, etc. (Roberts Brothers.)

CHENEY, JOHN VANCE. Born in the Genesee Valley, 1848, the son of Simeon Pease Cheney, he has been admitted to the bar, but is now in charge of the San Francisco Free Library. He is a musician, and his wife, a Stuttgart graduate, is his chosen critic. Volumes of verse, *Woodblooms and Thistle Drift*. (F. A. Stokes & Bro.)

CLARKE, SIMEON TUCKER. An eminent physician at Lockport, N. Y., son of the Rev. Nathan Sears Clark. He is a professor in Niagara College. Dr. Clark found recreation in poetry, and has given the public at least one touching sonnet. He has published *Josephine and other Poems*. (Rand & Avery.)

CLYMER, MRS. ELLA DIETZ. She is well known in New York's literary coterie, recently the president of Sorosis, active and influential in society. She has published four books of verse. (Allen & Co., London.)

COAN, DR. TITUS MUNSON. The head of the Bureau of Revision in New York; has contributed to the *Critic* and other periodicals.

COATES, FLORENCE EARLE. She is prominent in Philadelphia literary life, and has a pleasant home in Germantown; her husband is president of the Pennsylvania Academy of Fine Arts. *Morning* appeared in *Lippincott's*, and *Sappho* in the *Atlantic*.

COLEMAN, CHARLES WASHINGTON. A descendant of John Randolph, of Roanoke, he was born in Richmond, Va., 1862, and was educated at the University of Virginia. He lives in the old homestead of his family at Williamsburg. He has contributed to *Harper's Magazine*.

COLLIER, THOMAS S. Born in New York city in 1842. He went to sea when a mere lad, and soon joined the navy. He served until the war closed in 1864. The next year he settled in New London., Conn., where he now lives. He is the secretary of the New London County Historical Society. He published recently a volume of verse, *Song Spray*. (New London.) The sonnet *Not Lost* appeared in *A Masque of Poets*. (Roberts Brothers.)

CONE, MISS HELEN GRAY. A graduate of the New York Normal College, where she has recently been a teacher. She has written amusing society verse as well as serious poems. She has a new volume in hand; has published *Oberon and Puck*. (Cassell & Co.)

COOKE, MRS. ROSE TERRY. One who has been long known for entertaining prose and verse, juvenilia, etc. The sonnet *Dead Love* appeared in the *Atlantic*. *Poems*. (W. L. Gottsberger.)

"COOLIDGE, SUSAN" (MISS SARAH CHAUNCEY WOOLSEY). A popular author of stories and poems. She has printed *Verses*, and *A Few More Verses*. (Roberts Brothers.)

CORNWELL, HENRY S. An occasional contributor to periodicals. The *Katydid* is taken from the *Century*.

COOLBRITH, MISS INA DONNA. A native of Illinois, and now librarian in the Oakland, Cal., Free Library. She has published *A Perfect Day*. (Author's Edition.)

CRANCH, CHRISTOPHER PEARSE. Born in Alexandria, Va., in 1813, now a resident of Cambridge, Mass. He was educated for the ministry. His verse has been known for many years. *Ariel and Caliban*, *The Bird and the Bell*, etc., *The Æneid* (trans.). (Houghton, Mifflin & Co.)

CRANDALL, CHARLES HENRY. Born at Greenwich, Washington Co., N. Y., 1858. The sonnets *Waiting* and *Neilson* appeared in the New York *Tribune*, for which he has written since 1880.

CROSBY, MISS MARGARET. A young writer for the magazines. The sonnet *Sappho to Phaon* appeared in *Scribner's Magazine*.

CROSS, ALLEN EASTMAN. An Amherst College poet, now at Andover Seminary, born at Manchester, N. H., in 1864. The sonnet on Emma Lazarus appeared in the *Critic*.

CURRAN, MISS LULU. Her home is Roxbury, Mass. The picture in her sonnet may recall to some the imaginative drawings of Mr. Low.

CURTIS, GEORGE WILLIAM. Mr. Curtis, born in Providence, R. I. (1824), had a basis of farm experience for his career, having joined the Brook Farm enterprise in 1842, and subsequently labored on a farm at Concord, Mass., for eighteen months. He traveled extensively in later life, and did editorial work for the New York *Tribune* and *Putnam's Monthly* before settling down in the editorial management of *Harper's Weekly* and the "Easy Chair" of *Harper's Magazine*. His sonnet on the Rhode Island prisoner appeared first in *Recollections of the Jersey Prison Ship*, from the original manuscript of Captain Thomas Dring, one of the prisoners. (Morrisania, 1865, printed by Alvord.) It next appeared in *The Invasion of Canada in* 1775, including the Journal of Captain Simeon Thayer, describing Benedict Arnold's march to Quebec, edited by Edwin Martin Stone, Providence, R. I. (Knowles, Anthony & Co. 1867.) A third time it appeared in *The Journal of a Cruise in the Fall of* 1780 *in the Private Sloop of War Hope*, by Solomon Drowne, M. D., with notes by Henry T. Drowne, New York, 1872. (And we believe the usefulness of this sonnet is not ended.)

DANA, CHARLES A. The well-known veteran editor of the New York *Sun*, compiler of *The Household Book of Poetry*, is the author of the striking sonnet *Via Sacra*, whose sixteen lines have precedent in a few examples by Petrarca. This sonnet originally appeared in the great "transcendental" quarterly, *The Dial*, published in Boston, 1840-46, and notable for the contributions of Emerson, Margaret Fuller, Hawthorne, etc.

DAVENPORT, JAMES PIERPONT. A descendant of the famous legislator of Connecticut, celebrated by Whittier in his ballad about the *Dark Day*. When a motion was made to adjourn, as the Day of Judgment appeared to be at hand, this sturdy representative said he preferred to be found doing his duty, and moved that *candles be brought!* Mr. Davenport is a practical journalist on the New York *Tribune*, and clerk of one of the New York courts.

DAVENPORT, WILLIAM C. A young littérateur of Brooklyn; brother of the foregoing. He has published several poems in pamphlet form.

DAY, RICHARD EDWIN. One who is student, journalist, and poet; a writer on the Syracuse *Standard*, and author of a book of poems that was favorably reviewed by some of the best journals. (Cassell & Co.)

DAZEY, C. T. An occasional contributor, whose verse has a peculiar power, as is well shown in the sonnet *Storm Music*. Both sonnets appeared in the *Century*.

DE KAY, CHARLES. Born in Washington in 1848. He is now prominent in New York as a writer of magazine literature, as well as a member of various clubs and societies, president of the New York Fencing Club, etc. His poems include the volumes *Hesperus*, *The Vision of Esther*, *The Vision of Nimrod*, and *Love Poems of Barneval*, the latter abounding in amatory sonnets. (Charles Scribner's Sons.)

DENTON, FRANKLIN EVERT. An editor on the Cleveland *Sun*,

who has contributed verse to various periodicals. *Early Poems.* (William W. Williams.)

DODGE, MRS. MARY MAPES. The present editor of *St. Nicholas* is the daughter of Professor James J. Mapes, and the widow of William Dodge, a New York lawyer. For many years she was co-editor with Donald G. Mitchell on *Hearth and Home.* She is the author of *Hans Brinker's Silver Skates* and many favorite poems. *Along the Way.* (Charles Scribner's Sons.)

DORR, MRS. JULIA CAROLINE RIPLEY. Born in Charleston, S. C., in 1825. She is a daughter of William Young Ripley, and is the widow of Seneca R. Dorr, both of whom were largely interested in the marble quarries of Rutland, Vt., where she resides. She has written several novels besides her volumes of verse, and wrote the Gettysburg ode for the Vermont veterans. Her poem *The Fallow Field* has proved of precious worth to many an invalid. *Friar Anselmo, Afternoon Songs,* etc. (Charles Scribner's Sons.)

ELLET, MRS. ELIZABETH. The wife of Dr. Ellet, formerly a Professor of Chemistry in Columbia College. The sonnet appears in Caroline May's *American Female Poets.*

EGAN, MAURICE FRANCIS. Professor of English literature in the University of Notre Dame, Ind. The two sonnets have appeared in the *Century.* He has published *Songs and Sonnets.* (London.)

FAWCETT, EDGAR. Born in New York in 1847; a graduate of Columbia College, and a novelist and poet by profession. He is the author of a dozen novels, *An Ambitious Woman, Olivia Delaplaine,* etc. Mr. Fawcett has written sonnets on divers subjects and generally with fine appreciation of the capacity of the form. His published books of verse are *Fantasy and Passion* (Roberts Brothers), *Romance and Revery,* and *Song and Story* (Houghton, Mifflin & Co.).

FEARING, LILLIAN BLANCH. Miss Fearing is one of the Western army of poets whose voices reach Eastward. Her home is Chicago. She is the author of *The Sleeping World,* etc. (Anson, McClurg & Co.)

FELLOWES, CAROLINE WILDER. Resides in Hartford, and has contributed sonnets and other verse to the daily and weekly press, etc. The Dante sonnet was printed in the *Atlantic Monthly.*

FIELDS, ANNIE ADAMS. The wife of the late James T. Fields is an enthusiastic follower of letters, and an entertaining writer. The volume *Under the Olive* (Houghton, Mifflin & Co.) was more particularly an expression of grief. She has not made a second collection of poems. The sonnet selected appeared in *Scribner's Magazine.*

FORMAN, MRS. EMILY SHAW. This writer's poems on flowers have appeared under her initials in the *Atlantic* and other periodicals. The *Cactus*, one of her finest flower sonnets, appears in *Poems of Nantucket*, a collection by various authors, published by Henry S. Ayer. She has also issued a book of love sonnets, illustrated by Fidelia Bridges. (Prang & Co.) Mrs. Shaw is vice-president of the Boston Browning Club.

FOSTER, WILLIAM PRESCOTT. An attorney of Bar Harbor, Me., and a writer of considerable magazine verse. The sonnets quoted are taken from the *Century.*

GARRISON, WENDELL PHILLIPS. The son of William Lloyd Garrison. He is connected with *The Nation* and other periodicals, and is one of the authors of his father's biography. The notable sonnet on Lincoln's dream appeared in *Harper's Magazine*, the double sonnet in the *Century.*

GARRISON, WILLIAM LLOYD (1805-1879). The great anti-slavery agitator was not habitually a rhymer. In 1830 he was imprisoned in the Baltimore jail, and on this occasion he wrote the sonnet *The Free Mind*, on the walls of his cell. This is in strong contrast to the idea that the sonnet is but the emanation of an idle hour in a boudoir. The sonnet is printed in his *Life*, edited by his sons.

GATES, LEWIS. This sonnet was clipped from the *Harvard Advocate.*

GIBSON, WILLIAM. The sonnet *Pisa* appears in the *Atlantic Monthly.* The author was a late commander in the navy.

GILDER, JOSEPH B. Associated with Miss Jeannette L. Gilder as editor of the *Critic;* he has written stray bits of verse under the pen-name of *Randall Blackshaw.*

GILDER, RICHARD WATSON. Born in 1844; a son of the Rev. W. H. Gilder, captain of the 40th Regt., N. Y. Vols., who died at Brandy Station in 1864. Mr. Gilder is a brother of W. H. Gilder, the explorer, and of the *Critic* editors. Beginning journalism in Newark, he became editor of *Hours at Home* in 1869, and soon afterward was called to assist Dr. J. G. Holland in editing *Scribner's Monthly.* He succeeded the latter, who died in 1881, and has since been the editor of the magazine now known as the *Century.* He is the president of The Fellowcraft Club of New York. He has issued *The New Day*, *The Poet and his Master*, *Lyrics*, and *The Celestial Passion.* (The Century Co.)

GOODALE, MISS DORA READ. The younger of the Goodale

sisters, authors of *Apple Blossoms*, of *Sky Farm*, in the Berkshires. She was born in 1866. (G. P. Putnam's Sons.)

GOODALE, MISS ELAINE. Born in 1863. She is now doing active missionary and educational work among the Indians. (G. P. Putnam's Sons.)

GOODWIN, HENRY M. Resides at Olivet, Mich. Has printed occasional verse. *The Sistine Madonna* is now first printed.

GOODWIN, HOPESTILL. An occasional contributor. The sonnet is in Sharp's collection.

GREENE, HOMER. A lawyer at Honesdale, Pa., and author of the somewhat famous prize story, *The Blind Brother*. He was born in Ariel, Wayne Co., Pa., in 1853. The sonnet was first printed in the *Saturday Argus* of Scranton, Pa.

GUINEY, MISS LOUISE IMOGEN. Born in Boston in 1861, of French and Irish parentage, the only child of General P. R. Guiney. She graduated from Elmhurst Convent, Providence, R. I. Her poems appear frequently in high-class magazines. She is the author of *Brownies and Bogles*, the *Goosequill Papers*, *Songs at the Start*, and the *White Sail and other Poems*. (Houghton, Mifflin & Co.)

HALL, ELIZA CALVERT. Born in Bowling Green, Ky., in 1856; a contributor to *The Atlantic, Century, Scribner's, Lippincott*, etc. The sonnets cited appeared in the *Century*.

HAY, JOHN. Colonel Hay was born in 1838. He is a Brown graduate, and has had experience as a lawyer, soldier, diplomatist, editor (temporarily of the New York *Tribune*), and novelist. His greatest honor was that of being private secretary to Abraham Lincoln, whose historian, in association with Mr. Nicolay, he now is. He is credited with the authorship of the *Bread Winners*, and is widely known as the author of *Little Breeches, Jim Bludso*, and other *Pike County Ballads*. His tender sonnet is a fair example of his more refined verse, the only sonnet by him at my command, and recently published in *Scribner's Magazine. Poems*. (Houghton, Mifflin & Co.)

HAYNE, PAUL HAMILTON (1840–1887). Born in Charleston, S. C., he graduated from Charleston College, and soon after was given charge of a magazine started by Simms, Calhoun, Timrod and Legare. Ticknor & Co. published his first volume, when he was but twenty-five. During the war he was a Colonel on Governor Pickens's staff. He suffered ill-health for years, and died at "Copse Hill" among the pine woods. In the South he is sometimes alluded to as the Longfellow of that section. *Complete Poems*. (D. Lothrop & Co.) *Legends and Lyrics*. (J. B. Lippincott Co.)

HEAVYSEGE, CHARLES. A Canadian poet, now dead, author of *Jephthah's Daughter* and *Saul*. Mr. Sharp gives seven sonnets by this poet in his *American Sonnets*. The sonnets are, however, often irregular in form.

HENDERSON, WILLIAM J. A prominent literary and musical critic, now connected with the New York *Times*. The sonnet *Eve* first appeared in the *Century*. The other sonnet is taken from the New York *Times*.

HIBBARD, GEORGE A. A resident of Buffalo, New York. His sonnet appeared in the *Century*.

HIGGINSON, THOMAS WENTWORTH. Born in 1823, he was conspicuous as an anti-slavery advocate, and became the Colonel of the first regiment of freed slaves enlisted in the late war, in which he was wounded. He is now prominent as an author, essayist, woman-suffrage champion, president of the Boston Browning Club. etc. His books number a score. He published poems when a young man, and recently *The Afternoon Landscape*. (Longmans, Green & Co.)

HILLARD, MISS KATHARINE. Born in London of American parents, she was educated in Brooklyn. She had a poem printed when she was eleven, and wrote regularly for the press when she was seventeen. During a five years' sojourn in Italy she translated Dante's *Banquet* (Putnams), and has also contributed essays on French and English literature, sometimes over the pen name of *Lucy Fountain* (Charles Reade's heroine). The *Best Gift* appeared in *Harper's Magazine*.

HINCKLEY, ABBY. An occasional contributor. The sonnet appeared in the *Century*.

HOLLAND, JOSIAH GILBERT (1819-1881). Dr. Holland was the son of a Massachusetts farmer, and had little schooling. He became a pedagogue, afterward a graduate in medicine, but found his calling as an editor on the *Springfield Republican*. He was subsequently in charge of *Hours at Home*, and in 1870 became editor of *Scribner's Monthly*, which he edited until he died. The one quoted is perhaps his only sonnet, excepting one with some repellent features, written on President Garfield's death. He wrote numerous novels, sketches, and several long poems, besides shorter verse. (Charles Scribner's Sons.)

HOLMES, OLIVER WENDELL. Dr. Holmes was born in 1809, and now has a substantial fame on two continents as a poet and humorist, not to mention his novels, essays, and medical works. He has lectured at Harvard for many years, being himself a native of Cambridge. Though the author of a few excellent sonnets, he is most famous for his *Autocrat of the Breakfast-Table*, etc., and for lyrics of various moods, as, for instance, *The Chambered Nautilus* and *The One-Hoss Shay*. (Houghton, Mifflin & Co.)

HOUGHTON, GEORGE W. W. Born in 1850, has been an editor on several journals, and is now secretary of the *Christian Union* Company, and contributes regularly to that paper. He has issued *Niagara and other Poems*. (Houghton, Mifflin & Co.)

HOWELLS, WINIFRED. A gifted daughter, lately deceased, of the novelist, W. D. Howells. The *Century* first published her sonnet.

HUMPHREYS, COLONEL DAVID (1752–1818). He is reputed to be the first American to write a sonnet in fairly regular form. He was born in Connecticut, and served in the Revolutionary War as aide to Generals Putnam and Washington. He was secretary to the Peace Commission in 1784, and subsequently American Minister to Portugal and to Spain. He wrote verse at Yale, contributed to the *Anarchiad*, and published several works, including a poem on agriculture. In the War of 1812 he was made a Brigadier-General. His ordinary vocation was that of a manufacturer, and he had several such interests in Connecticut.

HUNTINGTON, WILLIAM REED. The present rector of Grace Parish, New York, was born in Lowell, Mass., 1838. He graduated at Harvard, and was rector of All Saints, Worcester, Mass., from 1862 to 1883. *Quinquaginta*, a book of fifty poems, edition of fifty copies, was issued in the author's fiftieth year, being published privately. The sonnet *Tellus* appeared in the *Century*.

"INNSLEY, OWEN." See "Jennison."

IRELAND, MARY E. A resident of Baltimore, Md., and author of stories, essays, and poems, translations from the German, juvenile books, etc.

JACKSON, HELEN MARIA FISKE [HUNT] (1831–1885). A daughter of Professor Nathan W. Fiske, of Amherst, Mass. She was married to Captain Edward B. Hunt in 1852, and, the latter dying, to William S. Jackson in 1875. She wrote the novel *Ramona*, besides many stories, essays, sketches of travel, and poems. The latter were highly esteemed by Emerson. In later years, she worked diligently for the welfare of the Indians in the West. She died at her home on Cheyenne Mountain, near Colorado Springs, Col. Several fine sonnets were written on her death. *Verses* and *Complete Poems*. (Roberts Bros.)

JENNISON, MISS LUCY WHITE ("Owen Innsley"). Born in Newton, Mass., in 1850. She has published considerably in periodicals; also a volume. (Damrell & Upham.)

JEWETT, MISS SOPHIA. See "Ellen Burroughs."

JOHNSON, ROBERT UNDERWOOD. The assistant editor of the *Century*, secretary of the American Copyright League, etc. He wrote the hymn sung at the laying of the corner-stone of the Washington Arch, in New York, on Decoration Day, 1890. His sonnets appeared in the *Century*.

JONES, EDITH. The author of occasional magazine verse, the one cited being taken from the *Century*.

JONES, MARIA W. A lady of Quaker family, living in Chicago, and a contributor to the *Century*.

KEMBLE, FRANCIS ANNE. Better known as "Fanny Kemble;" an author of varied gifts as well as a celebrated actress. She was the daughter of Charles Kemble, and was born in 1809. She resided at various times in New York city, at Lenox, and in the South. She wrote several plays, a story of her life on a Georgia plantation, and numerous poems which were published in Boston, 1859. She now lives in London.

KENYON, JAMES BENJAMIN. Born in Herkimer Co., N. Y., 1858, he has been for years a successful minister of the Methodist Episcopal Church, and is now located at Watertown, N. Y. Besides some early volumes, he has issued *Out of the Shadows* (J. B. Lippincott Co.), and *In Realms of Gold* (Cassell & Co.).

KIMBALL, HARRIET MCEWEN. Born in 1834, and resides at Portsmouth, N. H., her native town. She has published several volumes of verse. Her complete poems are just recently issued. (A. D. F. Randolph & Co.)

KING, EDWARD. For many years Paris correspondent of the *Evening Post*, N. Y. *Poems of the Orient*. (Kegan Paul & Co.)

KINNEY, MRS. ELIZABETH C. (1810–1889). The mother of E. C. Stedman, and a sister of William E. Dodge, the millionaire philanthropist and merchant. She was twice married — to Edmund B. Stedman and again to William B. Kinney. She accompanied her second husband when he was appointed minister to Italy in 1850. Her works are published by Houghton, Mifflin & Co.

LAIGHTON, ALBERT. The irregular but impressive sonnet on Night is by an early American writer, and is included in the Hunt-Lee collection. (Roberts Bros.)

LAMBORN, EMMA TAYLOR. The wife of Colonel C. B. Lamborn, of St. Paul, Minn., and a sister of Bayard Taylor. She contributes to prominent periodicals, and has published privately a *Book of Sonnets*.

LAMPMAN, ARCHIBALD. Is of German descent on both sides, though born in the County of Kent, a charming section of Canada. He is now twenty-nine years old, having been married three years, and is a clerk in the P. O. Department at Ottawa. Three years ago he published *Among the Millet*, etc. (Durie.)

LANIER, SIDNEY (1842-1881). A native of Macon, Ga., he served in the Confederate "Louisiana Tigers," and was captured in 1863, his prison experience prompting the book *Tiger-Lilies*. After the war he practiced law, and taught and lectured in various schools. He wrote the words of the cantata that was sung at the Centennial Exposition, 1876, also *The Science of Verse*, in which he applied the principles of music to verse. His poems are valued highly by many good critics. (Charles Scribner's Sons.)

LARCOM, LUCY (1826-1888). Born in Beverly, Mass. She was for a time an operative in the Lowell cotton mills. Here she first began to write, and attracted the attention of Whittier. For a number of years she edited *Our Young Folks*. Several collections of poetry, volumes of her own poems, and her complete poems have appeared. (Houghton, Mifflin & Co.) *The Woodthrush* is from the *Atlantic*.

LATHROP, GEORGE PARSONS. A versatile all-round man of letters and occasional poet, who has filled several editorial positions, and issued a number of books of prose. His most ambitious poem was an ode read at Gettysburg. He married Miss Rose Hawthorne, daughter of the great romancer. The two sonnets quoted appeared in *Scribner's Monthly*.

LAWTON, WILLIAM CRANSTON. An essayist and general contributor, who resides at Cambridge, Mass. *In Athens* and other sonnets appeared in the *Atlantic*.

LAYARD, MISS NINA F. A note has failed to reveal the personality of the author of the Snow sonnet which appeared in the *Century*.

LAZARUS, MISS EMMA (1849-1888). The daughter of a wealthy Hebrew, and brought in contact with fashionable society in New York, her devotion to literature was remarkable, and indicated her strong bent in that direction. A singing quality in her verse rendered her translations of Heine often as charming as the original. Her complete poems, now accessible in one volume, must always have peculiar interest, apart from her rare poetic gift, on account of her championship of the down-trodden Jews in Europe, as well as because of the sad cutting off of her valuable life. (Houghton, Mifflin & Co.)

LEARNED, WALTER. A young poet, who lives at the ancestral homestead in New London, Conn., and prints occasional verse in magazines. He has just published his first volume, *Between Times*. (F. A. Stokes & Bro.)

LIPPMANN, MISS JULIE MATHILDE. Born in Brooklyn in 1864, she still resides there. Her sonnets appeared in the *Century*. She has published a volume for children, *Through Slumbertown and Wakeland*. (Prang & Co.)

LONGFELLOW, HENRY WADSWORTH (1807–1882). He was born in Portland, Me., amid charming natural and social surroundings. A classmate of Hawthorne at Bowdoin, their friendship was life-long, and the world owes to Hawthorne the suggestion of *Evangeline*. As Professor of Literature at Harvard, a traveled student of almost every land and tongue, an ideal poet and gentleman, his career is a cherished legacy in America. He died at his home in Cambridge, Mass., March 24, 1882. Most of Mr. Longfellow's sonnets are the choice vintage of his ripest years, appearing in his later volumes, *Possibilities* being in the very latest, *In the Harbor*. His personality has called out a number of fine sonnets, including those by Holmes, Fawcett, Cone, and Morse. His poems, in various editions, are issued by Houghton, Mifflin & Co.

LORD, AUGUSTUS MENDON. Born in San Francisco, 1861; schooled at Boston, a graduate of Harvard and the Divinity School; now pastor of the First Congregational Church, Arlington, Mass. Has issued *A Book of Verses*. (Out of print.)

LOWELL, ANNA MARIA. Mrs. Lowell possessed a delicate fancy, which expressed itself in a number of sonnets and poems. Her death in 1853 is memorialized in Longfellow's *The Two Angels*. (Houghton, Mifflin & Co.)

LOWELL, JAMES RUSSELL. Mr Lowell was born in Cambridge in 1819, and still lives in his birthplace, "Elmwood," which was once occupied by Elbridge Gerry, the original "gerrymanderer" of political districts. Lowell graduated from the Harvard Law School, but his whole life has been devoted to literature, unless one excepts his period of duty as Minister at the Court of St. James. For some years he edited the *Atlantic Monthly*. To some it seems as if his fame rests strongest on *The Biglow Papers* or the series of *Odes*. To others he will come closest as the author of such poems as *The Courtin'*, *The Phœbe Bird*, *Longing*, etc., or such sonnets as *To Whittier*. Mr. Lowell's last volume, *Heartsease and Rue*, contains numerous sonnets. (Houghton, Mifflin & Co.)

LÜDERS, CHARLES HENRY. A young poet of Philadelphia, who contributes considerably to magazines. *Egypt* appeared in the Boston *Transcript*, and *The Haunts of the Halcyon* in *Scribner's Magazine*. He has issued one volume with a friend.

LUNT, ADELINE PARSONS. The widow of George Lunt is a

native and now a resident of Boston. She is a sister of Dr. T. W. Parsons, the poet. Her sonnet appeared in the Boston *Post*.

LUNT, GEORGE. Born in Newburyport in 1807, graduated from Harvard, 1824, and in 1848 was made U. S. District Attorney and removed to Boston. He subsequently edited the Boston *Courier* for several years. He issued several volumes of prose and books of verse in 1839, 1843, 1854. From 1877 until his death he lived at Scituate. *Complete Poems*. (Cupples, Upham & Co.)

MACE, FRANCES LAUGHTON. Born in Orono, Me., 1836. She was married, at nineteen, to Benjamin F. Mace, a lawyer of Bangor. In 1885 they removed to San Jose, Cal., where they now live. She wrote the poem called *Israfil*, which appeared with illustrations in *Harper's Magazine*. *Legends, Lyrics, and Sonnets*. (Damrell & Upham.) *Under Pine and Palm*. (Houghton, Mifflin & Co.)

MACDONALD, MARY NOEL. One of the group of early sonnet-writers; she was born in New York, contributed to the *Mirror*, *Columbian*, etc., and issued a volume of poems in 1845.

MARKHAM, CHARLES EDWIN. Born in Oregon, April 23, 1852, he passed his youth on a lonely cattle range in Central California. He attended the Pacific Methodist College, the State Normal School, where he graduated, and afterward studied at Christian College, Santa Rosa, where he became a member of the faculty. He has held positions in the educational department of his State, and has lectured on literary subjects. His verse is familiar to magazine readers. He is compiling two volumes of poems, also a prose volume. He lives now at Oakland, Cal. *The Cricket* is from the *Century*.

MARSH, JULIET C. *The Pines' Thought* appeared in the *Century*.

MASON, CAROLINE A. She was born in Marblehead, Mass., in 1823, and has published a number of sonnets, her only volume of verse, *Utterance*, being now out of print. The sonnets *May* and *June* appeared in the *Century*.

MASON, MARIE. The sonnets of this author have appeared mainly in *Scribner's Monthly*.

MASSEY, SUSANNA. Resides in Germantown, Pa. Her sonnet appeared in *Society*.

MATTHEWS, JAMES NEWTON. A citizen of the West (Mason, Ill.), Mr. Matthews' poems are frequently seen in the Eastern periodicals. He takes not a little interest in the sonnet form. His sonnet, *Death*, has been frequently quoted. He has published *Tempe Vale*. (C. H. Kerr & Co.)

MAY, CAROLINE. Has edited a selection from American woman poets, as well as written not a little verse. *Early Morn* is quoted from the *Century*. Her last volume of poems was issued by A. D. F. Randolph & Co.

McKAY, JAMES T. One of the poets who labor under the handicap of ill-health and yet achieve success. He has been unable to read or write since 1868. He was born in New York, 1843, and lives at Huntington, L. I. The *Thunder Cloud*, a striking sonnet, appeared in the *Atlantic*, and the *Whispering Gallery* in the *Manhattan*. He recently won a prize in a story competition in the *Youth's Companion*. He has published no volume yet.

McKENZIE, WILLIAM P. A young minister who resides at Auburn, N. Y. He published last year *Voices and Undertones*, which had a considerable sale, more especially in Canada.

MELLISH, JOHN H. Minister of the Congregational Church at North Scituate, R. I.

MITCHELL, LANGDON ELWYN. The sonnet on Decoration Day is taken from the *Century*, the other sonnet from the author's book, *Sylvia and other Poems*. (Brentano.)

MONROE, HARRIET. A daughter of Henry Stanton Monroe, a lawyer in Chicago. Her sonnet was first printed by the *Century*.

MORRIS, HARRISON S. A young poet of Philadelphia, well-known in its literary society. He has used the sonnet form frequently. Recently, he issued a volume with a friend entitled *A Duet in Lyrics*. (Author's Edition.)

MORSE, JAMES HERBERT. He was born at Hubbardston, Mass., in 1841, and graduated at Harvard. He is a member of the Century, the Author's, the Greek, and other New York clubs and societies. His volume, *Summer Haven Songs*, contains many sonnets. (G. P. Putnam's Sons.)

MOULTON, LOUISE CHANDLER. Mrs. Moulton was born in Pomfret, Conn., in 1835, and was a student at Mrs. Willard's famous seminary at Troy, N. Y. She was married to W. U. Moulton, a Boston publisher, in 1855. For a considerable period she wrote the Boston literary news for the New York *Tribune*. Her works include many stories as well as volumes of Poems. (Roberts Brothers.)

NOYES, CHARLES. Lives at Warren, Pa., and uses a *nom de plume* of an amusing contrast, *Charles Quiet*. He has published a volume called *Studies*.

O'DONNELL, MISS JESSIE F. A daughter of Hon. John O'Donnell, of Lowville, N. Y. Her muse has found expression in the Boston *Transcript* and elsewhere. In 1887 she published *Heart*

Lyrics. (G. P. Putnam's Sons.) She is now compiling the love poems of three centuries.

OSSOLI, SARAH MARGARET FULLER (1810-1850). One of the most gifted literary women of America, she held her own ground in assemblies of genius in Concord, Boston, and New York, and wrote extensively for the *Dial,* the *Tribune,* etc. Her friendships included such persons as Emerson, Greeley, Ripley, and Curtis. She was personally charming and a fine conversationalist, as well as a forcible writer and acute literary critic.

PARKER, THEODORE (1810-1860). The life of this clergyman, controversialist, and anti-slavery agitator is too dramatic and romantic to bear condensation. He was a voluminous author. His outspoken opinions brought him abundant abuse and indignities. The second sonnet quoted is unpublished, and is furnished from his diary by his literary executor, F. B. Sanborn. Born in Lexington, Mass., died in Florence, Italy.

PARSONS, DR. THOMAS WILLIAM. Born in Boston in 1819, he has seldom left his native place, though he spent a few years in foreign travel, resulting, in 1844, in *Ghetto di Roma,* reminiscences and impressions of Italy. He has published occasional poems of late.

PECK, SAMUEL MINTURN. The author of considerable society verse. His name is familiar to readers of the *Home Journal,* the *Century, Life,* etc. He recently published *Cap and Bells.* (F. A. Stokes & Bro.)

PERCIVAL, JAMES GATES (1795-1856). Kensington, Conn., was his birthplace. He was an accomplished linguist, a geologist, doctor, and editor, as well as poet, and one of the important forerunners in American literature. He also translated extensively. His report on the geology of Connecticut is a monumental work. His poems were published in 1826, and again in 1859. His sonnets have the courtly elegance and fine feeling of old-time poetry.

PERRY, MRS. LILLA CABOT. The wife of Thomas Sergeant Perry, a resident of Boston. She published recently the volume, *The Heart of the Weed.* (Houghton, Mifflin & Co.)

PIATT, JOHN JAMES. Born in 1835. Best known as the poet of the Ohio valley. He had a varied training as a journalist, having learned the rudiments of printing at the age of fourteen, and subsequently worked on the staffs of the Cincinnati *Commercial* and *Chronicle.* He has served in the Treasury Department, as clerk in the House of Representatives, Librarian of the House, and for the last half dozen years as United States Consul at Cork, Ireland. He has published numerous volumes of verse, some in conjunction with Mrs. Piatt, one with W. D. Howells (1860), and has edited a volume of the verses of George D. Prentice. His last volume appeared in Dublin. His sonnet, Gilder's, and Stoddard's make a notable trio on Lincoln. (Houghton, Mifflin & Co.)

PINNEY, REV. NORMAN. An early American writer. His sonnet is in the Hunt-Lee collection. (Roberts Brothers.)

POE, EDGAR ALLAN (1809–1849). The unhappy, saturnine poet of America was not a frequent writer of sonnets. The author of *The Raven* and *The Bells* evidently preferred more elastic stanzas. His sonnet *Silence* has a weird power, and yet is repellent and uncanny. The one quoted, *Science*, is, however, in several respects admirable. (W. J. Middleton.)

PONTE, C. E. DA. This sonnet is found in the Hunt-Lee collection of Sonnets, 1867. (Roberts Brothers.)

POWERS, HORATIO NELSON, D. D. Born in Dutchess Co., N. Y., in 1826, died in 1890. He was a graduate of Union College and of the General Theological Seminary. He was rector of a church at Pierpont-on-the-Hudson, having been over parishes at Bridgeport, Conn., Davenport, Iowa, Chicago, etc. For a long time correspondent of *L'Art*, he enjoyed the friendship of Philip Gilbert Hamerton, who dedicated a volume to him. He was also a friend of Bryant, Bayard Taylor, and others as prominent. Author of *Ten Years of Song*. (D. Lothrop & Co.)

PRESTON, MARGARET JUNKIN. She was born in 1835; the daughter of Rev. Dr. Junkin, once president of Lafayette College. She is the wife of Professor John T. L. Preston, of the Virginia Military Institute. She first wrote for *Sartain's Magazine*. The novel *Silverwood* is by her pen, and in her poem *Beechenbrook* she treats of life during the Civil War, in which contest she sided with her adopted State. Her popular poems include *Stonewall Jackson's Grave*, and *Slain in Battle*. Her volumes embrace *Old Songs and New* (1870), *For Love's Sake*, (1887), and *Colonial Ballads*. (Houghton, Mifflin & Co.)

REALF, RICHARD. A poet of undoubted talent; born in England, 1834, but spent the later years of a brief life in this country, and died in California, 1878. *Discord* appeared in *Harper's Magazine* with several others of his sonnets. His volume of verse was called *Guesses at the Beautiful*. Few volumes exist in this country, it having been published in England in 1852. He was an associate of John Brown in Kansas, and served from 1862 to 1866 in the United States Volunteers, and from 1868 to 1870 in the United States Civil Service. He was subsequently a lecturer and journalist. *Complete Poems*. (Charles W. Moulton.)

REESE, L. WOODWORTH. A young writer, a native of Maryland. She published *A Branch of May*, 1887. (Cushing & Bailey.)

RICHARDS, WILLIAM C. Born in London, 1818; graduated from Madison University, N. Y., in 1840. He has been in charge of churches in Providence and Pittsfield, and is now a resident of Chicago. He has published much stray verse, also *Science in Song* and other prose works, scientific, literary, and theological. A sonnet of his was erroneously ascribed to George Herbert, in Sanders' *Evenings with the Sacred Poets* (Randolph), p. 246. He has printed some fifty sonnets. *Monotones* appeared in *Harper's Magazine*.

RICKETSON, DANIEL. Mr. Ricketson lives at New Bedford, Mass., and is now in his seventy-sixth year. He enjoyed the friendship of Emerson, Thoreau, and Channing. He published in 1869, *An Autumn Sheaf*.

RILEY, JAMES WHITCOMB. A native of Greenfield, Ind., he is known as the "Hoosier Poet." His dialect, humorous and sentimental verse have become widely known. He began his career as a traveling showman, being the orator, actor, musician, artist, and sign-painter, all in one. Subsequently he followed journalism in Indianapolis, and now he travels, lectures, and recites. His latest book, *Old Fashioned Roses*, appeared in England. He has issued three other collections of verse. (The Bowen-Merrill Company.)

RIVES, AMÉLIE (MRS. JOHN ARMSTRONG CHANLER). Besides her novels, Mrs. Chanler has written considerable verse. As is well-known, she is still a young woman, and is a native of Virginia. Her sonnet was printed in the *Century*.

ROBERTS, CHARLES G. D. Born near Frederickton, the capital of New Brunswick, and there educated. He was the first editor of the Toronto *Week*, but is now Professor of Literature in King's College, Windsor, N. S. With Mr. Lampman he is among the most prominent of Canadian poets. The *Midwinter Thaw* appeared in a recent number of *Belford's Magazine*; the *Cow Pasture* was printed in the *McGill University Gazette*. He has published *Orion* (J. B. Lippincott Co.), and *In Divers Tones* (D. Lothrop & Co.).

ROBINSON, FANNY RUTH. An author of stories and poems, largely on domestic and religious themes, which have appeared for a number of years. The *Order for a Cameo* was printed in *Harper's Magazine*. The other sonnet is unpublished.

ROBINSON, HARRIET. The author of the *New Pandora* lives at Malden, Mass. Her sonnet was printed in the *Springfield Repub-*

lican. She has also issued a History of Massachusetts in the Woman Suffrage Movement.

RUBLE, ZULEMA A. A graduate of Smith College, Northampton, where she wrote the class play. She is now a teacher of Greek and Latin in a preparatory school, Cleveland, O.

SALTUS, FRANCIS SALTUS. Born in New York, 1849, he was buried in Sleepy Hollow Cemetery, Tarrytown, N. Y., in June, 1889. He was an extensive traveler, a versatile linguist, and a musician and musical student. According to his biographers, he left a mass of unpublished matter, the amount of which appears incredible. A volume of verse, *Honey and Gall*, appeared in 1873. *Selected Poems.* (Charles W. Moulton.)

SANBORN, FRANKLIN BENJAMIN. Born in 1841, a graduate of Harvard. He is the secretary of numerous charitable and scientific bodies. Has edited Channing's *Wanderer*, Alcott's *Sonnets*, Thoreau's *Life*, and the *Life and Letters* of John Brown. He was connected with the famous " Summer School " at Concord, Mass., where he lives.

SARGENT, EPES (1813–1880). A native of Gloucester, Mass., voluminous author of biographies, dramas, novels, and poems, and compiler of a cyclopædia of poetry. One of his best known poems is *A Life on the Ocean Wave*. In his varied career as journalist, man of letters, and man of society (for he belonged to numerous clubs), he had a wide acquaintance, and he left much abiding and influential literary work. *Songs of the Sea* (1847), and *Poems* (1858) are his volumes of verse.

SAVAGE, MINOT JACKSON (1841). A graduate of Bowdoin, and of Bangor Theological Seminary, he has held pastorates in California, Framingham, Mass., Hannibal, Mo., Chicago, and Boston. In the latter place he has charge of the Church of the Unity. Besides numerous works on social and religious topics, he has published a volume of poems (1882). (George H. Ellis.)

SAXE, JOHN GODFREY (1816–1887). This famous poet and humorist was born in Highgate, Vt. A lawyer by education, he was once Attorney-General of Vermont. He drifted into journalism and literature, and his fame will rest largely on his humorous poems, like *Riding on the Rail*, *Miss McBride*, etc. He is said to have remarked once on what he thought the unusual excellence of one of his sonnets. *Poems.* (Houghton, Mifflin & Co.)

SAXTON, ANDREW B. The author of considerable magazine verse of serious tone. He has liked the sonnet well enough to write about a hundred. He is now connected with the Oneonta, N. Y., *Herald.* *Midsummer* appeared in the *Century*.

SCOLLARD, CLINTON, was born in Clinton, N. Y., in 1860, and was educated at Hamilton College in that town, where he is now a professor of rhetoric and literature. He took a post-graduate course at Harvard, and has made several European trips. Besides an early volume, his books are *With Reed and Lyre* (D. Lothrop & Co.), and *Old and New World Lyrics* (F. A. Stokes & Bro.).

SCOTT, JOHN M. Born in Westmoreland Co., Pa., in 1855, he studied at Lafayette College, and was ordained to the ministry of the Baptist Church. He also teaches in the local Academy at his present place of residence, Sewickly, a suburb of Pittsburg. *A Marsh Melody* appeared in the *New Jerusalem Magazine*. The other sonnet is now first printed.

SHERMAN, FRANK DEMPSTER. Born in Peekskill, N. Y., 1860, he graduated at Columbia, and is now instructor in architecture at that college. His society verse is frequently seen in magazines. He has issued *Madrigals and Catches* (F. A. Stokes & Bro.), *Lyrics for a Lute* (Houghton, Mifflin & Co.).

SILL, EDWARD ROWLAND (1843-1887). A native of Windsor, Conn., he graduated at Yale and studied at the Harvard Divinity School. For eight years he was Professor of English Literature at the University of California. His closing years were shadowed by physical suffering, and his poems are frequently of the most grave sentiment. He issued *Poems*, and the *Hermitage*. For a time some of his poems in the *Atlantic* were signed "Andrew Hedbrooke." (Houghton, Mifflin & Co.)

SMITH, ELIZABETH OAKES. A native of Cumberland, Me., the author of several volumes, and a favorite contributor to the early magazines.

SPALDING, SUSAN MARR. The author of a considerable number of magazine poems. *Dear Hands* appeared in the *Atlantic*.

STEDMAN, EDMUND CLARENCE. Born in Hartford, Conn., in 1833. His father was Edmund B. Stedman and his mother a sister of William E. Dodge, and a relative of Channing. He is widely known both as a poet and as a critic ; and being a banker as well, and the author of *Pan in Wall Street*, he is often called the "banker-poet." During the war he was the correspondent in the field for the New York *World*. Besides volumes of criticisms on English and American poets, and several volumes of verse, he has lately compiled, with Miss Ellen M. Hutchinson, a Library of American Literature in eleven volumes. His poems, critical studies, etc., are issued by Houghton, Mifflin & Co. Mr. Stedman is president of the New York Authors' Club, a member of the Century Club, etc.

STOCKARD, HENRY JEROME. Born in 1860. He is now the County Superintendent of Public Instruction at Graham, N. C. His poems appear at intervals in magazines, etc.

STODDARD, RICHARD HENRY. The son of a sea-captain, he was born in Hingham, Mass., in 1825. He has been a clerk in the New York Custom House, City Librarian, and literary editor of the *Mail and Express*. A writer about the sonnet, he has written a number himself, though best known by his ballads, songs, and blank verse. The sonnet to Mary Bradley was published in the *Cosmopolitan* Magazine, and should be read in conjunction with the one by her. *Complete Poems*. (Charles Scribner's Sons.)

STORY, WILLIAM WETMORE. Born in 1819, this poet, painter, and sculptor has lived for many years in Italy. He lately published *Conversations in a Studio*. One of his sonnets, *Be of good cheer, ye firm and dauntless few*, was addressed to the early anti-slavery agitators. (Houghton, Mifflin & Co.)

TAIT, JOHN R. An early writer, whose sonnet appears in the Hunt-Lee collection.

TAYLOR, BAYARD (1825-1878). A native of Kennett Square, Penn., Mr. Taylor kep this charming home there, "Cedarcroft," to the end of his life. He wrote *Views Afoot* for the New York *Tribune* while traveling through Europe, and afterward filled conspicuous positions as a poet, critic, journalist, dramatist, and diplomat, and died while at Berlin as Minister to Germany. He translated Goethe's *Faust* in the original metre, and was the author of novels, *Prince Deukalion*, and many popular short poems, such as the *Song of the Camp*, and the *Bedouin Lover's Song*. He was among the first to write the sonnet considerably and well in this country. His poems, etc., are issued by Houghton, Mifflin & Co.

TAYLOR, BENJAMIN F. (1819-1887). Born in Lowville, N. Y., and a graduate of Madison University, he soon became literary editor of the Chicago *Evening Journal*, and was its war correspondent in the Union army. The University of California gave him the degree of LL. D. His prose as well as his poems is imaginative, and the London *Times* called him the Goldsmith of America. *Complete Poems*. 1887. (Chicago.)

THAXTER, MRS. CELIA. Born in Portsmouth, N. H., she has spent most of her life at "Appledore," her secluded home on the Isles of Shoals. Here, where the mails only come once a week, she has become attuned to the music of the sea, which sounds in many of her poems. (Houghton, Mifflin & Co.)

THAYER, JULIA H. A native of Keeseville, N. Y., but recently has been the preceptress of the Chicago Ladies' Academy, Morgan Park, Ill.

THAYER, STEPHEN HENRY. A New York poet, born in 1839, and now residing at Tarrytown. His verse, dealing mainly with national, domestic, and religious themes, includes a good proportion of sonnets. *Songs of Sleepy Hollow.* (G. P. Putnam's Sons.)

THOMAS, EDITH MATILDA. She was long a resident of Geneva, O., where her verse attracted the attention of Helen Hunt Jackson. She has had conspicuous success for a young poet. Her sonnets are numerous. *A New Year's Masque, Lyrics and Sonnets,* and *The Inverted Torch.* (Houghton, Mifflin & Co.)

THOMPSON, JAMES MAURICE. One who is familiarly known as an apostle of outdoor life, perhaps the latest prominent disciple of the admirable Roger Ascham in upholding the romantic traditions of archery. He has lived largely in Indiana and Georgia, but is now a conventionalized New Yorker and attached to the *Independent*. *Songs of Fair Weather.* (Houghton, Mifflin & Co.)

TILTON, THEODORE. Mr. Tilton's contributions to literature in prose and verse are well known and considerable. *Thou and I.* (Worthington.)

TIMROD, HENRY (1829–1867). He was born in Charleston, S. C., and had his genius nursed by poverty, sickness, and disappointment. His poems with memoir by his friend, Paul H. Hayne, were published in 1873. (E. J. Hale & Son.)

TOWNSEND, JAMES B. A well-known New York journalist, now manager of the Press News Association. *Ellen Terry* appeared in the New York *World.*

TROWBRIDGE, JOHN TOWNSEND. He was born in a log-cabin near Rochester, N. Y., in 1827, and in youth was initiated into all the pleasant and unpleasant experiences of a farm life. He subsequently taught school, after a time went to New York, and eventually achieved fame as a writer of boy's stories, novels, character poems, etc. *The Vagabonds,* etc. (Houghton, Mifflin & Co.)

TUCKERMAN, HENRY THEODORE (1813–1871). Born in Boston; made several voyages to Europe, visited Italy, etc., and partly regained his health. He wrote a large number of biographical, critical, and art essays, and many poems, such as *Love and Fame, The Apollo Belvidere,* etc. He spent his summers at Newport, where there is a memorial, in the Redwood Library, containing all his works. He published two volumes of poems. (Houghton, Mifflin & Co.)

TYRRELL, HENRY. A writer who has contributed verse to some of the best magazines. He is attached to *Frank Leslie's Newspaper*, New York. His sonnets appeared in the *Century*.

VERY, JONES (1813–1880). A unique genius, whose poems have the strength of sincerity and conscious inspiration. He believed himself the instrument of the Divine Power to a great extent, and so he speaks "as one having authority." He was born in Salem, Mass., and was the son of a ship-captain. He preached in Unitarian pulpits when his health allowed, meanwhile writing his poems and numerous sonnets, and visiting and corresponding with Emerson. He seemed more intimate with God and Nature than with man; yet he often puts the three-sided relationship in striking words and novel lights. Poems. (Houghton, Mifflin & Co.)

WALSH, HENRY C. The editor of *Lippincott's Magazine* issued a volume of verse in his college days which contains, among other things, *Love's Gold*.

WASSON, DAVID ATWOOD (1823–1887). This poet, of acknowledged genuineness, was a native of West Brooksville, Me. After a year at Bowdoin, he took a sea voyage for his health, subsequently studied law, and also attended the Bangor Theological Seminary. He ministered to the Independent Church at Groveland, Mass., but was disabled by ill health. In 1885–1886 he ministered to the society founded by Theodore Parker. Next he tried his hand in the Boston Custom House. He visited Germany, and finally settled at West Medford, Mass., and contributed general matter to the press. Refined ideality marks his poems, such as *Bugle Notes*, *Seen and Unseen*, and *Ideals*. The sonnet *Royalty* was included by Emerson in his *Parnassus*. (Lee & Shepard.)

WEBB, CHARLES HENRY ("JOHN PAUL"). His prose articles won wide celebrity in the *Tribune*. The one quoted was, until recently, the only sonnet Mr. Webb ever wrote. *Vagrom Verse*. (Houghton, Mifflin & Co.)

WEBSTER, DANIEL (1782–1852). The great orator's charming poem, *The Memory of the Heart*, was written in London, under date of November 19, 1839, and is published in *The Poets of New Hampshire*, compiled by Bela Chapin. (Charles H. Adams, publisher, Claremont, N. H., 1883.) Mr. Webster was a native of New Hampshire, and was educated at Exeter and at Dartmouth, where he allowed his poetical vein to crop out in the college papers. His career as an orator and statesman need not be commented on; though his fame sheds an unusual interest on the minutest particulars of his life — even to the writing of a sonnet.

The latter, which appears elsewhere is not a sonnet in structure, being a series of rhymed couplets.

WEEKS, ROBERT KELLEY (1840-1876). A native poet, whose volume was greeted as containing much promise; the author of the ballad, *How Roland blew the Horn*. (Henry Holt & Co.)

WHITING, CHARLES GOODRICH. Born in St. Albans, Vt., 1842. He has spent the years of his manhood — twenty-one — on the *Springfield Republican*, where he is a general writer and literary editor, as well as a partner. He published both prose and verse in the *Saunterer*. (Houghton, Mifflin & Co.)

WHITTIER, JOHN GREENLEAF. The Quaker poet was born in Haverhill, Mass., in 1807. His idylls of farm-life are founded on his experience as a country boy. He had no extensive education in schools. William Lloyd Garrison was the first to encourage his verse-writing, and welcomed the young man's poems to the *Free Press* and *Liberator*. The poet tried his hand at editing several papers, but ill-health forbade it, and he retired to Amesbury to enjoy his fame as the champion of the slave and the poet of "the plain people." He was selected to write the ode for the Centennial Exposition in 1876. *Complete Poems*. (Houghton, Mifflin & Co.)

WILCOX, ELLA WHEELER. A writer of much newspaper verse. She formerly resided in the West, but now lives in New York city. (Belford & Co.)

WILDE, RICHARD HENRY (1789–1849). Born in Dublin, Ireland; he came to America in 1797, and removed to Georgia, where he became Attorney-General of the State and a member of Congress. He spent six years in Florence, where he was so fortunate as to discover Giotto's portrait on the walls of the Barghello Palace. He studied Dante and Tasso, leaving an unfinished life of the former. One of his memorable poems was *My Life is like a Summer Rose*. Published *Hesperia*, Boston, 1867.

WILKINSON, WILLIAM C. A resident of Tarrytown, N. Y., an extensive traveler, and frequent writer on literary, historical, and scientific subjects, as well as of verse. He is now engaged on a long poem on an oriental subject. *The Open Polar Sea* appeared in *Scribner's* (now the *Century*), and is remarkable in that the two phases of a metaphor each occupy one sonnet.

WILLIAMS, FRANCIS HOWARD. A Philadelphia critic and journalist. The sonnet on *Decoration Day* appeared in *Harper's Weekly* with a double-page illustration. In conjunction with S. Decatur Smith he issued recently a volume of verse. He has also written several plays.

WILLIS, NATHANIEL PARKER (1806–1867). Born in Portland, Me., died at his country-seat, Cornwall-on-Hudson. He sprang from a family of printers, his father being the founder of the *Youth's Companion*. Willis graduated from Yale, and had a brilliant career as an editor, poet, and general writer. He was identified with the New York *Mirror*, and in his day one of the most noted of New York literary people. (Clark & Maynard.)

WILSON, ROBERT BURNS. A young author, a Kentuckian by birth, and a writer of considerable magazine verse. He published a volume, *Life and Love*. (Cassell & Co.)

WOODBERRY, GEORGE E. Born in Beverly, Mass., in 1855. A graduate of Harvard, he was professor in a Western college for a short period, but has returned to the East. He wrote the biography of Poe for the *Men of Letters Series*. Author of the *North Shore Watch*, etc. (Houghton, Mifflin & Co.) *At Gibraltar* appeared originally in the *Atlantic Monthly*.

ACKNOWLEDGMENT FOR ENGLISH SONNETS.

THE author acknowledges gratefully the kind permission of the authors, so far as they are living, as well as of the publishers, for the use of the English sonnets quoted in the introductory essay. Thanks are due, therefore, for the waiving of English copyright as follows: To Messrs. MacMillan & Co., — for sonnets by Lord Tennyson, Matthew Arnold, Miss Rossetti, Alexander Smith, and Mrs. D. M. Craik; Kegan Paul, Trench, Trübner & Co., — sonnets by Messrs. Dobson, Lang, Symonds, and Gosse; Chatto & Windus, — sonnet by Robert Buchanan; George Bell & Sons, — sonnet by E. A. Bowring; Ellis & Elvey, — sonnets by D. G. Rossetti; R. Bentley & Sons, — sonnet by Frances Anne Kemble.

INDEX OF FIRST LINES.

(To Sonnets in the Body of the Book.)

About the oak that framed this chair of old, 229.
A brow of stone and sunken eyes of stone, 245.
Across the brook of Time man leaping goes, 214.
Across thy sky the rifted clouds pursue, 312.
A few there are who to the troubled soul, 202.
After long days of dull perpetual rain, 285.
After the fierce midsummer, all ablaze, 309.
After the summer's fierce and thirsty glare, 202.
Age cannot wither her whom not gray hairs, 171.
A giant of awful strength, he dumbly lies, 164.
A high bare field, brown from the plough and borne, 263.
Ah me! that it has nearly passed away, 186.
Ah mournful Sea! yet to our eyes he wore, 268.
A land of Dreams and Sleep, — a poppied land! 286.
All hearts are not disloyal; let thy trust, 299.
All hushed the farm lands with a listening air, 240.
All night keen winds have scourged the frosty plain, 177.
Along the country roadside, stone on stone, 222.
Along the eastern shore the low waves creep, 201.
"A malformed giant!" Let us rather say, 278.
America, my mother and my queen, 108.
Amid the thunder of creation's fall, 186.
Am I not all alone? — The world is still, 253.
Among the thousand, thousand spheres that roll, 232.
A naked baby love among the roses, 295.
An Attic girl with garlands on her hair, 245.
"And thou, O River of to-morrow, flowing," 223.
And thou whose tresses like straw-colored gold, 295.
And thou art gone, most loved, most honored friend! 101.
And will the spirit falter and its fire, 247.
A patient, pensive silence fills the wood, 168.
A record of God's work, what He has done, 242.
Armed of the Gods! Divinest conqueror! 199.

Index of First Lines.

Around the cradle that thy childhood bare, 188.
Around the rocky headlands, far and near, 169.
As a fond mother when the day is o'er, 225.
As a wan weaver in an attic dim, 137.
As calmest waters mirror heaven the best, 267.
As, cleansed of Tiber's and Oblivion's slime, 230.
A sea of blossoms, golden as the glow, 274.
As early as the waning of July, 156.
As happy dwellers by the seaside hear, 290.
As in some deep pool, under shadowy skies, 270.
As little children in a darkened hall, 146.
As there she stood, that sweet Venetian night, 258.
A stranger lingered by Mahala's well, 207.
As those who sail in quest of quiet seas, 311.
As unto blowing roses summer dews, 303.
A thousand fans are fluttering the hot air, 127.
At last, beloved nature, I have met, 297.
At noon of night the goddess, silver-stoled, 273.
A vision fair you show me, that I deem, 254.
A voice that mocks a laughing mountain brook, 147.
A wealth of silence, that is all. The air, 128.
A wind of spring that whirls the feignèd snows, 141.
Ay, and thee, too, who wield'st a power divine, 114.
Ay, thou art welcome, heaven's delicious breath, 125.

Bayard, awaken not this music strong, 280.
Beecher! I will not any longer say, 151.
Behold I send thee to the heights of song, 244.
Behold! it is a draught from Lethe's wave, 182.
Behold the Maid and Mother, doubly blest, 178.
Believe me, dear, unyielding though I be, 177.
Bending above the spicy woods which blaze, 198.
Beside the ocean, wandering on the shore, 270.
Be thou my sun, and rise on every morn, 154.
Between thy frozen eyelids, in swift grace, 166.
Blank shadow here. The heights on either hand, 103.
Brave racer, who hast sped the living light, 140.
Bring no more flowers and books and precious things, 280.
But for thy gracious words, revered of men, 206.
But thou, To-morrow! Never yet was born, 160.

Call it not art; that sad, laborious name, 152.
Call me not dead when I, indeed, have gone, 176.
Can I forget that glorious autumn night, 106.

Champions of men with brawny fist and lung, 181.
Cherish thy Muse! for life hath little more, 252.
Come, blessed darkness, come and bring thy balm, 159.
Come, link thine arm in mine, good Poverty, 244.
Come not with wordy comfort, insincere, 249.
Creusa, in those idyll lands delaying, 300.

Day follows day; years perish; still mine eyes, 183.
Dashing in big drops on the narrow pane, 128.
Dear, amiable man, of soul sublime, 261.
Dear Love, I sometimes think how it would be, 178.
Dear witnesses, all luminous, eloquent, 181.
Deft hands called Chopin's music from the keys, 289.
Down the long hall she glistens like a star, 218.
Do you remember me, my glorified, 281.
Dreaming, he woke, our martyr President, 170.

Each counts his lot most grievous; his distress, 206.
Each day upon the yellow Nile, 't is said, 143.
Each Orpheus must unto the depths descend, 250.
Elegance floats about thee like a dress, 314.
England, I stand on thy imperial ground, 315.
Ensigns of empires flaunt thy flanking wall, 124.
Erelong I paced those cloisteral aisles, erelong, 165.
Even as the sculptor's chisel, flake on flake, 200.
Ever at night have I looked up for thee, 269.

Fair, fugitive, and few autumnal days, 281.
Fair month of roses! Who would sing her praise, 237.
Flame-hearted lover of the earth — great sun! 314.
Floating upon a swelling wave of sound, 220.
For twenty years did Nature wait without, 131.
For us he wandered through strange lands and old, 307.
Friend of the open hand, the genial eye, 194.
From my hill-circled home, this eve, I heard, 170.

"Give me the wine of happiness," I cried, 113.
Go forth in life, O friend, not seeking love! 120.
Go from me now; I will no longer feel, 205.
Gold of the reddening sunset, backward thrown, 228.
Go! read the patent of thy heritage, 109.
Grant me, O God! the glory of gray hairs! 135.
Grant me twice seven splendid words, O Muse, 293.
Great Father mine, deceased ere I was born, 283.

Had we been living in the antique days, 282.
Happy the man who has the poet's heart, 172.
Hark! sack-clothed nun, pressing the cloister stone! 152.
Hasten, soft wind, and when amid the gay, 256.
Hearts of eternity, hearts of the deep! 133.
He failed. He reached to grasp Hesperides, 192.
Here lies the gentle humorist who died, 223.
He sang one song and died, — no more, but that, 110.
He stood apart — but as a mountain stands, 258.
Here were the place to lie alone all day, 305.
Herewith I send you three pressed withered flowers, 100.
He 's not alone an artist weak and white, 129.
High walls and huge the body may confine, 172.
His cherished woods are mute. The stream glides down, 113.
His harp is silent; shall successors rise, 97.
How canst thou call my modest love impure, 115.
How many lives, made beautiful and sweet, 224.
How poor is all that fame can be or bring! 197.
How shall we know it is the last good-bye? 248.
How shrink the snows upon this upland field, 263.
How small a tooth hath mined the season's heart, 293.
How still the mountains! yet from steep to steep, 138.
How tenderly, spread to the sunset's cheer, 179.
Hush! through the sounds and through the troubled airs, 155.

I am the child of earth and air and sea, 121.
I cannot measure for thee, drop by drop, 182.
I cannot reach thee; we are so far, so far, 123.
Idle, and all in love with idleness, 306.
If, at the general judgment of the dead, 151.
If God speaks anywhere, in any voice, 288.
If he could say it, turning from the board, 257.
If I have ever told you all my heart, 94.
If like the torch flame which some Druid hoar, 107.
If on the clustering curls of thy dark hair, 253.
I found her walking in a lonely place, 249.
I give thee greeting — thou, my wedded heart, 291.
I grieve not that ripe knowledge takes away, 227.
I hasten homeward, through the gathering night, 190.
I know an isle, clasped in the sea's strong arms, 167.
I know not why I chose to seem so cold, 146.
I lie unread, alone. None heedeth me, 166.
I 'll call thy frown a headsman, passing grim, 116.
I looked to find a man who walked with God, 300.

Index of First Lines.   355

I love thee, O thou Beautiful and Strong, 114.
I miss thy face, dear friend, thy voice, thy hand, 256.
In dead, dull days I heard a ringing cry, 148.
In shimmering haze the landscape lay concealed, 209.
In the dim chamber whence but yesterday, 183.
In the white sweetness of her dimpled chin, 112.
Into the crystal chalice of the soul, 272.
I saw a child, once, that had lost its way, 236.
I saw a picture once by Angelo, 129.
I saw the lily pale and perfect grow, 122.
I saw the Spirit of the Night descend, 149.
I see the hard wind-ridden eastward hill, 264.
I shall behold, I hope I shall behold, 284.
I sometimes muse when my adventurous gaze, 162.
I sometimes wonder that the human mind, 104.
Is this a painting ? Are those pictured clouds, 111.
Is this the only tribute we should pay ? 296.
I stray with Ariel and Caliban, 235.
I think, ofttimes, that lives of men may be, 184.
It is a peaceful end of all desire, 239.
It is the place when life's long dream come true, 233.
It must be sweet, O thou, my dead, to lie, 143.
It shall be Eve's face, Carver, gleaming white, 265.
It was a stormy night in early spring, 118.
I walk beneath the tender, growing night, 313.
I woke and heard the thrushes sing at dawn, 136.
I wonder oft why God, who is so good, 122.
I would far rather wear upon my breast, 240.

Karnac, thy columns grand, in the moon's pale light, 209.

Last night I dreamed you kissed me on the lips, 147.
Last night in blue my little love was dressed, 305.
Lear and Cordelia! 't was an ancient tale, 117.
Less high, my thought, fly sweetly near the ground, 246.
Let fall the roses gently. It may be, 312.
Let me believe you, love, or let me die! 137.
Let me not lay the lightest feather's weight, 279.
Let no man say, *He at his lady's feet*, 213.
Life is too short, dear love, for unkind feeling, 102.
Light of dim mornings; shield from heat and cold, 187.
Like the eccentric wanderer of the skies, 179.
Like those grand heights of far-off northern lands, 237.

List! through dusk silence, warningly there steal, 153.
Little we know what secret influence, 284.
Lo, as sweet instruments of music play, 243.
Lo! I will hate my enemy, yet breathe, 294.
Lone in the sunrise of primeval day, 185.
Look where the sea, with swift resistless tide, 173.
"Love me or I am slain!" I cried, and meant, 276.
Love, touch my mouth with kisses as with fire, 205.
Love will outwatch the stars, and light the skies, 235.

Mean are all titles of nobility, 96.
'Mid forest trees I heard, one summer day, 275.
'Mid thirty centuries of dust and mould, 216.
Midway about the circle of the year, 272.
Mine be the force of words that tax the tongue, 261.
Most beautiful among the helpers thou! 289.
Most men know love but as a part of life, 296.
Mother of balms and soothings manifold, 212.
My ear can find no rest. The throbbing tide, 217.
My heart, forthlooking in the purple day, 208.
My heart was heavy, for its trust had been, 308.
My heaven-born soul! my body unconfined, 193.
My love for thee is like a wingèd seed, 215.
My soul goes wandering in the wilderness, 136.

Nay, friend, farewell! for if I loved you less, 94.
Near strange, weird temples, where the Ganges' tide, 267.
New England's poet, rich in love as years, 227.
No purer joy the glad midsummer holds, 168.
Night and its dews come silently to earth, 208.
Not for a rapture unalloyed I ask, 145.
Not like the brazen giant of Greek fame, 219.
Not to be conquered by these headlong days, 210.
Not while the fever of the blood is strong, 219.
Now at thy soft, recalling voice I rise, 213.

O clouds and winds and streams, that go your way, 120.
O Earth! thou hast not any wind that blows, 259.
O fair young queen, who liest dead to-day, 159.
O for a castle on a woodland height! 298.
Oft have I seen her when her artless art, 292.
Oft have I thought, musing, my love, on thee, 271.
O glorious tide, O hospitable tide, 180.

Index of First Lines.

O golden silence, bid our souls be still, 158.
O have you seen the scarlet pimpernel, 111.
Oh earth, oh dewy mother, breathe on us, 210.
Oh, for a breath of spicy woodland air, 130.
O highest, strongest, sweetest woman-soul! 176.
Oh, Love, thy sovereignty is great indeed, 264.
Oh, nature, take me home, and henceforth keep! 294.
Oh, not her gentle, silent forces most, 290.
Oh, you who love me not, tell me some way, 260.
Old age! I harbor thee a welcome guest, 105.
O messenger, art thou the king or I? 196.
Once, as I pondered o'er strange books, and sought, 266.
Once in an English woodland, where awoke, 165.
Once in the wave-girt garden of the world, 238.
Once more without you! — sighing, dear, once more, 287.
One cannot draw the bars against the friends, 199.
One weary night the baleful Crescent shone, 207.
On many a saddened hearth the evening fire, 191.
One stood upon the morning hills and saw, 103.
On the Lung' Arno, in each stately street, 173.
O restless throng, massed on the shovel prow, 153.
O Sleep, good mother of enchanting dreams, 252.
O solemn portal veiled in mist and cloud, 144.
O soul of fire within a woman's clay! 188.
O that some poet, with awed lips on fire, 260.
Oh, there are gentle souls on earth imbued, 285.
O thou great Friend to all the sons of men, 251.
Outwearied with the littleness and spite, 277.
O vale of Chester! trod by him so oft, 307.
O wanderer in unknown lands, what cheer? 248.
O white and midnight skies! O starry bath! 174.
O wholesome Death, thy sombre funeral car, 216.

Penelope sat weaving all the day, 135.
Pent in this common sphere of sensual shows, 184.

Rather, my people, let thy youths parade, 117.
Rest, hunted spirit: canst thou never sleep? 95.
"Rien," he wrote, because it chanced that day, 132.
River, that stealest with such silent pace, 222.
Room for our Poet in the immortal choir! 208.
Roughened and worn with ceaseless toil and care, 278.

Sad autumn, drop thy weedy crown forlorn, 287.

Science! true daughter of Old Time thou art! 255.
Sea-like in billowy distance, far away, 112.
Seems there a hand outstretched to bar the way? 109.
Self-awed with its own glory is the night, 155.
She flushed and paled and, bridling, raised her head, 241.
Shepherd with meek brow wreathed with blossoms sweet, 162.
She lies in that fair land where violets spring, 203.
She seemed an angel to our infant eyes! 279.
She softly sings, and paces to and fro, 189.
Ship, blest to bear such freight across the blue, 229.
Shrill oracle! proclaiming night by night, 144.
Sick of myself, and all that keeps the light, 99.
"Since Cleopatra died!" Long years are past, 187.
Sitting alone within this dusky glow, 123.
So long he walked a desert bleak and bare, 241.
Some are there spending greedy lives of toil, 303.
Some days in this prosaic, earnest life, 195.
So sails my soul for that pacific sea, 311.
So saith the Psalmist, with his eyes downcast, 150.
"So shalt thou never tread the weary ways," 189.
Soul, art thou thirsty, art thou yearning, lone? 266.
So you have wondered at me, — guessed in vain, 277.
"Speak tenderly! for he is dead," we say, 156.
Spectre of stone! that from thy ocean bed, 231.
Stand, thou great bulwark of man's liberty! 118.
Stay where thou art, thou need'st not farther go, 302.
Stern be the pilot in the dreadful hour, 254.
Still unto thee, my brightest, fairest, best, 255.
Storm had been on the hills: the day had worn, 313.
Summer is routed from her rosy plains, 119.
Superb and sole upon the plumèd spray, 212.
Sweet Poesy, most shy and gentle maid, 247.
Swift, through some trap mine eyes have never found, 214.

Take all of me, — I am thine own, heart-soul, 262.
Take of the maiden's and the mother's sigh, 134.
That eyes which pierced our inmost being through, 131.
That regal soul I reverence in whose eyes, 304.
That thou art high above me I have found, 95.
That which is noblest in the noblest men, 246.
The bird sits spelled upon the lithe, brown wrist, 217.
The circling hills of woods and clouds snow-white, 203.
The darkness brings no quiet here, the light, 211.
The daughter of a king, how should I know, 196.

Index of First Lines.

The day has past, I never may return, 133.
The eyes of night soft closing to their rest, 150.
The frost is out, and in the open fields, 302.
The gorgeous blossoms of that magic tree, 286.
The holiest of all holidays are those, 224.
The increasing moonlight drifts across my bed, 99.
The keeper of the Concord Light is dead, 120.
The merchant clouds that cruise-the sultry sky, 292.
The month of carnival of all the year, 198.
The music dwells upon its dying chord, 299.
The old, old wonder of the lengthening days, 106.
The old wine filled him and he saw with eyes, 161.
The piping of our slender, peaceful reeds, 190.
The prison ship, — a tomb of living men, 149.
There as she sewed, came floating through her head, 193.
There came a breath out of a distant time, 200.
Therefore I trust, although to outward sense, 309.
Therefore I dare reveal my private woe, 218.
There is a time between our night and day, 157.
There lurks a deadly beauty in the air, 154.
There were no roses till the first child died, 161.
The saddest hour of anguish and of loss, 310.
The sea is never quiet: east and west, 160.
"These rugged wintry days I scarce could bear," 226.
The skillful listener, methinks, may hear, 134.
The speech that day doth utter and the night, 175.
The stars are glittering in the frosty sky, 185.
"The sworder by the sword shall fall," I said, 158.
The tree of faith, its bare, dry boughs must shed, 308.
The twilight is the morning of his day, 234.
The unfailing starlight falls upon the plain, 230.
The wisest man could ask no more of Fate, 228.
They talk of short-lived pleasure — be it so, 126.
They wait all day, unseen by us, unfelt, 157.
Thine eyes shall see the light of distant skies, 125.
This bronze doth keep the very form and mould, 175.
This is the deep profound that imports man, 306.
This is the earth He walked on; not alone, 174.
This is the face that shone when Greece was free, 139.
This man, whose homely face you look upon, 282.
This were a boon all others far excelling, 145.
Thou art the friend and comrade, Poesy, 102.
Thou art the rock of empire, set 'mid seas, 315.
Thou art the same, my friend, about whose brow, 259.

Thou Child-Soul sister of the Loving Ones, 98.
Though I recall no word, no glance, no tone, 119.
Though Love loves well all things of outward grace, 271.
Thou intimate, malign, benumbing power, 142.
Thou need'st not rest; the shining spheres are thine, 301.
Thou wast not robbed of wonder when youth fled, 141.
Through the Cathedral of thy finished song, 257.
Throughout the world in vain, in vain they sought, 232.
Thy beauty fades, and with it, too, my love, 301.
Time's wonted ravage shall not touch my love, 304.
'T is wrought in heirlooms of our country's lore, 105.
To fawn and pander to our own conceit, 226.
To look upon the face of a dead friend, 132.
To me thou cam'st the earliest lamp of light, 251.
To stand within a gently-gliding boat, 231.
Touched with the delicate green of early May, 101.
Tradition's favoring verdict would express, 163.
Trained in the holy art whose lifted shield, 191.
Truth: So the frontlet's older legend ran, 192.
Turn with me from the city's clamorous street, 121.
Two, sauntering, hand in hand, one happy day, 140.

Upon the dreamy upland aureoled, 238.
Upon the silver beach the undines dance, 220.
Upon the storm-swept beach brown broken weeds, 167.

Weary with pondering many a weighty theme, 298.
We count them happy who have richly known, 108.
We must be nobler for our dead, be sure, 107.
We oft are sorrowful, yet have no word, 130.
We strive to shield our lives as years advance, 138.
What footstep but has wandered free and far, 163.
What honey in the year's last flowers can hide, 140.
What is diviner than the peace of foes! 201.
What is more large than knowledge and more sweet, 211.
What is it you are whispering, solemn woods? 215.
What is my lady like? thou fain would'st know, 204.
What is this mystic, wondrous hope in me, 269.
What lies beyond we ask not. In that hour, 233.
What matter, though the world be alien cold, 291.
What need have I to fear — so soon to die? 276.
What though the cities blaze, the ports be sealed, 115.
What though you lie like the still pool of rain, 221.
When Avon's Bard his sweetest music scored, 127.

Index of First Lines.   361

When days were long, and o'er that farm of mine, 288.
When first I met you, little milk-white flower, 265.
When from the vaulted wonder of the sky, 93.
When I beneath God's radiant beams of grace, 274.
When I do hear the changeful trumpet blow, 243.
When in thy glass thou studiest thy face, 171.
When I remember with what buoyant heart, 97.
When Love is dead, who writes his epitaph ? 142.
When she comes home again! A thousand ways, 262.
When sleep's soft thrall with dawn of day is breaking, 239.
When St. Cecilia, soul of song and fire, 234.
When such a spirit away from earth has fled, 164.
When the tired bee is slumbering in his cell, 221.
When to soft Sleep we give ourselves away, 98.
Where are the Poets unto whom belong, 225.
Which was it of the whirling orbs of night, 297.
While men pay reverence to mighty things, 100.
While in these spacious fields is my sojourn, 180.
"Whom the gods love die young," we have been told, 283.
Who nearer Nature's life would truly come, 96.
Why art thou troubled, oh my cherished friend, 195.
Why dost thou hail with songful lips no more, 273.
Why here on this third planet from the sun, 194.
Winged mimic of the woods! thou motley fool ! 310.
Winged wanderer from clover meadows sweet, 275.
With acclamation and with trumpet tone, 242.
Within a sluggish pool I saw a bank, 250.
Within the shadow of ourselves we stand, 236.
With sails full set, the ship her anchor weighs, 197.
With the mild light some unambitious star, 116.
With whirring wings that heavenward would aspire, 148.
Working as erst by law, not miracle, 124.

Yea, rock him gently in thine arms, O Deep! 204.
Yes, cross in rest the little, snow-white hands, 139.

www.ingramcontent.com/pod-product-compliance
Lightning Source LLC
Chambersburg PA
CBHW030357230426